D1267832

THE POEMS OF LAURA RIDING

LAURA (RIDING) JACKSON

THE POEMS OF
LAURA RIDING

A New Edition of the 1938 Collection

PERSEA BOOKS, INC.
New York

International Standard Book Number: 0–89255–044–9

Library of Congress Catalog Card Number: 79–91169

First American edition

Printed in Great Britain

To

Schuyler Brinckerhoff Jackson

who knew, and exerted himself to his
extreme to serve, the beneficent duty
that words lay upon us, and help us
to exert ourselves to serve

The poems in this edition are collected from the following books:—

The Close Chaplet (Hogarth Press).
Love as Love, Death as Death (Seizin Press).
Poems: A Joking Word (Jonathan Cape Ltd.).
Though Gently (Seizin Press).
Twenty Poems Less (Hours Press).
Poet: A Lying Word (Arthur Barker Ltd.)

Voltaire (Hogarth Press).
Laura and Francisca (Seizin Press).
The Life of the Dead (Arthur Barker Ltd.).

Epilogue, Volumes I, II and III (Seizin Press and
Constable & Co.)
and from work not published previously
to the 1938 edition.

CONTENTS

The arrangement of the poems duplicates that of the first edition. The order in which those of the main sections appear is predominantly chronological. The three long supplementary poems ('Histories') are distinct in time and character, and of marginal significance in the whole.

POEMS OF IMMEDIATE OCCASION

POEMS OF FINAL OCCASION

POEMS CONTINUAL

HISTORIES

APPENDIX

INTRODUCTION

THE preface I wrote for the first presentation of this collection of poems (it was published in 1938) gives an account of poetry unqualifiedly loyal to the actuality of poetry as a tradition of linguistic composition in forms intended for oral or written delivery, of a level of expression above all common levels of expression, and also above the heights of linguistic distinction attainable in learned discourse, philosophic disquisition, the exposition of religious feelings and ideas, the narration of real events or imagined life-experiences for meeting varieties of mentally dignified human interest. Until twentieth-century literary modernism effected a spiritual alteration in the conception of the nature of poetry, the poetic level of linguistic expression has never been treated as other than of a decreed unique height of linguistic and spiritual distinction, except as the basic tradition of poetry has been liberalized in intellectually purposeful literary play, or where the tradition has been morally neglected or trifled with while the outer trappings of poetic distinction were maintained as professional identification. In becoming a poet in the century's first quarter of poetic modernism, I assumed the character of a modern in the freedom with which I, cheerfully, dispensed with the literary conventionalities of poetic idiom, and forged me a poetic diction out of natural standards of diction-excellence, shaped to the requirements of the special concerns of poetry.

As to what the special concerns of poetry are, the tradition provides no definitions. It presents *itself* as the definition of them, with the burden of proof put upon the poet of justifying the implicit meaning of the tradition as the union of the highest human concerns within the bounds of poetic expression. Thus it is that the general human weakness of want of distinctness of conception of the highest human concerns has been endowed in poetry with supplementary strength: poetry, that is, identifies commitment to its mode of expression with a commitment to exclusive preoccupation with these concerns, and in so doing represents itself as a plane of sensibility on which spiritual height of being is concretely realizable. In my choosing the rôle of poet, I recognized this traditional allocation by poetry to itself of an area of experience of an immediate, absolute, life-purifying quality of spirituality, and I accepted poetry without reservation as having demarcated this area as potentially occupiable in distinct forms of consciousness, real functions of being, exactly congruous translation of the occupation of it into words. While other poets were endeavoring to fashion poetry into a compromise between an adapting of the historic conception of human spirituality to modern humanistic sophistication and a preservation of the historical identity of poetry as a highly honored literary function, I had not the least difficulty in uniting the traditional character of poetry as an active literature of spirituality with the dignities of modern intellectuality. But these were attached, for me, to scruples of linguistic verity, not to doctrinaire enlightenment-opinion.

I was religious in my devotion to poetry. But in saying this I am thinking of religion as it is a dedication to, a will to know and make known, the ultimate knowledge, a will to think, to be, with truth, to voice, to live articulately by, the essentialities of existence. Poetry made itself the secular twin of religion. But its secularity has not been of a 'worldly' cast. Rather than endeavoring to serve as a ritual of spirituality symbolic of the religiously serious, a process of metaphorical imitation of it, a mere *art*, it has, except in vulgar conception and practice, endeavored to serve as an area for the exercise of spiritual consciousness as a directly, personally possessed human function, not just a derivative of a mysterious condition of spiritual blessedness. Poetry, that is, made itself a charter of the internal, personally independent spirituality of the human being. Where religion dealt with the separation of a spiritual part from the mixed body-and-soul, or mixed body-and-mind, with soul as intermediating factor, poetry gave the spiritual element the rôle of a·teaching presence in the complex composition of the individual human being. Poetry may be described as an institution devoted to the pursuit of spiritual realism, in relation to religion as an institution devoted to the pursuit of spiritual idealism. For those to whom the spiritual nature of the human being calls for literal expression, living fulfilment, there presses a sense of a necessity of choice between poetry and religion—the quality of the urgency determines the choice.

The vision of the spiritual offices of poetry that I describe in the preface to the 1938 edition of these poems (which is to be found in this book's appendix) presents the case of the choice of poetry, as against that of spiritual solution of religious futurizing, in all its intensity of identification of the poetic order of spiritual fulfilment with practical truth. I took poetry at its face-value as turning upon human life, through all the untrustable weather of time, a steadily shining countenance, promise of the words all yearned to hear from one another, a promise delivered in the eloquent appearance of being the prelude to the speaking of them. I put religious trust in the predictiveness of poetry as an immediacy, not a future, in the making. I believed in the possibility of a transformation, through poetic apprehension of the spiritual function of language and the natural force of the life-breath of the word-animating human mind, of ordinary human verbal intercourse into a spiritually expressive, a spiritually successful, order of human existence.

I treated the profession of literal sincerity of being that poetry spoke on behalf of human beings generally as a commitment backed by an intention implicit in human nature. I *began* with this reading of the significance of poetry in my adoption of it as my life-work's path. Making my way steadily in this path, I came eventually to where I found poetic utterance arrested even in its being poetic utterance: it adumbrated a potentiality that was not developable *within it*, its limit of achievement *was* the adumbration of the potentiality. I ended, in my movement in the poetic path, at no-end. The success of my exploration of the possibilities of poetic utterance, that the early *Collected Poems* exemplified, was a success of predictive truth: nothing has been achieved in it except the exemplification of the nature of poetry as truth qualified by the limits of prediction.

My sincerity as a poet was a sincerity of spiritual literalness of faith in the truth-potentiality of words embodied in the spiritual creed of poetry. *If* poetry could not comprise transcendence from immediacies of predictive eloquence to realities of immediate truth of word in which it surpassed its historical identity as a literary area of utterance, its value would prove itself inevitably to be—*to have been no more than*—a course of utterance in which what was said was said in isolation from the influences of common, prevailing modes of verbal expression. Poets were free to suit their mode of verbal expression to the dictates of their individual sense of what choice and arrangement of words fitted their meaning. But the privilege of individual freedom of word that poetry bestowed could not be itself a warranty of truth of word. For the freedom was qualified by a limitation of poetic utterance to conventionalities of form that restricted the operation of thought and the rhythmic course of its expression within recitative or song-like patterns.

The price of poetic freedom of word was poetry's having the identity of a mode of verbal expression outside the norms of expression that language, as the common human possession, seemed to ordain to be natural, 'ordinary' practice—its automatic, self-regulating functional technique. That there was, in the *difference* of poetic expression from 'ordinary' expression, the key to the *natural* in language, the use of words according to a principle of truth inspiring the relationship of understanding existing between human minds and language as their common instrument of self-corroboration, no poet of honorable linguistic sensitivity cannot have felt.

I must concentrate on report of how it was with me, in my sense of what the difference of the poetic expression from 'ordinary' expression betokened as to the *right* linguistic norm, the linguistically real natural correspondent with the humanly real natural.

There has come to be a false weight of authority attached to the term 'ordinary', in contexts of reference to human behavior, practices, modes of feeling and thought, as indicating the humanly 'natural'. This 'ordinary' signifies no more than what human beings fall into the way of doing, feeling, thinking, *saying*, etc., without individual action of intelligent choice. The choice is imitative of what has become prevalent as the assumed choice of a nebulously conceived 'everyone'. This falling into the 'ordinary' is not the same as a collectively instinctive hitting upon the suitably human in any element or feature of human-behavior performance, capability, disposition. It is a sinking down, from failure to achieve a common level of sensitive realization and fulfilment of the suitably human, in the expressive forms of life, to a common level of general indulgence of one another, by human beings, in a variable less than successful achievement of the true quality of the human, collectively or individually. Wherever 'ordinary' connotes a lower level in the quality of anything of human

mode, the connotation allows of the possibility of a not entire-
ly salutary difference from the ordinary in what belongs to a
human level of higher grading—a something not altogether
natural. The necessity of resolving the conflict between the
poetic ideal of the linguistic natural and the commonplace
verbal procedure as representing the linguistic natural was a
fundamental element of my sense of my responsibility as a
poet.

The difference of the poetic use of words was precious: the
difference must be served with a devout separate-keeping of
the poetic and the non-poetic verbal practice. But the poetic
ideal was not an emblem of difference. It was evocative of a
proper human standard of rightness of word—the happy
natural. Poetic verbal practice, the serving of the poetic ideal,
must be in the service of this standard. Such a conception as
this—mine—of the poetic course, such a location of the level
of poetic word-use, carried in its implications energies of
commitment to a mode and an objective of poetic verbal
practice in which the conception of poetry as a category of
literary composition, and as a level of word-use categorically
higher than the 'ordinary', was transcended in all the major
aspects of serious personal preoccupation. The poetic course
became for me more and more, as I dedicated to it my faith
in the good significance of human existence, and my powers,
a course in which to unite, with all my virtue of compre-
hensive, personally general, sincerity of dedication, the
intellectual, the moral, the spiritual trails of the journey to
truth—to the plane of utterance on which human speaking
spoke the language of being with a full, universal explicitness
of sense.

The scope of my preoccupations as a poet is of a breadth,
a spaciousness of subject-matter content, that does not con-
form to the stock critical notion of the general as matter of
reference, in poetry. Matter of general reference has been
conventionalized both in poetic practice and critical evaluation
as the appropriate for treatment on special rhetorical planes
of emotional elevation or with intellectually intricate devices
of symbolization. That the general, in my poetic work, is
treated as existent to natural thought, and experience of
feeling, and properly within expression-reach of the regular
resources of language, without intensive resort to metaphoric

and symbolic improvizations, has provoked rampant characterization of it as 'abstract', and 'obscure', in meaning. It has been denounced as the work of one who is no poet at all—an extreme example of the violation of Blake's description of the poetic requisite: 'minute particulars'. And I have been accused, with teasing intent, of endeavoring to renew the poetic gospel of Matthew Arnold. The accusation has serious point.

For Arnold, poetry was the level of the higher moral criticism, the engagement by 'man' in speech 'in which he comes nearest to being able to utter the truth'. The poet has ideas 'on man, on nature, and on human life' that the 'distinctive character of superiority' he possesses, under the 'immutably fixed laws of poetic beauty and truth', empower him to propagate with an elevating, generally inspiring, influence. Poetry's attributes—the attributes of the 'best' poetry—were all associated, for Arnold, with the higher potentialities of human nature, intelligence, moral and spiritual consciousness. His gospel was, essentially, educative, a scriptural ideal of 'culture' that would raise the sights of human aspiration above the 'average man' level. The *difference* of poetry from the 'ordinary' in the standards of pitch of mind, and soul, and *diction*, was an absolute, for him: human nature must, as it were, transcend itself, achieve difference from itself, by subjecting itself to the influence of poetry as the moral voice of its higher part. Arnold was probably the last critic-and-poet of the modern cultural *ancien régime* to fly a banner of moral hope against the evidence of the development of a widening vacancy, in modern visions of standards of human aspiration, between belief in a human capability of attainment to excellencies and the gospel of a new regime of cultural intelligence that made sceptic suspicion of all ideality a canon of intellectually superior common-sense. In my poetic work and critical writing, I have indeed flown a banner of moral hope in the midst of wide-spreading cultural new-regime advances in the down-levelling, in human intellectual self-appraisal, of the moral and spiritual credit of human intellectuality itself.

The accusation that my thinking was, in my commitment to poetry, and is, generally along the lines of Matthew Arnold's preachment of the uses of poetry for human cultural salvation, does both Arnold and myself the injustice of rating us as simpletons of an intellectually highfalutin literary piety served by a priesthood invested with powers of raising the spiritual sights of the human commonalty. Arnold was himself a poet. But he had none of the religiose megalomania that made Blake—for instance—a politician of a paradise answering to his personal sense of moral superiority. Arnold had a real cause, a cause outside himself, for his literature-and-poetry-based moral evangelism.

Arnold saw a wasting of the intellectual will, in his time, and a general succumbing to the interest of the practical aspects of human existence, and reiterated the implicit message of poetry that there was a better seeing, better understanding and feeling and speaking, within the compass of human attainment than the 'ordinary' human version of intelligent evaluation of human experience. The 'ordinary', the commonplace, under-standings and values had become expanded, in the moderni-zation of intellectual custom and the emotionality of moral and spiritual concerns, into dangerous competitors of the older distinctly supernatural areas of human preoccupation. Arnold made an appeal for a new priority of the higher energies of human intelligence, the higher spiritual instincts of which poetry had been the moral patron, to redeem modern humanity from modern intellectual simplifiers of its spiritual problems. He was right in judging human sensibility, the integrity of human mentality itself, to be in a crisis condition. But what he prescribed was only an athletically earnest, a vigorously sincere, version of literary gospel. It perpetuated an aristocratic tradition, a higher-lower level-distinction in human aspiration and attainment, a superiority in human mentality and sensibi-lity that should be capable of determining the dominant trend in human behavior by standards of custom. Contemporary literary critics who mind their intellectual p's and q's do not, however, lightly make Matthew Arnold a mockable emblem of morally noble literary high-mindedness, irrelevant to the requirements of contemporary critical sophistication.

In my own envisioning of poetry as an area in which might be realized full excellence in the articulate exercise of the human powers of understanding and self-understanding, full embodiment of intelligent being in truth-rendering words, I differed from such a commitment of faith in poetry as Arnold's in that I did not identify poetry with a fixed actuality, an achieved realization, an effectual continuum of expressive verbal imaging of the human spiritual desideratum. I identified it with an objective of which it itself was not the ultimate reality of attainment of it. By the terms of literary tradition, the values of poetry are those of a level of personal sensibility and expressive capability that is not one of common human habitation, though a level to which human beings in their common character can be elevated for the enjoyment of experiences of special imaginative presence in it. The terms of my perception of the nature of poetry were terms of human, not categorically literary, value. For me, the significance of the potentiality demonstrated in poetry of a difference from the ordinary, the common, practice in human linguistic functioning went beyond a call to promote dedicated concern with and prizing the poetic performance and the special, different-from-the-ordinary kind of verbal experience it made available. The potentiality carried for me implications of a general human potentiality secreted in the poetic demonstration.

I viewed the poetic performance as having an underlying commitment to an endeavor to open up language in its entire breadth and depth to human expressive capability in *its* entire breadth and depth. As a poet and an advocate of poetry, I looked to what might be achieved, from the vantage of poetic difference in word-use, through the organized preoccupation of poetic word-use with the different, towards the discovery of a rule of true, not merely familiar, wording in the given nature of language. I labored, as a poet, to bring the poetic endeavor out from the climate of the mere different in wording into an air of utterance in which the ring and spirit and mental movement of true wording and that of familiar wording coincided in a non-differentiability, a quality of human and linguistic universalness. I think that *Collected Poems* reveals my course as a poet to have been such a course, and reveals also how my commitment to poetry and my commitment to a universal linguistic solution befitting the general dignity of being human went as far as they could go together.

I did not know when I put the final touches to *Collected Poems* for the 1938 edition that I had reached a limit in the possibility of holding these commitments within one frame of endeavor. Several years passed before I understood this. What I have called my renouncing of poetry was the outer manifestation of an inner experience of discovery that I could not take what was essentially an argument of hope I felt it mine to make any further within the linguistic allowances of poetry: and there was further to go. The universal linguistic solution hangs suspended in poetry, and, so long as it does, human beings cannot know what kind of beings they are, cannot speak themselves with whole consciousness of their being speaking beings, and what this lays upon them to require of themselves.

Poetry bears in itself the message that it is the destiny of human beings to speak the meaning of being, but it nurses it in itself as in a sacred apartness, not to be translated into the language of common meanings in its delivery. I was able to achieve in my poems a use of words that paid respect to the poetic motive of difference in word-use and respect at the same time to language as essentially one with itself, not divided into levels of meaning. But the constraints that the poetic techniques of difference impose on word-use limit the speaking-range and the meaning-effectuality of language to a miniature human and linguistic universalness. My kind of seriousness, in my looking to poetry for the rescue of human life from the indignities it was capable of visiting upon itself, led me to an eventual turning away from it as failing my kind of seriousness.

My renouncing of poetry became known gradually, though I made only one public statement on it in print. This was in the 'fifties, in a supplementary volume of *Twentieth Century Authors*. In the early 'sixties I offered an explanation of it to introduce a reading (not by myself) of some poems of mine for a B.B.C. broadcast. The renouncing has been treated in a few conventionally serious literary quarters largely as the product of a quirk in my thinking entitled to respect because of the patent seriousness of my work in general, and of my thinking before and after the renouncing. I have found unfriendly resentment lurking under friendly manifestations towards my later view of poetry, with persons having—as poets or critics, or as both—a stake in poetry as necessarily an ever-surviving, self-renewing, field of performance. There has been but little recognition of the respect paid by me to the underlying motivations of poetry, in my post-renunciation commenting on the limitations imposed on the potentialities of language by poetry in its very dedication to the linguistic best as an altogether different form of linguistic expression from those of ordinary kind. A tribute of the early 'seventies of Mr Roy Fuller, who is not friendly to my general course of thought, is worthy of note. It is that I did not 'rat' on poetry in renouncing it.

There has been no recognition at all of the unchallengeable logic of my linguistic position, in the time of my working linguistically as a poet, and in my later working without affiliation with any categorically literary position. This is, that the objective of the linguistic best must eventually comprise a practical realization of the objective that transcends the division of the human linguistic possibilities into a mode of verbal practice at a general human level of linguistic expression and a mode at an absolute remove of difference from it in excellence-distance. Such a best in linguistic expression would unite the effect of truth, the essence of the good in language, with the effect of perfect sincerity of being, the essence of the good in the human, the personal, form of life. I believe this position to be quite plainly described in the preface to a selection from my *Collected Poems* first published in 1970 in England, and in 1973 in the United States (*Selected Poems: In Five Sets*). (Portions of it are reproduced in the appendix to this book.) The reasonableness of a condition of practice in which the ordinary fulfils 'best' precepts of the good in word-use, as being as natural to human linguistic sensitivity as 'best' precepts of the good in personal behavior are to natural human moral sensitivity, can be ignored only where concern in matters of language has become a morally inert sophistication, accepting the diffuseness of linguistic sensitivity characteristic alike of the contemporary ordinary linguistic life of people and of contemporary prose and poetic literary custom as the modern linguistic *natural*.

Sophisticated critical obeisance to the diffuse in verbal practice in poetry has taken the form of a lauding of it as a style that properly incorporates 'everyday speech' in the poetic expression-mode. The degeneration of the 'language' of poetry into a compound of super-ordinary 'ordinary language' and enough features of the categorically poetic in linguistic expression to give the identity of poetry to the super-mongreloid compositional results has acquired the character, in the self-protective politics of the latest schools of modern literary criticism, of progress into a modern poetic naturalness that makes the term 'modernist' fit only for the archaic, in modern poetic production. 'Modernism', in poetry, has been pronounced, in the judgement-councils of these schools, to be passé. This is a manifesto of advocacy of a new poetic linguistic naturalness in which the nature of poetry and the nature of language are thinned in a squeaky blend that voices neither. I feel the re-offering of my *Collected Poems* at this time has the special use of affording a fresh modern view of the nature of poetry and the nature of language in conjunctive relation, to the possible in a natural united voicing of them.

I am regarding the explanatory references made to my poems themselves presented in the appendix, excerpted from a reading I made for the Lamont Library at Harvard University, as adequate specific commentary on them for this book, which is designed by the publisher and myself to serve mainly for making available again the original *Collected Poems*. It is no part of our design to provide substantial accompaniment of bibliographical data. What poems have been reproduced in the successive volumes of poems of which *Collected Poems* was the last, and what was omitted, and what revisions are to be found, from volume to volume, will be noted in a general bibliography now in preparation. This will include references to the large number of early poems of mine, published in magazines, never subsequently reproduced. (There is consideration of publishing these as a supplement to this bibliography.) I am planning to present in the appendix one of those early poems, for the stamp upon it of American location. My husband pronounced it, upon first seeing it, as uniquely of all my poems, a veritable American item. (Americana)

I was, indeed, an American poet. My birth-placement and scene of growing-up have had effect in the personal mood of my life and work. In my responses, to the course of circumstances, I am unreservedly open to impression, my feelings frank in the quality of their occurrence in me, and ready for call upon them to manifest themselves; I am prompt in my responses of feeling, in the American manner of treating what

is immediately there as personally immediate. But this dispo-
sition is not, with me, a peculiarity marking behavior; it does
not take the form of a distinct typicality. It is generalized
into, assimilated by, my natural constitution, which is rather
free of typicality-bents. My individual character inclines to the
general in the forms in which it expresses itself. This might be
viewed as a propensity to conventionalism. I attend literally to
the observance of proprieties of word-meaning. In my poetic,
and in my other, writing, I am given to maintaining a serene
(though it might seem prim, or on the other hand, anxious)
hold on the reins of consistency. None of this spells me as
American, but neither does it spell me as non-American.

I have had, I have, queer things said of me. Allen Tate,
providing commentaries on American poets in the 'forties
for information-service for points abroad, described me, with
veiled implications, as an 'international' poet 'who happens
to write in English'. In recent time an English literature pro-
fessor at an English university of whom an undergraduate
student drawn to interest in my work asked his view of it
pronounced me to her 'a madwoman'. Another literary pro-
fessional personage has it that those who try to see the world
through my eyes succumb to crippling mental artificialities—
well-satisfied, he, within the security of something he calls
his world. Perhaps it will steady those who, having met with
queer things said of me, anticipate the experience of reading
in this book with some uneasiness, if I quote a comment
made by an American reviewer of it (John Holmes) at the
time of its first publication: '. . . She refreshes one's under-
standing of the plainest words, so providing excitement of a
rare sort in poetry . . .'. This argues that the world of my eyes,
and my words, is the world of all of us, the better known for
report of it in the language of my vision.

But another American reviewer (whom I was subsequently
to meet, and, in time, to marry—Schuyler B. Jackson), having
commented that I wrote 'in a language in which every word
carries its fullest literate meaning', let the cat of trouble-ahead
out of the bag with: 'For this reason, language that would
seem clear in Shakespeare or Mother Goose may seem obscure
in Laura Riding'. He faced the fact, with the deadly word
'obscure', that there would be many to carp, and, worse, even
pretenders at understanding, false friends to the sense made

with my words, condescenders for the distinction of not being fazed by them. There is but little in the records or environment of professional critical or otherwise special opinion of poets and poems to give heart to readers of my poems for exerting themselves to make close acquaintance with them. They must find heart for this largely in themselves.

Perhaps those about to begin to read here will like to have me tell them, for send-off cheer, what someone not of the professional literary world, but yet of scholarly status, I know to have advanced to a person confessing to him a certain wonderment at long, still unshaken attachment to my work, my way of work, writing, poetic or other. 'It is a way of life for you,' he said, 'as for me.' I am sure he meant: 'It takes us on, and on, to hope of something.' This applies to what was intended in these poems: to take us on, and on, as far as poems could take.

LAURA (RIDING) JACKSON

POEMS OF MYTHICAL OCCASION

FORGOTTEN GIRLHOOD

Into Laddery Street

The stove was grey, the coal was gone.
In and out of the same room
One went, one came.
One turned into nothing.
One turned into whatever
Turns into children.

But remember the coal was gone.
Old Trouble carried her down
To her cellar where the rags were warm.

And turned her sooner
Than had her mother
Into one of the Laddery children,
And called her Lida
For short and for long,
For long, for long.

In Laddery Street
Herself

I am hands
And face
And feet
And things inside of me
That I can't see.

What knows in me?
Is it only something inside
That I can't see?

Children

Children sleep at night.
Children never wake up
When morning comes.
Only the old ones wake up.
Old Trouble is always awake.

Children can't see over their eyes.
Children can't hear beyond their ears.
Children can't know outside of their heads.

The old ones see.
The old ones hear.
The old ones know.
The old ones are old.

Toward the Corner

One, two, three.
Coming, Old Trouble, coming.
The organ-grinder is turning,
The children are sing-songing,
The organ grinder is stopping,
The children are hum-coming,
Coming, Old Trouble, coming.

One, two three.
Coming, Old Trouble, coming.
The bakeshop is sugar-crusting,
The children are window-tasting,
The bakeshop is shop-shutting,
The children are sugar-dreaming,
The children are sugar-stealing,
Coming, Old Trouble, coming.

One, two three.
Coming, Old Trouble, coming.
Father Bell is evening-praying,
The night is empty-falling,
The rats are out,
The birds are in,
Coming, Old Trouble, coming.

One, two, three.
One, two, three.
Coming, Old Trouble, coming.
Somebody's dead, who can it be?
Old Trouble, is it you?

Then say so, say so.
One, two, three,
Into the great rag-bag you go.
Going, Old Trouble, going.

Around the Corner

But don't call Mother Damnable names.
The names will come back
At the end of a nine-tailed Damnable Strap.
Mother Damnable, Mother Damnable,
Good Mother Damnable.

Home, thieves, home.
Mother Damnable waits at her counting-table.
Thieves do the thieving,
But she does the counting.
Home, thieves, home.

Home Sparkey, home Dodo, home Henry, home Gring.
With Dodo I kiss,
With Henry and Gring
I go walking and talking,
With Sparkey I sing.

Then along comes Mother Damnable.
Off, thieves, off.
'Such nonsense is disgraceful among thieves.
Off, wench, off.'

A Second Away

One, two, three, four, more,
Knock at the door,
Come in, come in,
Stir the stew,
Warm love up
In a wooden pot
And serve it hot
With a wooden spoon.

Rap, rap,
Come in, come in,
Love's the only thing
That deceives enjoyably.
Mother Mary and her Magdalenes,
We don't care a curse how much we're deceived
Or deceive.

Hey, Lida,
Away, away,
On a hobby horse
That is wooden together
With everything else
But Lida, Lida.

Hey, hey,
Away, away,
Until Lida falls off
At any next turning.

At any next turning
Off may come falling
Lost lady with question-marks
All over her nose,
All over her nose.

All the Way Back

Bill Bubble in a bowler hat
Walking by picked Lida up.
Lida said 'I feel like dead.'
Bubble said
'Not dead but wed.'
No more trouble, no more trouble,
Safe in the arms of Husband Bubble.

A rocking-chair, a velvet hat,
Greengrocer, dinner, a five-room flat,
Come in, come in,
Same old pot and wooden spoon,
But it's only soup staring up at the moon.

Have you heard about Bubble?
He was called away
To fight for his country
And got stuck in the chimney.
Then hey, Lida, away
On a hobby left over from Yesterday.

One, two, three,
Mother and Moon and Old Trouble and me.
How happy we'll be
Together and all raggedy.
I'm not a full yard,
Old Trouble's not a full inch,
The moon's a hole
And mother's a pinch.
The rest is tatters,
But to rag-pickers
Faults are perfection's faults,
And only perfection matters.

INCARNATIONS

Do not deny,
Do not deny, thing out of thing.
Do not deny in the new vanity
The old, original dust.

From what grave, what past of flesh and bone
Dreaming, dreaming I lie
Under the fortunate curse,
Bewitched, alive, forgetting the first stuff . . .
Death does not give a moment to remember in

Lest, like a statue's too transmuted stone,
I grain by grain recall the original dust
And, looking down a stair of memory, keep saying:
This was never I.

PRIDE OF HEAD

If it were set anywhere else but so,
Rolling in its private exact socket
Like the sun set in a joint on a mountain . . .
But here, nodding and blowing on my neck,
Of no precedent in nature
Or the beauties of architecture,
Flying my hair like a field of corn
Chance-sown on the neglected side of a hill,
My head is at the top of me
Where I live mostly and most of the time,
Where my face turns an inner look
On what's outside of me
And meets the challenge of other things
Haughtily, by being what it is.

From this place of pride,
Gem of the larger, lazy continent just under it,
I, the idol of the head,   .
An autocrat sitting with my purposes crossed under me,
Watch and worry benignly over the rest,
Send all the streams of sense running down
To explore the savage, half-awakened land,
Tremendous continent of this tiny isle,
And civilize it as well as they can.

HOW BLIND AND BRIGHT

Light, visibility of light,
Sun, visibility of sun.
Light, sun and seeing,
Visibility of men.

How blind is bright!
How blind is bright!

Eyes looking out for eyes
Meet only seeing, in common faith,
Visibility and brightness.

Night, invisibility of light,
No sun, invisibility of sun,
Eyes in eyes sheltered,
Night, night and night.
All light, all fire, all eyes,
Wrapt in one conference of doubt.

Eyes not looking out for eyes
Look inward and meet sight
In common loneliness,
Invisibility and darkness.

How bright is blind!
How bright is blind!

BECAUSE I SIT HERE SO

Because I sit here so,
Drooping and parched under this sun of sorrow,
I know
Somewhere
A flower or another like me
Hidden in a rare chance of difference
Wonders and withers unaccountably.

And if I sit here so,
Kindred and interlinked in circumstance
With others like me
Wherever I have been to dream—

And if I sit here so?

Stir me not,
Demons of the storm.
Were I as you would have me,
Astart with anger,
Gnawing the self-fold chain
Until the spell of unity break,
Madness would but thunder
Where sorrow had once burned,
A sun to smile in
And sit waiting under.

Because I sit here so,
Initiating in unrebellion
The perpetual ring
Of who are like me,
Death laughs along with us
And wears this garland of
Another and another dying
Alone, alike, and always.

SEVERAL LOVE-STORIES

The formulas of recognition
Apply themselves to memories.
There's where,
There's when,
There's there.

Yes, a nice time.
I met three fishermen out on the bay
Who couldn't understand language.
I found a mercadon—
What's a mercadon?—
And dined with native nobility,
But there's no place like home!

Yes, true-love—not travel.
It was a sky
Not·just to look at
But prove—
If possible,
If possible.

I went up of love,
I fell down of loves.
There's no place like home!

Townsfolk, untwirl these casings
From Paris and Heaven.

THE MASK

Cover up,
Oh, quickly cover up
All the new spotted places,
All the unbeautifuls,
The insufficiently beloved.

With what? with what?
With the uncovering of the lovelies,
With the patches that transformed
The more previous corruptions.

Is there no pure then?
The eternal taint wears beauty like a mask.
But a mask eternal.

THE SIGNATURE

The effort to put my essence in me
Ended in a look of beauty.
Such looks fanatically mean cruelness
Toward self; toward others, sweetness.

But ghostly is that essence
Of which I was religious.
Nor may I claim defeat
Since others find my look sweet
And marvel how triumphant
The mere experiment.

So I grow ghostly,
Though great sincerity
First held a glass up to my name.
And great sincerity claim
For beauty the live image,
But no deathly fame:
The clear face spells
A bright illegibility of name.

CHLOE OR . . .

Chloe or her modern sister, Lil,
Stepping one day over the fatal sill,
Will say quietly: 'Behold the waiting equipage!'
Or whistle Hello and end an age.

For both these girls have that cold ease
Of women overwooed, half-won, hard to please.
Death is one more honour they accept
Quizzically, ladies adept

In hiding what they feel, if they feel at all.
It can scarcely have the importance of a ball,
Is less impressive than the least man
Chloe, smiling, turns pale, or Lil tweaks with her fan.

Yet, they have been used so tenderly.
But the embarrassment of the suit will be
Death's not theirs. They will avoid aggression
As usual, be saved by self-possession.

Both of them, or most likely, Lil,
No less immortal, will
Refuse to see anything distressing,
Keep Death, like all the others, guessing.

YES AND NO

Across a continent imaginary
Because it cannot be discovered now
Upon this fully apprehended planet—
No more applicants considered,
Alas, alas—

Ran an animal unzoological,
Without a fate, without a fact,
Its private history intact
Against the travesty
Of an anatomy.

Not visible not invisible,
Removed by dayless night,
Did it ever fly its ground
Out of fancy into light,
Into space to replace
Its unwritable decease?

Ah, the minutes twinkle in and out
And in and out come and go
One by one, none by none,
What we know, what we don't know.

THE NUMBER

The number is a secret,
How many elements assemble
To pronounce *Alive*—
And leave *Alive* to count places,
The conference adjourned
And the ghosts inaccurate,
Scattering poor memories.

Calamity if they remember
And long counting of fingers.
No sooner known the number,
There is division to prove the whole,
But never reassembling.
The elements are many
As they were in meeting.
The ghosts reminded,
The commemoration of the scene
Is man parading myriadly,
A precise madness distributing
Alive to ghosts accurately.

CHRYSALIS

Golden to itself it lay,
Its dreams as grains in twinkle-twinkle,
Inward only, to my eyes grey,
Mere cotton, mere butterfly to be.

The time of premonition is thought.
Long before flying, in my thought it flew,
On that day on a tree-side
An old butterfly was new,
Clung wet with fright to its wings.

I blew more fright upon it,
Helped it shudder dry.
Because it could not cry
Stuttering it flew among the vines.
Among the vines my own eyes failed.
'Come away,' they said,
'Out of sight is dead.'

SO SLIGHT

It was as near invisible
As night in early dusk.
So slight it was,
It was as unbelievable
As day in early dawn.

The summer impulse of a leaf
To flutter separately
Gets death and autumn.
Such faint rebellion
Was lately love in me.

So slight, it had no hope or sorrow,
It could but choose
A passing flurry for its nuptial,
Drift off and fall
Like thistledown without a bruise.

THE TILLAQUILS

Dancing lamely on a lacquered plain,
Never a Tillaquil murmurs for legs.
Embrace rustles a windy wistfulness,
But feels for no hands.
Scant stir of being, yet rather they
Unfulfilled unborn than failing alive,
Escaping the public shame of history.

Once only two Tillaquils nearly a man and woman
Violated a hopeless code with hope,
Slept a single dream seeming in time.
'Come,' he cried, coaxing her,
'Stairs stream upward not for rest at every step
But to reach the top always before Death.'
'Softly,' she whispered,
'Or two Tillaquils will wake.'

Death they passed always over and over,
Life grew always sooner and sooner.
But love like a grimace
Too real on Life's face
Smiled two terrified dreams of Tillaquils
Tremblingly down the falling flights;
Who saved themselves in waking
The waste of being something
And danced traditionally
To nothingness and never;
With only a lost memory
Punishing this foolish pair
That nearly lived and loved
In one nightmare.

TAKE HANDS

Take hands.
There is no love now.
But there are hands.
There is no joining now,
But a joining has been
Of the fastening of fingers
And their opening.
More than the clasp even, the kiss
Speaks loneliness,
How we dwell apart,
And how love triumphs in this.

LUCRECE AND NARA

Astonished stood Lucrece and Nara,
Face flat to face, one sense and smoothness.
'Love, is this face or flesh,
Love, is this you?'
One breath drew the dear lips close
And whispered,
'Nara, is there a miracle can last?'
'Lucrece, is there a simple thing can stay?'

Unnoticed as a single raindrop
Broke each dawn until
Blindness as the same day fell.
'How is the opalescence of my white hand, Nara?
Is it still pearly-cool?'
'How is the faintness of my neck, Lucrece?
Is it blood shy with warmth, as always?'

Ghostly they clung and questioned
A thousand years, not yet eternal,
True to their fading,
Through their long watch defying
Time to make them whole, to part them.

A gentle clasp and fragrance played and hung
A thousand years and more
Around earth closely.
'Earth will be long enough,
Love has no elsewhere.'

And when earth ended, was devoured
One shivering midsummer
At the dissolving border,
A sound of light was felt.
'Nara, is it you, the dark?'
'Lucrece, is it you, the quiet?'

THE NIGHTMARE

Of the two flowers growing
Each one side of the wall,
Which would the hungry child
In her nightmare
Pick to wear
If she did not fall
Frightened from the wall?

One was real,
One was false.
Both were same.

While she wavered they withered.
They died.
Hunger went.
There is no more a wall.
The nightmare is morning.
The child says, over-remembering:
Mother, the strangest thing,
Two flowers asleep,
One flower I saw, one I didn't,
One was alive, one was dead.
I was so hungry to be hungry.
Now I'll never know this way or that way,
Just because of breakfast and being awake.

THE SAD BOY

Ay, his mother was a mad one
And his father was a bad one:
The two begot this sad one.

Alas for the single boot
The Sad Boy pulled out of the rank green pond,
Fishing for happiness
On the gloomy advice
Of a professional lover of small boys.

Pity the lucky Sad Boy
With but a single happy boot
And an extra foot
With no boot for it.

This was how the terrible hopping began
That wore the Sad Boy down
To a single foot
And started the great fright in the province
Where the Sad Boy became half of himself.

Wherever he went thumping and hopping,
Pounding a whole earth into a half-heaven,
Things split all around
Into a left side for the left magic,
Into no side for the missing right boot.

Mercy be to the Sad Boy,
Mercy be to the melancholy folk
On the Sad Boy's right.

It was not for clumsiness
He lost the left boot
And the knowledge of his left side,
But because one awful Sunday
This dear boy dislimbed
Went back to the old pond
To fish up the other boot
And was quickly (being too light for his line)
Fished in.

Gracious how he kicks now—
And the almost-ripples show
Where the Sad Boy went in
And his mad mother
And his bad father after him.

MORTAL

There is a man of me that sows.
There is a woman of me that reaps.
One for good,
And one for fair,
And they cannot find me anywhere.

Father and Mother, shadowy ancestry,
Can you make no more than this of me?

THE QUIDS

The little quids, the monstrous quids,
The everywhere, everything, always quids,
The atoms of the Monoton,
Each turned an essence where it stood,
Ground a gisty dust from its neighbours' edges,
Until a powdery thoughtfall stormed in and out—
The cerebration of a slippery quid enterprise.

Each quid stirred.
The united quids
Waved through a sinuous decision.
The quids, that had never done anything before
But be, be, be, be, be—
The quids resolved to predicate,
To dissipate themselves in grammar.

Oh, the Monoton didn't care,
For whatever they did—
The Monoton's contributing quids—
The Monoton would always remain the same.

A quid here and there gyrated in place-position,
While many turned inside-out for the fun of it.
And a few refused to be anything but
Simple unpredicated copulatives.
Little by little, this commotion of quids,
By ones, by tens, by casual millions,
Squirming within the state of things,
The metaphysical acrobats,
The naked, immaterial quids,
Turned in on themselves
And came out all dressed—
Each similar quid of the inward same,
Each similar quid dressed in a different way,
The quids' idea of a holiday.

The quids could never tell what was happening.
But the Monoton felt itself differently the same
In its different parts.

The silly quids upon their learned exercise
Never knew, could never tell
What their wisdom was about,
What their carnival was like,
Being in, being in, being always in
Where they never could get out
Of the everywhere, everything, always in,
To derive themselves from the Monoton.

ENOUGH

One sleep, one stirring,
Were one life enough
Were they enough one life.

One is so many, so many,
Innumerably, more and more wearily,
Never quite, never quite.

Will beauty, can beauty,
Allay the deficiency?
(Never quite, never quite.)

The lagging, the dying,
The more and more of the many,
The less of the one,
Until the diverse dwindling
Is none:
After the death,
What can go on?

Still the lagging
Of life now less than nothing,
An approaching
More ineffusively
A sum.

ROOM

Whatever is before goes behind.
Each makes room for the next of kind.
The unborn beggars cry 'Unfed'
Until all are born and dead.
Death is the crumb
To which they come;
God the division of it,
The nothing and no more of it
When the procreative doom
Stops making room—
The name of charity
By which to be is not to be.

AFTERNOON

The fever of afternoon
Is called afternoon,
Old sleep uptorn,
Not yet time for night-time,
No other name, for no names
In the afternoon but afternoon.

Love tries to speak but sounds
So close in its own ear.
The clock-ticks hear
The clock-ticks ticking back.
The fever fills where throats show,
But nothing in these horrors moves to swallow
While thirst trails afternoon
To husky sunset.

Evening appears with mouths
When afternoon can talk.
Supper and bed open and close
And love makes thinking dark.
More afternoons divide the night,
New sleep uptorn,
Wakeful suspension between dream and dream—
We never knew how long.
The sun is late by hours of soon and soon—
Then comes the quick fever, called day.
But the slow fever is called afternoon.

NO MORE ARE LOVELY PALACES

No more are lovely palaces
And Taj-Mahal is old.
The listening tenements,
The wakeful entertainments,
Waited wide and many ages
For the spirits of the promises
That more than men would come,
Would come the visitants evoked
By lovely palaces
And such emblazoned places
Men would never light for men.

A little surer now you know
They do not come the way you go.
And better build you and more soberly—
Houses fitter for you to leave
Than to receive
The more than haughty hosts
Of the imperishable ghosts,
That swing death's doors
And suck you into topless palaces,
Untrembling on the blowing bluish spaces,
Where you gasp out your gratitude
And say breathless:
Heaven's hand is not gentle,
The lovely palaces were too lovely,
True lavish is the terrible.

GOAT AND AMALTHEA

I have been assaulted by the moths
Thick in my eyes and throat many a night
When the thought of Amalthea was
Tall flame in the grimy wick.
Then I have blown the light out
And not remembered.
It is better to be dark with Amalthea
Than give her over to the moths and bats.

And Amalthea does not marvel that I can laugh
Or open my eyes to other eyes so brightly
Or strum upon my tongue
My best ballads over so merrily.

She fell of no plague or passion.
She was only swift, so swift, they say,
She ran till she stood still
As a bell swung round more than rings,
And was alive and dead in one day.
When the day went she was dead most fully.
She knew all.

I have come with Amalthea in my veins
Into a fifth season. Time is more than slow.
For winter is over, yet I see no summer.
Now it is always snow.

But I am love of her and I am now.
And she is death of me and she was long ago.
The centuries I weep her bring us nearer.
Yet we can never touch.
For Amalthea in her former time
Shall weep me longer.

THE VIRGIN

My flesh is at a distance from me.
Yet approach and touch it:
It is as near as anyone can come.

This vestiary stuff
Is a true relic,
Though I have never worn it,
Though I shall never be dead.

And the possession?
The violence will be over,
A forgotten passion,
Before I learn of it.

TO A LOVELESS LOVER

1.

How we happened to be both human,
Of the material of the machine . . .

The one original substance is one.
Two is two's destruction.
But love is the single word wherein
The double murder of the machine
Is denied
In one suicide . . .

Long very long ago,
A time unthinkable,
We loved each other.

Greet an old doubt
With contemporary conviction—
Lest going you give me lovelessness
And the accursed courage for a close.

2.

Did I surprise too truly, then,
Your all too prompt anticipation,
Tear down the wall of self,
Expose the terror of fulfilment?

As from a balcony,
Applaud the way I build the wall again.

3.

The requisite spot of anguish having shown
Upon my cheek the growth of the disease
From the internal infection of the bone
To the full epidermal fever, please
Proceed as you intended, in the tone
With which your parting sonnet tried to freeze
My too unliterary passion to stone.

Though love is not yet dead, your lyric crow,
Smelling the near-corruption, may come and perch
In antecedent mourning, not to sing
But consecrate to your pedantic church
His ultra-polite yet energetic wing
That flaps your piety incognito.

4.
The cycle of revenge comes round,
Your expiation ties in me.

Mercy, mercy for me
Who would only suffer,
Who would never sin.
The righteous are transfixed
While sinners are swept round to judgement.
Mercy, mercy for me where I stand
A bigot of forgiveness.

DRUIDA

Above Druida, below Druida,
Round Druida when she loved,
The air and earth,
The grass and clouds,
Were golden, were laden,
Not with love—oh, less ethereal
Her radiation—
But with him heavily.

Her trance of him was timeless.
Her space of him was edgeless.
But meagre was the man,
He took ambition.
He heard a clock,
He saw a road.
When the clock struck,
Where the road began,
He called farewell to Druida.

A hundred huts heard the cry.
The heavy earth, the heavy air,
Lightened, melted.
The man was gone.
Druida laughed.
Follow him, follow him,
A hundred sisters said.

Druida followed.
Not to bless him, not to curse him,
Not to bring back the bridegroom,
But to pass him like a blind bird
Seeing all heaven ahead.

She follows him, she follows him,
A hundred sisters said,
Standing at their doors while the man fled
And Druida smiled along.

Druida found the sky.
Earth was but imagination,
Love but self-alienation,
Man but a lover not love.

She has passed him, she has passed him,
A hundred sisters cried.
And the man turned back.
And a hundred passions welcomed him
In a hundred huts.

BACK TO THE MOTHER BREAST

Back to the mother breast
In another place—
Not for milk, not for rest,
But the embrace
Clean bone
Can give alone.

The cushioning years
Afraid of closer kiss
Put cure of tears
Before analysis;
And the vague infant cheek
Turned away to speak.

Now back to the mother breast,
The later lullaby exploring,
The deep bequest
And franker singing
Out of the part
Where there is no heart.

AS WELL AS ANY OTHER

As well as any other, Erato,
I can dwell separately on what we know
In common secrecy,
And celebrate the old, adoréd rose,
Retell—oh why—how similarly grows
The last leaf of the tree.

But for familiar sense what need can be
Of my most singular device or me,
If homage may be done
(Unless it is agreed we shall not break
The patent silence for mere singing's sake)
As well by anyone?

Mistrust me not, then, if I have begun
Unwontedly and if I seem to shun
Unstrange and much-told ground:
For in peculiar earth alone can I
Construe the word and let the meaning lie
That rarely may be found.

JOHN AND I

Begin the story with a man; curtail
The matter of his hair and hands and eyes.
The simple character will be enough
For bearing out the name—pass by the flesh,
Since this is but a tale and therefore clean
Of the decay that dresses up the soul.
Then tell the wife and woman at one stroke
And let the detail lie uncut upon
The monument of this small artifice.
There was a man to be delivered of
His wife as of a poor witch of the shades
Of plausibility. The unasked help
Of that old fury, accident, sufficed.
She died or was devoured in one swift night
She ripped apart and sewed herself into,
A weighted sack that never bubbled once,
And sank. Perceive him madder than before,
With nothing but a nasty vacancy
In the dark, gangrened spot upon his brain
That she had occupied—repudiation,
But nothing more: an itching, empty sore
That better had been left incurable.
The uselessness of words about this case
Is obvious. The literary end
Establishes a certain calm in us,
If not in him; and he may stop, fall out,
For all we know or care, where we leave off.
And yet, if this is death, how listlessly,
How indecisively, the sentence drops,
And not through pity but embarrassment,
The provocation seeming trivial.

Then strip the narrative of mystery
And let it shiver out the meaning like
A naked foetus parted from its womb:
This way a character becomes a man
Impossible to end in words or their
Equivalent in silence. Therefore find
The fellow a good name. John makes a frame

That any not too fanciful idea
Or man can fit into . . . . And John looked out,
Deduced his world and wisdom from the sins
And freaks of creatures not designedly
Alive, but born just in the course of things;
Construed his house among the others. . . .
He was a man as far as he could see,
And where he could not, I, his chronicler,
Began. The woman, among other things,
Confused the issue—yet it was as bad
After her going, for there seems to be
Nothing for me to talk about. A touch
Of night falls upon both of us. John sleeps,
Or else I sleep, my words obscure my words.
I have not done and yet I can't go on—
The articles that make us two divide us,
I am aware only of certain rules
By which he's rhetoric and I a fool,
The one who sets the problem, frets and loves,
While John evades, equivocates, evades.

There was an insufficiency in me
To which no one but John could minister,
A hunger no mere man could satisfy.
If I infringed upon the laws of art
By making John outlast himself till now,
It was to save him from the consequence
Of his genetic artfulness and falseness—
Defection, malice and oblivion.
The laws of art? Could I not alter them?
The reason I must call the passion dead
Lies in an insufficiency in him
That leaves me stranded in a half-told tale.
His name is cold. Life feels the loss when death
Takes off a man, and not at all the corpse;
And so with John and me. Nor do I weep
Or yet deny, confronted with the shame
Of a but literary authorship,
That John and I are better off like this.

LYING SPYING

(Lying spying what men say of dead men,
What men say of me—
I can't remember anything.
Why can't I remember
What I alive knew of death
I dead know nothing of?)

'Poor John, John, John, John, John,'
Said the parson as he perched
On the sharp left discomfort
Of John John's tombstone—
John, John, John, John, John.

Cobbler on the right
Hammered out the memory
Of the nails of John's soles.
Mercer in the middle
Remembered the measure
Of John's extraordinary shroud.

But no further the parson, the cobbler, the mercer,
Lying spying
In the graveyard,
Where night fell deeper darker,
Dead men mumbled, might be mumbling,
Something secret about life.

Lying spying
John, John, John, John, John,
Parson, cobbler, mercer, parson.

PRISMS

What is beheld through glass seems glass.

The quality of what I am
Encases what I am not,
Smoothes the strange world.
I perceive it slowly,
In my time,
In my material,
As my pride,
As my possession:
The vision is love.

When life crashes like a cracked pane,
Still shall I love
Even the strange dead as the living once.
Death also sees, though distantly,
And I must trust then as now
A prism—of another kind,
Through which one may not put one's hands to touch.

POSTPONEMENT OF SELF

I took another day,
I moved to another city,
I opened a new door to me.
Then again a last night came.
My bed said: 'To sleep and back again?'
I said: 'This time go forward.'

Arriving, arriving, not yet, not yet,
Yet yet arriving, till I am met.
For what would be her disappointment
Coming late ('She did not wait').
I wait. And meet my mother.
Such is accident.
She smiles: long afterwards.
I sulk: long before.
I grow to six.
At six little girls in love with fathers.
He lifts me up.
See. Is this Me?
Is this Me I think
In all the different ways till twenty.
At twenty I say She.
Her face is like a flower.
In a city we have no flower-names, forgive me.
But flower-names not necessary
To diary of identity.

THE LULLABY

Every poor fellow reminds me of my father.
With worse luck than that
He reminds me of my father
With worse luck than he had.
Which means me
Who have better luck than my father had
Because it is worse than bad.

Every fine fellow reminds me of me.
Good luck is hard come by.
It is not that innocency
Of how luck befalls.
It is a bad luck weary,
A worse luck turned into destiny,
A knowledge of bad luck
And with bad luck seamy.

A poor fellow knows a poor fellow.
A fine fellow knows a poor fellow and a fine fellow,
A poor fellow and a poor fellow.
Every poor fellow reminds me of me.
Every fine fellow reminds me of my father.

And it is not to be forgotten:
All luck is luck,
My father's or mine.
He was a poor fellow.
His bad luck was perhaps no luck.
I am a fine fellow.
My good luck is perhaps no luck.
All luck is perhaps no luck.
All luck is luck or perhaps no luck.

For is this a way to divide,
By poorness and fineness,
By pity and pride?
Comparison of luck is how
All babies cry.
Mother! Cease rocking, promising,

Let us all choke
Rather than sob asleep
With pout of luck on every lip
Resentful birth renewing.

HELEN'S BURNING

Her beauty, which we talk of,
Is but half her fate.
All does not come to light
Until the two halves meet
And we are silent
And she speaks,
Her whole fate saying,
She is, she is not, in one breath.

But we tell only half, fear to know all
Lest all should be to tell
And our mouths choke with flame
Of her consuming
And lose the gift of prophecy.

HELEN'S FACES

Bitterly have I been contested for,
Though never have I counted numbers—
They were too many, less than all.
And kindly have I warded off
Contest and bitterness,
Given each a replica of love,
Beguiled them with fine images.

To their hearts they held them.
Her dear face, its explicitness!
Clearly, of all women, the immediate one
To these immediate men.

But the original woman is mythical,
Lies lonely against no heart.
Her eyes are cold, see love far off,
Read no desertion when love removes,
The images out of fashion.

Undreamed of in her many faces
That each kept off the plunderer:
Contest and bitterness never raged round her.

THE TIGER

The tiger in me I know late, not burning bright.
Of such women as I am, they say,
'Woman, many women in one,' winking.
Such women as I say, thinking,
'A procession of one, reiteration
Of blinking eyes and disentangled brains
Measuring their length in love.
Each yard of thought is an embrace.
To these I have charms.
Shame, century creature.'
To myself, hurrying, I whisper,
'The lechery of time greases their eyes.
Lust, earlier than time,
Unwinds their minds.
The green anatomy of desire
Plain as through glass
Quickens as I pass.'

Earlier than lust, not plain,
Behind a darkened face of memory,
My inner animal revives.
Beware, that I am tame.
Beware philosophies
Wherein I yield.

They cage me on three sides.
The fourth is glass.
Not to be image of the beast in me,
I press the tiger forward.
I crash through.
Now we are two.
One rides.

And now I know the tiger late,
And now they pursue:
'A woman in a skin, mad at her heels
With pride, pretending chariot wheels—
Fleeing our learned days,
She reassumes the brute.'

The first of the pursuers found me.
With lady-ears I listened.
'Dear face, to find you here
After such tiger-hunt and pressing of
Thick forest, to find you here
In high house in a jungle,
To brave as any room
The tiger-cave and as in any room
Find woman in the room
With dear face shaking her dress
To wave like any picture queen . . .'
'Dear pursuer, to find me thus
Belies no tiger. The tiger runs and rides,
But the lady is not venturous.
Like any picture queen she hides
And is unhappy in her room,
Covering her eyes against the latest year,
Its learning of old queens,
Its death to queens and pictures,
Its lust of century creatures,
And century creatures as one woman,
Such a woman as I,
Mirage of all green forests—
The colour of the season always
When hope lives of abolished pleasures.'

So to the first pursuer I prolonged
Woman's histories and shames,
And yielded as became a queen
Picture-dreaming in a room
Among silk provinces where pain
Ruined her body without stain—
So white, so out of time, so story-like.
While woman's pride escaped
In tiger stripes.

Hymn to the hostage queen
And her debauched provinces.
Down fell her room,
Down fell her high couches.
The first pursuer rose from his hot cloak.

'Company,' he cried, 'the tiger made magic
While you slept and I dreamt of ravages.
The queen was dust.'
And Queen, Queen, Queen,
Crowded the Captain's brain.
And Queen, Queen, Queen,
Spurred the whole train
With book-thoughts
And exploits of queen's armies
On gold and silver cloth.
Until they stumbled on their eyes,
Read the number of the year,
Remembered the fast tiger.

The tiger recalled man's fear
Of beast, in man-sweat they ran back,
Opened their books at the correct pages.
The chapter closed with queens and shepherdesses.
'Peace to their dim tresses,'
Chanted the pious sages.

And now the tiger in me I knew late.
'O pride,' I comforted, 'rest.
The mischief and the rape
Cannot come through.
We are in the time of never yet
Where bells peal backward,
Peal "forget, forget".'

Here am I found forgotten.
The sun is used. The men are in the book.
I, woman, have removed the window
And read in my high house in the dark,
Sitting long after reading, as before,
Waiting, as in the book, to hear the bell,
Though long since has fallen away the door,
Long since, when like a tiger I was pursued
And the first pursuer, at such and such a date,
Found how the tiger takes the lady
Far away where she is gentle.
In the high forest she is gentle.

She is patient in a high house.
Ah me, ah me, says every lady in the end,
Putting the tiger in its cage
Inside her lofty head.
And weeps reading her own story.
And scarcely knows she weeps,
So loud the tiger roars.
Or thinks to close her eyes,
Though surely she must be sleeping,
To go on without knowing weeping,
Sleeping or not knowing,
Not knowing weeping,
Not knowing sleeping.

THE RUGGED BLACK OF ANGER

The rugged black of anger
Has an uncertain smile-border.
The transition from one kind to another
May be love between neighbour and neighbour;
Or natural death; or discontinuance
Because, so small is space,
The extent of kind must be expressed otherwise;
Or loss of kind when proof of no uniqueness
Confutes the broadening edge and discourages.

Therefore and therefore all things have experience
Of ending and of meeting,
And of ending that much more
As self grows faint of self dissolving
When more is the intenser self
That is another too, or nothing.
And therefore smiles come of least smiling—
The gift of nature to necessity
When relenting grows involuntary.

This is the account of peace,
Why the rugged black of anger
Has an uncertain smile-border,
Why crashing glass does not announce
The monstrous petal-advance of flowers,
Why singleness of heart endures
The mind coupled with other creatures.
Room for no more than love in such dim passages
Where between kinds lie only
Their own uncertain edges.

This such precise division of space
Leaves nothing for walls, nothing but
Weakening of place, gentleness.
The blacker anger, blacker the less
As anger greater, angrier grows;
And least where most,
Where anger and anger meet as two
And share one smile-border
To remain so.

POEMS OF IMMEDIATE OCCASION

ECHOES

1.
Since learning all in such a tremble last night—
Not with my eyes adroit in the dark,
But with my fingers hard with fright,
Astretch to touch a phantom, closing on myself—
I have been smiling.

2.
Mothering innocents to monsters is
Not of fertility but fascination
In women.

3.
It was the beginning of time
When selfhood first stood up in the slime.
It was the beginning of pain
When an angel spoke and was quiet again.

4.
After the count of centuries numbers hang
Heavy over the unnumbered hopes and oppress
The heart each woman stills beneath her dress
Close to the throat, where memory clasps the lace,
An ancient brooch.

5.
It is a mission for men to scare and fly
After the siren luminary, day.
Someone must bide, someone must guard the night.

6.
If there are heroes anywhere
Unarm them quickly and give them
Medals and fine burials
And history to look back on
As weathermen point with pride to rain.

7.
Dire necessity made all,
Made the most frightful first,
Then less and less dire the need
Until in that world horrors were least
And haunting meant never to see ghosts.

8.
Intelligence in ladies and gentlemen
And their children
Draws a broad square of knowledge
With their house walls.
But four corners to contain a square
Yield to an utmost circle—
The garden of the perpendicular is a sphere.

9.
Need for a tragic head,
Though no occasion now to grieve,
In that mere mental time
When tears are thought of and none appear.

10.
The optician, in honour of his trade,
Wore the most perfect spectacles ever made,
Saw his unspectacled mother and father
And all his unspectacled relatives with anger,
On holidays for spite never went home
But put away his spectacles to visit Rome,
And indulged his inherited astigmatism
As the vacation privilege of an optician,
Squinting up at the Cathedral
As the Romans thought cultivated and natural.

11.
'I shall mend it,' I say,
Whenever something breaks,
'By tying the beginning to the end.'
Then with my hands washed clean
And fingers piano-playing

And arms bare to go elbow-in,
I come to an empty table always.
The broken pieces do not wait
On rolling up of sleeves.
I come in late always
Saying, 'I shall mend it.'

    12.
Gently down the incline of the mind
Speeds the flower, the leaf, the time—
All but the fierce name of the plant,
Imperishable matronymic of a species.

    13.
The poppy edifices of sleep,
The monotonous musings of night-breath,
The liquid featureless interior faces,
The shallow terrors, waking never far.

    14.
Love at a sickbed is a long way
And an untastable thing.
It hangs like a sickroom picture
And wears like another's ring.
Then the guarded yawn of pain snaps,
The immeasurable areas of distress
. . . . . . collapse . . .

    15.
. . . cheated history—
Which stealing now has only then
And stealing us has only them.

    16.
Now victory has come of age,
Learned in arts of desolation,
Gifted with death, love of decline,
Hunger of waste and fresh corruption.
And here it softens and laments,
Mourns fallen enemies, kisses the razed cities,
Hovers where sense has been,
In a ravished world, and calls the pities.

17.
Forgive me, giver, if I destroy the gift!
It is so nearly what would please me,
I cannot but perfect it.

18.
'Worthy of a jewel,' they say of beauty,
Uncertain what is beauty
And what the precious thing.

19.
And if occasionally a rhyme appeared,
This was the illness but not the death
So fear-awaited that hope of it
Ailing forgetfulness became.

20.
In short despite of time, that long despite of truth
By all that's false and would be true as true,
Here's truth in time, and false as false,
To say, 'Let truth be so-and-so
In ways so opposite, there's no
Long-short of it to reason more.'

21.
Between the word and the world lie
Fading eternities of soon.

22.
When a dog lying on the flagstones
Gazes into the sea of spring,
The surface of instruction
Does not ripple once:
He watches it too well.

23
Love is very everything, like fire:
Many things burning,
But only one combustion.

24.
My address? At the cafés, cathedrals,
Green fields, marble terminals—
I teem with place.
When? Any moment finds me,
Reiterated morsel
Expanded into space.

25.
Let us seem to speak
Or they will think us dead, revive us.
Nod brightly, Hour.
Rescue us from rescue.

26.
What a tattle-tattle we.
And what a rattle-tattle me.
What a rattle-tattle-tattle-rattle we-me.
What a rattle-tattle.
What a tattle-rattle.
What a we.
What a me.
What a what a
What a
What

HOSPITALITY TO WORDS

The small the far away
The unmeant meanings
Of sincere conversation
Encourage the common brain of talkers
And steady the cup-handles on the table.
Over the rims the drinking eyes
Taste close congratulation
And are satisfied.

Happy room, meal of securities,
The fire distributes feelings,
The cross-beam showers down centuries.
How mad for friendliness
Creep words from where they shiver and starve,
Small and far away in thought,
Untalkative and outcast.

ONE SELF

Under apparel, apparel lies
The recurring body:
O multiple innocence, O fleshfold dress.

One self, one manyness,
Is first confusion, then simplicity.
Smile, death, O simultaneous mouth.
Cease, inner and outer,
Continuous flight and overtaking.

AN AGELESS BROW

This resolve: with trouble's brow
To forswear trouble and keep
A surface innocence and sleep
To smooth the mirror
With never, never,
And now, now.

The image, not yet in recognition, had grace
To be lasting in death's time, to postpone the face
Until the face had gone.
Her regiments sprang up here and fell of peace,
Her banners dropped like birds that had never flown.

And her arrested hand, clasping its open palm,
Pressed on from finger to finger
The stroke withheld from trouble
Till it be only ageless brow,
A renunciatory double
Of itself, a resolve of calm,
Of never, never, and now, now.

THERE IS MUCH AT WORK

There is much at work to make the world
Surer by being more beautiful.
But too many beauties overwhelm the proof.
Too much beauty is Lethe.

The succession of fair things
Delights, does not enlighten.
We still know nothing, nothing.
Beauty will be truth but once.

Exchange the multiplied bewilderment
For a single presentation of fact by fairness;
And the revelation will be instantaneous.
We shall all die quickly.

THE DEFINITION OF LOVE

The definition of love in many languages
Quaintly establishes
Identities of episodes
And makes the parallel
Of myth colloquial.

But, untranslatable,
Love remains
A future in brains.
Speech invents memory
Where there has been
Neither oblivion nor history.
And we remembering forget,
Mistake the future for the past,
Worrying fast
Back to a long ago
Not yet to-morrow.

MANY GENTLEMEN

Many gentlemen there are born not babes.
They will be babes, they will be babes
In the shades.
They will dribble, they will babble,
They will pule in pantomime
Who were not babes in baby time.

Of such infant sorrow
Will they whimper
On Diotima's bosom
In the shades to-morrow:
Many gentlemen, many gentlemen frowning,
But not Socrates simpering among these,
Who was well weaned of her honey
In his prime and needs no pap now,
Having then long with baby eyes
Smiled upward to her learned brow.

THE POETS' CORNER

Soldierly at last, for the lines
Go marching on.
And happily may they rest beyond
Suspicion now, the incomprehensibles—
It was mere loveliness.
And loveliness?
Death has an understanding of it
Loyal to many flags.

SUNDAY

Sky scanned the mind and found behind
Holes in the mind, more mind behind,
Clouds to provide appearances of thought.

'Dear Sister!' it cried,
'One kiss!'
The bland outrage
Spread over both as one,
Whispering 'This is heaven.'

'Oh, no,' said the populations
Getting out of bed into slippers,
'What lovely weather!
To-day is Sunday!'

A PREVIOUS NIGHT

A previous night is now,
Its passion without desire,
In the mind, a commonplace
Of not forgetting,
On the tongue, an automatic sentiment.
The allegiance is: it was so.
The treason: I survive.

I have my history present like this,
As I have my body,
Employ memory like limbs,
Without repine to move away,
Look down, seem where I was.

And of such furious standstill
I may escape at last to when
No previous night is now,
Time having caught up somehow.

THE DEVIL AS FRIEND

Too late for peace
Your peace is ever late,
And farewell and alas,
Outrageous blarneyman
Who hated falsehood
Better than truth loved.
Good-bye, and never greeting.

See how his antics multiply
To this fresh ancient theme—
Ours is the endless judgement-day,
His the corrupt new endless years.

LIFE-SIZE IS TOO LARGE

To the microscopy of thinking small
(To have room enough to think at all)
I said, 'Cramped mirror, faithful constriction,
Break, be large as I.'

Then I heard little leaves in my ears rustling
And a little wind like a leaf blowing
My mind into a corner of my mind,
Where wind over empty ground went blowing
And a large dwarf picked and picked up nothing.

THE MAP OF PLACES

The map of places passes.
The reality of paper tears.
Land and water where they are
Are only where they were
When words read *here* and *here*
Before ships happened there.

Now on naked names feet stand,
No geographies in the hand,
And paper reads anciently,
And ships at sea
Turn round and round.
All is known, all is found.
Death meets itself everywhere.
Holes in maps look through to nowhere.

FOOTFALLING

A modulation is that footfalling.
It says and does not say.
When not walking it is not saying.
When saying it is not walking.
When walking it is not saying.
Between the step and alternation
Breathes the hush of modulation
Which tars all roads
To confiding heels and soles and tiptoes.
Deep from the rostrum of the promenade
The echo-tongued mouth of motion
Rolls its voice,
And the large throat is heard to tremble
While the footfalls shuffle.

It says and does not say.
When the going is gone
There is only fancy.
Every thought sounds like a footfall,
Till a thought like a boot kicks down the wall.

DEATH AS DEATH

To conceive death as death
Is difficulty come by easily,
A blankness fallen among
Images of understanding,
Death like a quick cold hand
On the hot slow head of suicide.
So is it come by easily
For one instant. Then again furnaces
Roar in the ears, then again hell revolves,
And the elastic eye holds paradise
At visible length from blindness,
And dazedly the body echoes
'Like this, like this, like nothing else.'

Like nothing—a similarity
Without resemblance. The prophetic eye,
Closing upon difficulty,
Opens upon comparison,
Halving the actuality
As a gift too plain, for which
Gratitude has no language,
Foresight no vision.

THE TROUBLES OF A BOOK

The trouble of a book is first to be
No thoughts to nobody,
Then to lie as long unwritten
As it will lie unread,
Then to build word for word an author
And occupy his head
Until the head declares vacancy
To make full publication
Of running empty.

The trouble of a book is secondly
To keep awake and ready
And listening like an innkeeper,
Wishing, not wishing for a guest,
Torn between hope of no rest
And hope of rest.
Uncertainly the pages doze
And blink open to passing fingers
With landlord smile, then close.

The trouble of a book is thirdly
To speak its sermon, then look the other way,
Arouse commotion in the margin,
Where tongue meets the eye,
But claim no experience of panic,
No complicity in the outcry.
The ordeal of a book is to give no hint
Of ordeal, to be flat and witless
Of the upright sense of print.

The trouble of a book is chiefly
To be nothing but book outwardly;
To wear binding like binding,
Bury itself in book-death,
Yet to feel all but book;
To breathe live words, yet with the breath
Of letters; to address liveliness
In reading eyes, be answered with
Letters and bookishness.

ELEGY IN A SPIDER'S WEB

What to say when the spider
Say when the spider what
When the spider the spider what
The spider does what
Does does dies does it not
Not live and then not
Legs legs then none
When the spider does dies
Death spider death
Or not the spider or
What to say when
To say always
Death always
The dying of always
Or alive or dead
What to say when I
When I or the spider
No I and I what
Does what does dies
No when the spider dies
Death spider death
Death always I
Death before always
Death after always
Dead or alive
Now and always
What to say always
Now and always
What to say now
Now when the spider
What does the spider
The spider what dies
Dies when then when
Then always death always
The dying of always
Always now I
What to say when I
When I what
When I say

When the spider
When I always
Death always
When death what
Death I says say
Dead spider no matter
How thorough death
Dead or alive
No matter death
How thorough I
What to say when
When who when the spider
When life when space
The dying of oh pity
Poor how thorough dies
No matter reality
Death always
What to say
When who
Death always
When death when the spider
When I who I
What to say when
Now before after always
When then the spider what
Say what when now
Legs legs then none
When the spider
Death spider death
The genii who cannot cease to know
What to say when the spider
When I say
When I or the spider
Dead or alive the dying of
Who cannot cease to know
Who death who I
The spider who when
What to say when
Who cannot cease
Who cannot
Cannot cease

Cease
Cannot
The spider
Death
I
We
The genii
To know
What to say when the
Who cannot
When the spider what
Does what does dies
Death spider death
Who cannot
Death cease death
To know say what
Or not the spider
Or if I say
Or if I do not say
Who cannot cease to know
Who know the genii
Who say the I
Who they we cannot
Death cease death
To know say I
Oh pity poor pretty
How thorough life love
No matter space spider
How horrid reality
What to say when
What when
Who cannot
How cease
The knowing of always
Who these this space
Before after here
Life now my face
The face love the
The legs real when
What time death always
What to say then
What time the spider

THAT ANCIENT LINE

Old Mother Act and her child Fact-of-Act
Lived practically as one,
He so proud of his monomaniac mother,
She so proud of her parthenogenetic son.

After her death he of course
With his looks and education
Lived on the formal compliments
That other phrases paid him;
And had, of his economy, one daughter
Who remarkably resembled
Her paternal and only grandmother.

Indeed, between Act and Matter-of-Fact
Was such consanguineous sympathy
That the disappearance of the matronymic
In the third generation of pure logic
Did not detract from the authority
Of this and later versions
Of the original progenitive argument.

Long flourished that estate
And never died that self-engendering line out.
Scion followed after scion
Until that ancient blood ran nearly thin.
But Verily, In Truth and Beyond Doubt
Renewed the inheritance—and And So On.

OPENING OF EYES

Thought looking out on thought
Makes one an eye.
One is the mind self-blind,
The other is thought gone
To be seen from afar and not known.
Thus is a universe very soon.

The immense surmise swims round and round,
And heads grow wise
Of marking bigness,
And idiot size
Spaces out Nature,

And ears report echoes first,
Then sounds, distinguish words
Of which the sense comes last—
From mouths spring forth vocabularies
As if by charm.
And thus do false horizons claim pride
For distance in the head
The head conceives outside.

Self-wonder, rushing from the eyes,
Returns lesson by lesson.
The all, secret at first,
Now is the knowable,
The view of flesh, mind's muchness.

But what of secretness,
Thought not divided, thinking
A single whole of seeing?
That mind dies ever instantly
Of too plain sight foreseen
Within too suddenly,
While mouthless lips break open
Mutely astonished to rehearse
The unutterable simple verse.

THOUGH IN ONE TIME

Though in one time
Occur such unlike incidents
As my quickening of substance
And yours or yours,
Close questioning of our prompt elements
Tells nothing,
Baffling replies the baffled shrug.
Yet continue the comparison of names
And signs, searching of eyes,
Hands and the blurred records.
A same bewilderment of mind
Marries our proximate occasions,
Yet perhaps no more tokens
Than a colliding of the rapt—
Coincidence precipitate
Of zealous purposes
That for impatience
Left their sealed messages behind.

Then I think these are not lame excuses,
I think we are not much disgraced
In these our second reasons,
In these our new credentials,
By which we justify encounter
With a bewildering accuracy.

ORIGINALLY

Originally being meant
In us no sense of us.
No guiding sense meant
Minds ruled by hearts,
Those brash foreminds
Minds questioning and answered:
'This way, death following.'

Hearts faded, minds knew,
Death led from chaos
Into sense of us,
And no remembrance
Save death behind.

If now seems little known
Of joys of origin,
It is that there were none.

THE WIND SUFFERS

The wind suffers of blowing,
The sea suffers of water,
And fire suffers of burning,
And I of a living name.

As stone suffers of stoniness,
As light of its shiningness,
As birds of their wingedness,
So I of my whoness.

And what the cure of all this?
What the not and not suffering?
What the better and later of this?
What the more me of me?

How for the pain-world to be
More world and no pain?
How for the old rain to fall
More wet and more dry?

How for the wilful blood to run
More salt-red and sweet-white?
And how for me in my actualness
To more shriek and more smile?

By no other miracles,
By the same knowing poison,
By an improved anguish,
By my further dying.

DING-DONGING

With old hours all belfry heads
Are filled, as with thoughts.
With old hours ring the new hours
Between their bells.
And this hour-long ding-donging
So much employs the hour-long silences
That bells hang thinking when not striking,
When striking think of nothing.

Chimes of forgotten hours
More and more are played
While bells stare into space,
And more and more space wears
A look of having heard
But hearing not:
Forgotten hours chime louder
In the meantime, as if always,
And spread ding-donging back
More and more to yesterdays.

YOU OR YOU

How well, you, you resemble!
Yes, you resemble well enough yourself
For me to swear the likeness
Is no other and remarkable
And matchless and so that
I love you therefore.

And all else which is very like,
Perfect counterfeit, pure almost,
Love, high animation, loyal unsameness—
To the end true, unto
Unmasking, self.

I am for you both sharp and dull.
I doubt thoroughly
And thoroughly believe.
I love you doubly,
How well, you, you deceive,
How well, you, you resemble.
I love you therefore.

GROWTH

The change of self in wide address of self
To use of self in the kind wideness
Of sense-experience: this loses,
Though memory has
One lasting integration—
The steady growth of death.

And so the habit of smile alters.
And so the hair in a new parting falls.
Can recognition be
Past loss of hour-by-hour identity?
Where is the self that withered
And the self that froze?
How do the rising days succeed to vacancy?

The days are in a progress,
As death in a steady growth,
From no to no and yes.
And from there to there and here
Needs no more proof or witness
Than the legs that stopped.
And if the legs themselves have doubt,
Self will the progress prove
With progress, the legs will move,
The smile alter, the hair
In a new parting relapse,
And the mind pause upon
A more mature perhaps.

GRACE

This posture and this manner suit
Not that I have an ease in them
But that I have a horror
And so stand well upright—
Lest, should I sit and, flesh-conversing, eat,
I choke upon a piece of my own tongue-meat.

ALL NOTHING, NOTHING

The standing-stillness,
The from foot-to-foot,
Is no real illness,
Is no true fever,
Is no deep shiver;
The slow impatience
Is no sly conscience;
The covered cough bodes nothing,
Nor the covered laugh,
Nor the eye-to-eye shifting
Of the foot-to-foot lifting,
Nor the hands under-over,
Nor the neck and the waist
Twisting loose and then tight,
Right, left and right,
Nor the mind up and down
The long body column
With a know-not-why passion
And a can't-stop motion:
All nothing, nothing.

More death and discomfort
Were it
To walk away.
To fret and fidget
Is the ordinary.
To writhe and wriggle
Is the usual;
To walk away
Were a disgrace,
Were cowardice,
Were malice,
Would leave a mark and space
And were unbeautiful
And vain, oh, it were vain,
For none may walk away—
Who go, they stay,
And this is plain
In being general.

What, is their suspense
Clownish pretence?
What, are their grimaces
Silly-faces
And love of ghastilness? *ghastliness*
What, is their anxiety and want
Teasing and taunt?
This scarcely,
This were a troublesome
Hypocrisy.

No, the twisting does not turn,
The stamping does not steam,
Nor the impatience burn,
Nor the tossing hearts scream,
Nor the bones fall apart
By the tossing of the heart,
Nor the heads roll off
With laugh-cough, laugh-cough,
Nor the backs crack with terror,
Nor the faces make martyr,
Nor love loathe
Nor loathing fondle
Nor pain rebel
Nor pride quarrel
Nor anything stir
In this stirring and standstill
Which is not natural,
Which is not trivial,
Not peaceful, not beautiful,
Altogether unwoeful,
Without significance
Or indeed further sense
Than going and returning
Within one inch,
Than rising and falling
Within one breath,
Than sweltering and shivering
Between one minute and the next
In the most artless
And least purposeful
Possible purpose.

LAST FELLOWS

Who have survived the time extreme,
The breaking, the last knot,
The day to be remembered
Or forgotten and all else forgotten,
These are the derelict, the chosen,
The older than the old,
The sane who know their kind by madness,
By the too sane look.

What is the love between them?
Talk in silence, luck in evil-boding,
Thought endless, speech used,
Fate in their stiff hearts,
The never-to-be-said on their still breaths,
As conversation between angels.

It is a dull bright day,
Clear doom as clouds of fortune.
It is north, south, east, west,
Equator, poles, meridians.
It is a map but no geography.
It is a place but not a space.

Do they sit down to meals,
Stand up to names,
Speak of to-morrow, yesterday, to-day,
Say yes and no and keep a body
To sometimes rest the brain?

They do, and they do not,
However it would please you.
Yours is the dying word and testament,
They do but after come,
Inherit of your havoc.

SEA, FALSE PHILOSOPHY

Foremost of false philosophies,
The sea harangues the daft,
The possessed logicians of romance.
Their swaying gaze, that swaying mass
Embrace in everlasting loss—
Sea is the spurned dust
Sifted with fine renunciation
Into a metaphor,
A slow dilution.

The drifting rhythms mesmerize
The speechless book of dreams.
The lines intone but are not audible.
The course is overtrue and knows
Neither a wreckage nor a sequel.

Optimisms in despair
Embark upon this apathetic frenzy.
Brains baffled in their eyes
Rest on this picture of monotony
And swoon with thanks.
Ah, hearts whole so peculiarly,
Heaven keep you by such argument
Persuaded and unbroken,
Heaven keep you if it can
As visions widen to a watery zero
And prophecy expands into extinction.

BY CRUDE ROTATION

By crude rotation—
It might be as a water-wheel
Is stumbled and the blindfolded ox
Makes forward freshly with each step
Upon the close habitual path—
To my lot fell a blindness
That was but a blindedness,
And then an inexpressive heart,
And next a want I did not know of what
Through blindedness and inexpressiveness
Of heart.

To my lot fell
By trust, false signs, fresh starts,
A slow speed and a heavy reason,
A visibility of blindedness—these thoughts—
And then content, the language of the mind
That knows no way to stop.

Thus turning, the tragedy of selfhood
And self-haunting smooths with turning,
While the worn track records
Another, and one more.

To my lot fell
Such waste and profit,
By crude rotation
Too little, too much,
Vain repetition,
The picture over-like,
Illusion of well-being,
Base lust and tenderness of self.

Fall down, poor beast,
Of poor content.
Fly, wheel, be singular
That in the name of nature
This creaking round spins out.

IT HAS BEEN READ BY ALL

It has been read by all
That a pleasure-party met death
At high speed, and that a child
Before its mother's eyes a corpse reappeared
Instantly following the crash,
And that such a one, held venerable,
Went, like a commoner, mad in a money-rout,
And that the daughter of an earl, consumptive,
Lives by her own labour, a parlour-maid.

A public pain distresses the public epidermis,
A tremor passes as if through the one body—
The one body, cumbersome fond Titaness.

But instantly following the tremor
The reading heart returns to toast,
Having fluttered in self-pity
And felt its beat with curiosity.

SLEEP CONTRAVENED

An hour was taken
To make the day an hour longer.
The longer day increased
In what had been unfinished.
Another hour from sleep was taken,
Till all sleep was contravened,
Yet the day's course
More long and more undone.

And the sleep gone.
And the same day goes on and on,
A mighty day, with sleeplessness
A gradual evening toward soon lying down.

Soon, soon.
And sleep forgotten,
Like: What was birth?
And no death yet, the end so slowly,
We seem departing but we stay.

And if we stay
There will be more to do
And never through though much is through.
For much keeps the eyes so much open,
So much open is so much sleep forgotten,
Sleep forgotten is sleep contravened,
Sleep contravened is so much longer mind,
More thought, more speaking,
Instead of sleep, blinking, blinking,
Blinking upright and with dreams
Same as all usual things,
Usual things same as all dreams.

FINALLY

Finally bigness turned into the sun.
Hotter and hotter then made man.
Bigness reduced itself to someone:
The little giant with the big mind,
The sage who finally.

The big dunce with the little sieve
Whose passion is to sift and sift
Until triumphant he can stand
With an empty sieve in his hand.

WORLD'S END

The tympanum is worn thin.
The iris is become transparent.
The sense has overlasted.
Sense itself is transparent.
Speed has caught up with speed.
Earth rounds out earth.
The mind puts the mind by.
Clear spectacle: where is the eye?

All is lost, no danger
Forces the heroic hand.
No bodies in bodies stand
Oppositely. The complete world
Is likeness in every corner.
The names of contrast fall
Into the widening centre.
A dry sea extends the universal.

No suit and no denial
Disturb the general proof.
Logic has logic, they remain
Locked in each other's arms,
Or were otherwise insane,
With all lost and nothing to prove
That even nothing can live through love.

POEM ONLY

Poem talking silence not dead death
Security not from danger drowning
Only from fear and fearlessness
Lasting weakness stronger than prompt strength

Pale health like tranquil mourning
Mourning nothing or rejoicing
Wholeness without whole
Whole of wholeness

Self-pitiless illumination
A shrunken world no pride no after-shame
Inhospitable welcome deaf the door
To who is not within.

Cruel if kind and kind if cruel
And all if nothing.

RHYTHMS OF LOVE

1.
Woman, reviling term
Of Man unto the female germ,
And man, reproach of Woman
In this colloquy,
Have grown so contrary
That to have love
We must combine chastely next
Among the languages
Where calling is obscene
And words no more than mean.

2.
'Yes!' to you is in the same breath
'No! No!' to Death.
And your 'Yes! Yes!' to me
Is 'No!' to Death once angrily.
The Universe, leaning from a balcony,
Says: 'Death comes home to me
Covered with glory, when with such love.'
But such love turns into another stair.
Death and the Universe are an earlier pair.

3.
Dark image of my mind,
Shadow of my heart,
Second footfall and third
Partner of my doubleness
And fourth of this—
Love stops me short of counting to the end
Where numbers fail and fall to two,
Then one, then nothing, then you.

4.
Our months astonish, as meals come round.
So late! so soon!
We cry waterily like a pair of pigeons
Exclaiming whenever nothing happens
But commotion inwardly irises their bosoms.
And little more we know.

Our mouths open wide, our breath comes quick,
We gape like the first ones
And look to magic.

5.

In these embraces glamour
Comes early and is an early go-er.
After we have fictitiousness
Of our excess
All will be as before.
We shall say: Love is no more
Than waking, smiling,
Forcing out 'good morning',
And were it more it were
Fictitiousness and loving.

6.

You bring me messages
From days and years
In your time-clouded eyes
And I reply to these
And we know nothing of each other
But a habit, and this is ancient.
How we approach is hidden in a dream.
We close our eyes, we clutch at bodies,
We rise at dream's length from each other
And love mysteriously and coldly
Strangers we seem to love by memory.

7.

A brick and mortar motley,
A heart and mind confusion,
Built this Academy
And this Instruction.
We wag to bells
And wear the cap too high,
The gothic Axiom of Joy.
We know which jingling spells
Which understanding, but jingling
Is all our understanding.
Like dunces we still shall kiss
When graduated from love-making.

NEARLY

Nearly expressed obscurity
That never was yet but always
Was to be next and next when
The lapse of to-morrow into yesterday
Should be repaired at least till now,
At least till now, till yesterday—
Nearly recaptured chaos
That truth, as for a second time,
Has not yet fallen or risen to—
What news? And which?
You that never were yet
Or I that never am until?

FAITH UPON THE WATERS

A ghost rose when the waves rose,
When the waves sank stood columnwise
And broken: archaic is
The spirituality of sea,
Water haunted by an imagination
Like fire previously.

More ghost when no ghost,
When the waves explain
Eye to the eye

And dolphins tease,
And the ventriloquist gulls,
Their angular three-element cries.

Fancy ages.
A death-bed restlessness inflames the mind
And a warm mist attacks the face
With mortal premonition.

ADVERTISEMENT

Have arrived at this interrogatory.
Would know, for private information only.
Knowledge informs the what of the what.
For seventy-six years, six months, seventeen days,
Have studied what for what,
Spoken of what to what,
Am now tired of what
And know not what
For all the what have read or written
Since was who.
What is what is what.
That's that. Am no wiser
For all that, for being wise.
Would now know for private information only.
Would like now to know who.
Am who:
Would be obliged to be informed of others.
So far each who whom have encountered
Has been which.
Would be obliged to hear from who are who,
Pleased to meet you, glad to know you.
Have quantity guaranteed self
Willing affiliate with private party.
Will not ask name, publisher, address.
Confidence given and taken free of charge
And treated with the strictest confidence.
Would like to know who's who and who is who.
Respond in person.
Inquire within.
Frankness or secrecy
Need not apply.
No correspondence about what I mean.
No branch establishments.
Am just plain who
Who would respectfully inquire
Thanking you in advance
Who is yours most sincerely
                              who.

DEAR POSSIBLE

Dear possible, and if you drown,
Nothing is lost, unless my empty hands
Claim the conjectured corpse
Of empty water—a legal vengeance
On my own earnestness.

Dear creature of event, and if I wait the clock,
And if the clock be punctual and you late,
Rail against me, my time, my clock,
And rightfully correct me
With wrong, lateness and ill-temper.

Dear scholar of love,
If by your own formula
I open heaven to you
When you knock punctually at the door,
Then you are there, but I where I was.

And I mean that fate in the scales
Is up, down, even, trembling,
Right, wrong, weighing and unweighing,
And I mean that, dear possible,
That fate, that dear fate.

O VOCABLES OF LOVE

O vocables of love,
O zones of dreamt responses
Where wing on wing folds in
The negro centuries of sleep
And the thick lips compress
Compendiums of silence—

Throats claw the mirror of blind triumph,
Eyes pursue sight into the heart of terror.
Call within call
Succumbs to the indistinguishable
Wall within wall
Embracing the last crushed vocable,
The spoken unity of efforts.

O vocables of love,
The end of an end is an echo,
A last cry follows a last cry.
Finality of finality
Is perfection's touch of folly.
Ruin unfolds from ruin.
A remnant breeds a universe of fragment.
Horizons spread intelligibility
And once more it is yesterday.

THROE OF APOCALYPSE

And in that shrill antithesis of calm
The goaded brain is struck with ague,
By a full moon of waste sublimely sweats.

Relent not, divine hatred,
In this convulsive prime.
You are enchanted against death
By that you are but death
And nothing but death can love or know.
Nor yet can mourn, except by mocking,
Crushed zeal, tired verse, bruised decoration,
Or any agony of blemish—
Except by vengeful imitation.

IN NINETEEN TWENTY-SEVEN

1.

In nineteen twenty-seven, in the spring
And opening summer, dull imagination
Stretched the dollish smile of people.
Behind plate-glass the slant deceptive
Of footwear and bright foreign affairs
Dispelled from consciousness those bunions
By which feet limp and nations farce—
O crippled government of leather—
And for a season (night-flies dust the evening)
Deformed necessity had a greening.

Then, where was I, of this time and my own
A double ripeness and perplexity?
Fresh year of time, desire,
Late year of my age, renunciation—
Ill-mated pair, debating if the window
Is worth leaping out of, and by whom.

If this is ghostly?
And in what living knowledge
Do the dressed skeletons walk upright?
They memorize their doings and lace the year
Into their shoes each morning,
Groping their faulty way,
These citizens of habit, by green and pink
In gardens and smiles in shops and offices;
Are no more real than this.

2.

And they are vast preliminaries:
Cohorts of hours marching upon the one
That must reduce and tell them.
Much must pass to be much vain—
Many minor and happy themes
For one unhappy major dissolution.

The calendar and clock have stopped,
But does the year run down in time?

While time goes round? Giddying
With new renewal at each turning?

Thus sooner than it knows narrows
A year a year a year to another.
The season loses count, speeds on.
But I, charmed body of myself,
Am struck with certainty, stop in the street,
Cry 'Now'—and in despair seize love,
A short despair, soon over.
For by now all is history.

Do we not live? We live. And love? We love.
But I? But you? We are but we.
A long table lies between us
Of talk and wood.
The best is to go out.
'Unpleasant weather,' banks and bakers say,
'But fine weather promised for to-morrow.'
To-morrow is when? This question
Turns heaviness of hours into affection:
Home for a place to lean an elbow.

3.

Fierce is unhappiness, a living god
Of impeccable cleanliness and costume.
In his intense name I wear
A brighter colour for the year
And with sharp step I praise him
That unteaches ecstasy and fear.
If I am found eating, loving,
Pleasure-making with the citizens,
These are the vigours learned of newspapers:
By such formalities I inhale
The corrupt oxygen of time
And reconstruct a past in which to wait
While the false curve of motion twitches straight.

Love me not less, next to myself
Most unloyal of the citizens,
That I thus worship with

The hourly population.
For by such looseness
I argue you with my tight conscience
And take you for so long, an empty term,
An irony of dearness.
And this is both love and not love,
And what I pledge both true and not true,
Since I am moved to speak by the season,
Bold and shy speed and recession,
Climax and suspension.

   4.

Had I remained hidden and unmoved,
Who would have carried on this conversation
And at the close remembered the required toast
To the new year and the new deaths?
Oh, let me be choked ceremoniously
With breath and language, if I will,
And make a seemly world of it,
And live, if I will, fingering my fingers
And throwing yesterday in the basket.
I am beset with reasonableness,
Swallow much that I know to be grass,
Tip as earth tips and not from dizziness.
But do not call me false.
What, must I turn shrew
Because I know what I know,
Wipe out the riverfront
Because it stinks of water?
I cannot do what there is not to do.
And what there is to do
Let me do somewhat crookedly,
Lest I speak too plain and everlasting
For such weather-vanes of understanding.

   5.

Therefore, since all is well,
Come you no nearer than the barrel-organ
That I curse off to the next square
And there love, when I hear it not.
For I have a short, kind temper

And would spare while I can.
While the season fades and lasts
I would be old-fashioned with it.
I would be persuaded it is so,
Go mad to see it run, as it were horses,
Then be unmaddened, find it done,
Summon you close, a memory long gone.

So I am human, of much that is no more
Or never was, and in a moment
(I must hurry) it will be nineteen twenty-eight,
An old eternity pleading refutal.

SECOND-DEATH

Far roam the death-faces
From the face-shaped lockets,
The small oval tombs of truth,
In second-death, the portrait sadness.

Long hunger the death-faces to know
Who was once who and hear hello
And be remembered as so-and-so
Where albums keep
Death like a sleep.

First-death, life unlikeness,
Second-death, life-likeness
And portrait sadness,
Continuous hope and haunting,
Reality stricken
With homesickness.

FOR-EVER MORNING

'Time's Conscience!' cried the allerion.
'How great the thrustlecock and thistle,
How small the lily and the lion,
How great and small and equal all,
How one and many, same and sorted,
How not unchanged and not distorted!'

And the money was made of gold,
And the gold was made of money,
And the cause of the quarrel was nothing,
And the arguers stopped counting
At how much, how many, one and plenty,
And peace came and was the same.

If then, if now, then then, now now,
No more and always and thus and so,
To not believe, to not doubt,
To what, to wit, to know and not-know,
To eat evenly of fire and snow,
To talk, loud and soft, to not-talk.

But when was last night?
Oh, just before the cock crew.
And when did the cock crow?
Oh, just after remembrance flew.
And when did remembrance fly?
Oh, just as the chandler sat down to die.

REJOICE, LIARS

Rejoice, the witch of truth has perished
Of her own will—
Falling to earth humanly
And rising in petty pain.

It was the last grandeur,
When the witch crashed
And had a mortal laming.

And quick heart turned to blood
Those fires of speculation
Where she burned long and coldly.

Away, flattery, she has lost pride.
Away, book-love, she has a body.
Away, body-love, she has a death
To be born into, an end to make
Of that eternity and grandeur
In which a legend pines till it comes true—
When fawning devil boasts belief
And the witch, for her own honour,
Takes on substance, shedding phantomness.

BEYOND

Pain is impossible to describe
Pain is the impossibility of describing
Describing what is impossible to describe
Which must be a thing beyond description
Beyond description not to be known
Beyond knowing but not mystery
Not mystery but pain not plain but pain
But pain beyond but here beyond

AND THIS HARD JEALOUSY

And this hard jealousy against me
Of you a not sour advocate—
It means I think a time of when,
A time of not, when sourly
Because of not you plotted sourly
Against—as if against myself,
My not, as if against me.

I think it means.
When with a shade of me
A time of not I spelt
When greedily against a shade
You argued argue,
And this jealousy.

It meant I think I thought it means
A shade that guarded shared myself
To later and with fury fade
Into a hovering time of not.

And this hard jealousy against me
If now a time of when were,
And that hard jealousy against her
When with a shade she spelt.

IN DUE FORM

I do not doubt you.
I know you love me.
It is a fact of your indoor face,
A true fancy of your muscularity.
Your step is confident.
Your look is thorough.
Your stay-beside-me is a pillow
To roll over on
And sleep as on my own upon.

But make me a statement
In due form on endless foolscap
Witnessed before a notary
And sent by post, registered,
To be signed for on receipt
And opened under oath to believe;
An antique paper missing from my strong-box.
A bond to clutch when hail tortures the chimney
And lightning circles redder round the city,
And your brisk step and thorough look
Are gallant but uncircumstantial,
And not mentionable in a doom-book.

ALL THE TIME

By after long appearance
Appears the time the all the time
Name please now you may go.

By after love time and she knows
And he says rose
Unless unless if not.

Or if if sometimes if
How like myself I was
Among the salt and minutes.

CELEBRATION OF FAILURE

Through pain the land of pain,
Through tender exiguity,
Through cruel self-suspicion:
Thus came I to this inch of wholeness.

It was a promise.
After pain, I said,
An inch will be what never a boasted mile.

And haughty judgement,
That frowned upon a faultless plan,
Now smiles upon this crippled execution,
And my dashed beauty praises me.

THEN WHEREFORE DEATH

Death, removal of names, disappearance
Of flesh, furtherance, discrepancy—
Who worships this,
What thing of abased calling
Prays for equality?

Humanity lives by ambition
And by fortune dies:
Commemorative leafiness and intertreeing
Of conversant ranks in death it has;

No death. Then wherefore grief,
Pang of democracy?
Since we do not kill our dead,
But bury?

COME, WORDS, AWAY

Come, words, away from mouths,
Away from tongues in mouths
And reckless hearts in tongues
And mouths in cautious heads—

Come, words, away to where
The meaning is not thickened
With the voice's fretting substance,
Nor look of words is curious
As letters in books staring out
All that man ever thought strange
And laid to sleep on white
Like the archaic manuscript
Of dreams at morning blacked on wonder.

Come, words, away to miracle
More natural than written art.
Tou are surely somewhat devils,
But I know a way to soothe
The whirl of you when speech blasphemes
Against the silent half of language
And, labouring the blab of mouths,
You tempt prolixity to ruin.
It is to fly you home from where
Like stealthy angels you made off once
On errands of uncertain mercy:
To tell with me a story here
Of utmost mercy never squandered
On niggard prayers for eloquence—
The marvelling on man by man.

I know a way, unwild we'll mercy
And spread the largest news
Where never a folded ear dare make
A deaf division of entirety.

That fluent half-a-story
Chatters against this silence
To which, words, come away now

In an all-merciful despite
Of early silvered treason
To the golden all of storying.

We'll begin fully at the noisy end
Where mortal halving tempered mercy
To the shorn utterance of man-sense;
Never more than savageries
Took they from your bounty-book.

Not out of stranger-mouths then
Shall words unwind but from the voice
That haunted there like dumb ghost haunting
Birth prematurely, anxious of death.
Not ours those mouths long-lipped
To falsity and repetition
Whose frenzy you mistook
For loyal prophetic heat
To be improved but in precision.

Come, words, away—
That was an alien vanity,
A rash startling and a preening
That from truth's wakeful sleep parted
When she within her first stirred story-wise,
Thinking what time it was or would be
When voiced illumination spread:
What time, what words, what she then.

Come, words, away,
And tell with me a story here,
Forgetting what's been said already:
That hell of hasty mouths removes
Into a cancelled heaven of mercies
By flight of words back to this plan
Whose grace goes out in utmost rings
To bounds of utmost storyhood.

But never shall truth circle so
Till words prove language is
How words come from far sound away

Through stages of immensity's small
Centering the utter telling
In truth's first soundlessness.

Come, words, away:
I am a conscience of you
Not to be held unanswered past
The perfect number of betrayal.
It is a smarting passion
By which I call—
Wherein the calling's loathsome as
Memory of man-flesh over-fondled
With words like over-gentle hands.
Then come, words, away,
Before lies claim the precedence of sin
And mouldered mouths writhe to outspeak us.

AS TO A FRONTISPIECE

If you will choose the portrait,
I will write the work accordingly.
A German countenance
I could dilate on lengthily,
Punctilio and passion blending
To that slow national degree.

Or, if you wish more brevity
And have the face in mind—
A tidy creature, perhaps American—
I could provide a facile text,
The portrait being like enough
To stand for anyone.

But if you can't make up your mind
What poetry should look like,
What name to call for,
I think I have the very thing
If you can read without a picture
And postpone the frontispiece till later.

That is, as you may guess,
I have a work but, I regret,
No preliminary portrait.
Yet, if you can forgo one,
We may between us illustrate
This subsequent identity.

JEWELS AND AFTER

On the precious verge of danger
Jewels spring up to show the way,
The bejewelled way of danger,
Beautied with inevitability.

After danger the look-back reveals
Jewels only, dangerlessness,
Logic serened, unharshed into
A jewelled and loving progress.

And after danger's goal, what jewels?
Then none except death's plainest,
The unprecious jewels of safety,
As of childhood.

TALE OF MODERNITY

1.

Shakespeare knew Lust by day,
With raw unsleeping eye.
And he cried, 'All but Truth I see,
Therefore Truth is, for Lust alone I see.'

By night Lust most on other men
Its swollen pictures shone.
And the sun brought shame, and they arose
Their hearts night-stained, but faces lustless.

They in the sun to themselves seemed well.
The sun in guise of Truth gave pardon.
Hypocrisy of seeming well
Blamed the sore visions on bed and night.

But Shakespeare knew Lust by day,
By day he saw his night, and he cried,
'O sexual sun, back into my loins,
Be night also, as you are.'

2.

Shakespeare distinguished: earth the obscure,
The sun the bold, the moon the hidden—
The sun speechless, earth a muttering,
The moon a whispering, white, smothered.

Bishop Modernity, to his spent flock cried,
'She is illusion, let her fade.'
And she, illusion and not illusion,
A sapphire being fell to earth, time-struck.

In colour live and liquid and earth-pale,
Never so near she, never so distant.
Never had time been futured so,
All reckoning on one fast page.

Time was a place where earth had been.
The whole past met there, she with it.
Truth seemed love grown cool as a brow,
And young as the moon, grown girl to self.

3.

Bishop Modernity plucked out his heart.
No agony could prove him Christ,
No lust could speak him honest Shakespeare.
A greedy frost filled where had been a heart.

And that disdainful age his flock,
Resolved against the dream-delight
Of soft succession another world to that,
Like women slipping quiet into monk-thoughts,

Went in triumph of mind from the chapel,
Proud interior of voided breast,
To Heaven out, or Hell, or any name
That carnal sanctity bestows.

Home they went to heartless memories of wives
And appetites of whoredoms stilled
In lustful shaking off lust,
Of knowledge-gall, love's maddening part.

4.

Bishop Modernity in the fatal chapel watched
And end-of-time intoned as the Red Mass
Of man's drinking of the blood of man:
In quenched immunity he looked on her

Who from the fallen moon scattered the altar
With thin rays of challenged presence—
The sun put out there, and the lamps of time
Smoking black consternation to new desire.

Then did that devilish chase begin:
Bishop Modernity's heart plucked out
In old desire flew round against and toward her—
And he but shackled mind, to pulpit locked.

Which stirred up Shakespeare from listening tomb,
Who broke the lie and seized the maid, crying,
'Thou Bishop Double-Nothing, chase thy soul—
Till then she's ghost with me thy ghostly whole!'

MIDSUMMER DUET*

First Voice
    O think what joy that now
    Have burst the pent grenades of summer
    And out sprung all the angry hordes
    To be but stuttering storm of bees
    On lisping swoon of flowers—
    That such winged agitation
    From midge to nightingale astir
    These lesser plagues of sting and song
    But looses on the world, our world.

    O think what peace that now
    Our roads from house to sea go strewn
    With fast fatigue—time's burning footsounds,
    Devilish in our winter ears,
    Cooled to a timeless standstill
    As ourselves from house to sea we move
    Unmoving, on dumb shores to pledge
    New disbelief in ills to come
    More monstrous than the old extremes.

Second Voice
    And what regret that now
    The dog-star has accomplished wholly
    That promise April hinted with
    Faint blossom on her hungry branches,
    And pallid hedgerow shoots?
    Exuberance so luscious
    Of fruit and sappy briar
    Disgusts: midsummer's passion chokes
    'No more!'—a trencher heaped too high.

    And O what dearth that now
    We have sufficient dwelling here
    Immune to hopes gigantical
    That once found lodgement in our heart.
    What if less shrewd we were

*The Second Voice is Robert Graves. See appendix.

And the Dog's mad tooth evaded not—
But quick, the sweet froth on our lips,
Reached at fulfilments whose remove
Gave muscle to our faith at least?

First Voice
Let prophecy now cease
In that from mothering omens came
Neither the early dragon nor the late
To startle sleeping errantries
Or blaze unthinkable futures.
The births have not been strange enough;
Half-pestilential miseries
At ripeness failed of horrid splendour.
Our doomsday is a rabbit-age
Lost in the sleeve of expectation.

Let winter be less sharp
In that the heats of purpose
Have winter foreflight in their wings,
Shaking a frostiness of thought
Over those aestive fancies
Which now so inwardly belie
(Their fury tepid to our minds)
The outward boast of season—
We need not press the cold this year
Since warmth has grown so honest.

Second Voice
Let talk of wonders cease
Now that outlandish realms can hold
No prodigies so marvellous as once
The ten-year-lost adventurer
Would stretch our usual gaze with.
The golden apple's rind offends
Our parks, and dew-lapped mountaineers
Unbull themselves by common physic.
There comes no news can take us from
Loyalty to this latter sameness.

Let the bold calendar
Too garrulous in counting

Fortunes of solar accident
Weary, and festive pipes be soft.
Madness rings not so far now
Around the trysting-oak of time;
Midsummer's gentler by the touch
Of other tragic pleasures.
We need not write so large this year
The dances or the dirges.

First Voice
But what, my friend, of love—
If limbs revive to overtake
The backward miles that memory
Tracks in corporeal chaos?
Shall you against the lull of censoring mind
Not let the bones of nature run
On fleshlorn errands, journey-proud—
If ghosts go rattling after kisses,
Shall your firmed mouth not quiver with
Desires it once spoke beauty by?

And what of beauty, friend—
If eyes constrict to clear our world
Of doubt-flung sights and ether's phantom spaces
Cobwebbed where miserly conceit
Hoarded confusion like infinity?
If vision has horizon now,
Shall you not vex the tyrant eyes
To pity, pleading blindness?

Second Voice
But what, my friend, of death,
That has the dark sense and the bright,
Illumes the sombre hour of thought,
Fetches the flurry of bat-souls?
Shall you not at this shriven perfect watch
Survey my death-selves with a frown
And scold that I am not more calm?
Shall you not on our linking wisdoms
Loathe the swart shapes I living wear
In being dead, yet not a corpse?

And what of jest and play-
If caution against waggishness
(Lest I look backward) makes my mood too canting?
Shall you not mock my pious ways,
Finding in gloom no certain grace or troth,
And raise from moony regions of your smile
Light spirits, nimbler on the toe,
Which nothing are—I no one?

First Voice
Suppose the cock were not to crow
At whitening of night
To warn that once again
The spectrum of incongruence
Will reasonably unfold
From day's indulgent prism?

Second Voice
Suppose the owl were not to hoot
At deepening of sleep
To warn that once again
The gospel of oblivion
Will pompously be droned
From pulpit-tops of dream?

First Voice
And shall the world our world have end
In miracles of general palsy,
Abject apocalyptic trances
Wherein creature and element
Surrender being in a God-gasp?

Both Voices
Or shall the world our world renew
At worn midsummer's temporal ailing,
Marshal the season which senescence
Proclaimed winter but we now know
For the first nip of mind's hereafter?

POEMS OF FINAL OCCASION

AS MANY QUESTIONS AS ANSWERS

What is to start?
It is to have feet to start with.
What is to end?
It is to have nothing to start again with,
And not to wish.

What is to see?
It is to know in part.
What is to speak?
It is to add part to part
And make a whole
Of much or little.
What is to whisper?
It is to make soft
The greed of speaking faster
Than is substance for.
What is to cry out?
It is to make gigantic
Where speaking cannot last long.

What is to be?
It is to bear a name.
What is to die?
It is to be name only.
And what is to be born?
It is to choose the enemy self
To learn impossibility from.
And what is to have hope?
Is it to choose a god weaker than self,
And pray for compliments?

What is to ask?
It is to find an answer.
What is to answer?
Is it to find a question?

THE JUDGEMENT

The judgement is prepared.
In every respect it is exact and just.
Then why no doom,
Why no deliverance?

The judgement is prepared,
It was prepared,
It never failed to be,
Should ever the rightful cause
Speak at the rightful bar:
A coincidence that has not yet astounded,
Or one so close that it did not astound—
And properly now afterwards
Runs on as now before.

And properly some in agitation go,
As if the very end were,
And some in dullard peace,
As if it ever had been,
And some in artfulness,
As if it had or had not,
Both and either, which or which.
And properly, however—
The judgement being fixed
In every multiplied respect,
And full in every separate article,
Though silent with unhurriedness
And disregard of lateness.

AND I

And I,
And do I ask,
How long this pain?
Do I not show myself in every way
To be happy in what most ravages?

When I have grown old in these delights,
Then usedness and not exclaiming
May well seem unenthusiasm.

But now, in what am I remiss?
Wherein do I prefer
The better to the worse?

I will tell you.
There is a passing fault in her:
To be mild in my very fury.
And 'Beloved' she is called,
And pain I hunt alone
While she hangs back to smile,
Letting flattery crowd her round—
As if I hunted insult not true love.

But how may I be hated
Unto true love's all of me?
I will tell you.
The fury will grow into calm
As I grow into her
And, smiling always,
She looks serenely on their death-struggle,
Having looked serenely on mine.

EARTH

Have no wide fears for Earth:
Its universal name is 'Nowhere'.
If it is Earth to you, that is your secret.
The outer records leave off there,
And you may write it as it seems,
And as it seems, it is,
A seeming stillness
Amidst seeming speed.

Heavens unseen, or only seen,
Dark or bright space, unearthly space,
Is a time before Earth was
From which you inward move
Toward perfect now.

Almost the place it is not yet,
Potential here of everywhere—
Have no wide fears for it:
Its destiny is simple,
To be further what it will be.

Earth is your heart
Which has become your mind
But still beats ignorance
Of all it knows—
As miles deny the compact present
Whose self-mistrusting past they are.
Have no wide fears for Earth:
Destruction only on wide fears shall fall.

REGRET OF WAR WAYS

Can truth lose charm,
Can love turn back to history?
The faithful follow with sad eyes
The retreat of the old Enemy.

Peace tastes as if defeat
In those battle-fed mouths
Which long no other glut knew
Than banquets to the brave.

Vanished the hosts of lies
That by the gracious standard
They hotly persecuted
With righteous war wraths.

And, loyal to vexedness,
They fret away the sweetened light,
Mourning the bitterness and flash
As ghosts the living mourn.

ALL THINGS

All things that wake enjoy the sun—
All things but one—
All things except the sun—
The sun because the sun.

An observation of my girlhood.
I now speak less equivocally
And yet more guardedly.

All things that wake enjoy the sun—
All things but one—
All things except the sun—
The sun because
All things once sun were
Which more and more was
The pride that could not be
Except looked back on
By all things become
One, one and one
Unto death's long precision.

All things that wake enjoy the sun.
All things remember not having been,
When waking was but sun to be,
And sleeping was but sun to be,
When life was life alone once—
Deathless, all-instantaneous,
Begun and done in one
Impossibility of being sun,
Death's too proud enemy—
All things enjoy to watch
The pride that could not be,
The largeness against death—
All things enjoy to watch this
From death where life is
As lasting as it little is.

An observation of my—
What shall I call such patience
To look back on nature,
Having already looked enough
To know the sun it is which was,
And the sun again which was not,
By nights removed from days,
By nights and days, by souls
Like little suns away toward
Dreams of pride that could not be—
What shall I call such patience—
An observation of my agedness—
Death's long precision while
All things undo themselves
From sunhood, living glory
That never, never was—
Because the sun.

FURTHER DETAILS

The reward of curiosity
In such as you are
(Statisticians of doubt)
Is increased cause for curiosity,
And the punishment thereof,
To be not a cat.

I shall inform you truthfully,
And you will hear philosophically,
And more words will be required,
And you shall have them.

There is no end of information
Where there is no end of intelligence
By which to comprehend
Always somewhat.

As through a stained-glass vision
The simple instantaneous light
Is gradual and shy as God.

That is, as much remains to be described
As you have ear for.
And you have not only a live ear
But an immortal mind.

Assuming by your finical attention
That you allow the whole and ask
A mere enumeration of parts,
I shall avoid all argument.
In the general thing, we agree,
In the particulars you are well-disposed.

I shall pay you the humane compliment
Of not beginning at the beginning—
Which is the procedure with cats,
That love to start with nothing
And start again of sudden ending.

May you be long in dying.
Is this not your wish?

THE WAY IT IS

It falls to an idiot to talk wisely.
It falls to a sot to wear beauty.
It falls to many to be blessed
In their shortcomings,
As to the common brute it falls
To see real miracles
And howl with irksome joy.

Many are the confusions that fall,
Many are the inspired ones.
Much is there indeed contrary,
Much is there indeed wonderful.
A most improbable one it takes
To tell what is so,
And the strangest creature of all
To be natural.

AND A DAY

The course of a day is never steady.
The hours experiment with pain and pleasure.
By bedtime all you know is giddiness.
But how long is a day?
Some say as long as love.
But love leaves off early,
Before to-morrow and death set in.
How long has day on day been?
Some say for ever.
But starting from when?

From no sooner than first when
Eyes opened far and saw not all—
From no later than last when
Was time for no more than a day,
A day of guessing:
How long is it permitted
So little done so much to call?

THE FATES AND THE MOTHERS

We, the befallen fates,
We are known and necessitous
To all but the children.
And to them we are words:
We are death, not befallen.
We are justice, not swift.
We are knowledge, not ominous.

And their mother is a meanwhile.
She teaches them the game Self,
How to spin out suspense
By a winner and a next game:
While we, the fates to befall,
Keep our same watch of nearness
And unpredictableness.

To the children is given a mother,
To make them strong in days.
To the mother is given a dark spirit—
He brings the nights on.
From long time to long hell
Runs the story delaying
Death, the true story.

To the mother is given a lover—
Time gives the demon, Future.
But the father is the immediate
Angel of impatience.
Her very womb is a man,
And she but a meanwhile.

And the children are but a never.
And we are but the present
From which date back all deaths
To the past of all meanwhiles—
An order of shortcoming
Rising toward an ebb
Like children agedly
Prolonging childhood.

WHO

But whose house or head
Or intimate or ruling presence?
Am I by a ticket of identity,
Like any other lifetime?
But suppose no house or head
Or actuality called mine?
Then am I by a broomstick
As when I rode and was not,
Unlike any other lifetime.

The answer concerns you, I think,
Your prosperity, not mine.
When you could spare me but a broomstick,
You were but a poor world
That must grudge me even a broomstick.
Now you are bolder to possess yourselves,
And I am nearly what I am,
As nearly as I may be
In a generous world of others.

CYCLES OF STRANGENESS

When a tree falls
A tree only dies only.
When a rock crumbles
Rock only dies not only.
When a man dies
Man dies:
It is death indeed.
No further the change
From sea or tree
To rock or man
Who changes all to man
But may not man change
Without death indeed.
For later than himself
Comes God which is not
Save as death tarries
Or as woman pities.
Think you this strange?
But think you not woman strange,
And strange as death indeed,
Stranger than God-you?

But to change to flies—
They which so prettily annoy
And with subdued regret
See themselves scarcely killed,
Scarcely alive, scarcely dead.
Or of moths, how if turned outdoors
Next morning with goodbye,
A gratitude beyond their will
Humanizes the unasked release,
And an emotion reels away.
Such insincere hysterias
Or terrorless philosophies
Show nature's suave proficiency in man.
Have you not seen swallows
By the sea flash themselves
High and down more knowingly

Than even the hyperbolic air
Can render bird-veritable?

But suppose in that same sea
A man turns human-hearted
And—as an angel walking earth
In heavenly difference from once mortal gait
Might in a sudden doubt of self
Be man and instantly a corpse
Inhuman, nature's meanest same—
Dives into languid foretime
To be connatural with fish:
That's drowning, and a fish
A better man, gliding like man
Manwards, and with mournful fins,
Lest uncommemorated pass
The near-strange funerals of flies.

THE TIME BENEATH

In the premortuary tomb
Of ancient time—
Who does not lie there,
A mummy not yet born?
Who does not lie there,
Who lives?
Except mock-creatures in wild numbers
The upper air usurping
While the great dead still sleep?

But when the great dead at last live,
What are those deep worlds then?
When beauty rises from the blackened queens
And the lachrymatory vessels sparkle
With tears from unbound eyes
That grieve sincerely how they lay
Long closed?

They are the pit of future then,
Where cautious souls that never risked name
Lie down in ghastly triumph of will
And dream of grandeur never lost
To the ancient test of death.

THE FACT

While discovery is the fact,
Sea-skill and the way to find,
Flee, land, more inland,
Even to the devil's bosom, loneliness.

Which cannot comfort,
But which cannot give a foreign name
Or make you other than desolate.

Yet be not undiscoverable,
Except where land seen is mere sailor's fancy,
Not native strangeness.

For if you be a true unknown,
Discovery must fade into you
And the foreign name translate,

And the discoverer succeed the devil,
Even unto loneliness—
To comfort by it,
By it call you known.

SCORNFUL OR FOND INFINITY

Greater is to lesser
As many is to one—
Breaths of breath.

An infinity of lack describes
The indescribable moment of enough.
And this is not comparison,
Only a proved equality
Of much and little.

Nor even singleness
Impossible to sum,
Unless infinity but scorn is
Rather than to add up slowly
The one and one and one
That singleness of one makes millionish—
Unless infinity is only time
And thinks the moment to outnumber
Which weightless keeps the scales
In such eternal balance of
Unnumbered one against
The moment upon moment that bears down,
In mathematical spite
Or fond amazement, the other way.

THE COURTESIES OF AUTHORSHIP

Now that you have read of,
You will want to see.
I can only take you to the spot
And let you not see.
Then you may choose freely
Between my book and your eye.
You will undoubtedly prefer your eye,
To not see for yourself.
I shall be delighted to withdraw my book
In favour of your however blind eye.
But I will not withdraw my book
In favour of any words of yours,
In favour of a time-tongued eloquence.
This may be yet an early hour for seeing,
But it is a late hour for telling of,
And I will not be indistinct
That the confounded may distribute
Confusion like a cheaper gold.

Not even the insensible shroud
Can money of such coining buy you.
Loud naked fools you'll go to death,
Flying the rags of shamelessness
To advertise your faith in gifts.
You'll call the same large wants,
And still the same large courtesies
Between the author and the reader
Shall perfectly adjudicate,
And the writing of the book suffice
To give to those who do not read
A thank-you for such proof of need.

THEN FOLLOWS

Then follows a description
Of an interval called death
By the living.
But I shall speak of it
As of brief illness.
For it lasted only
From being not ill
To being not ill.

It came about by chance—
I met God.
'What,' he said, 'you already?'
'What,' I said, 'you still?'
He apologized and I apologized.
'I thought I was alone,' he said.
'Are you displeased?' I said.
'I suppose I should not be,' he said.
A dove hopped out of his sleeve
And muted well in his palm.
Frowning, he wrung its neck.
'Are there any more of you?' he said,
Tears in his eyes, but politely.
'As many as you care to meet,' I said.
Tears falling, he said politely,
'I can't wait, but remember me to them.'

Here was an awkward moment
Worthy of my awkwardness at last.

A Prince once kissed my cheek, saying,
'Accept the only homage possible
From a vulgarian.'
And I did not protest.
But that was in a dream,
And the fellow only democratic-royal.
This was a more far-reaching
Crisis of deportment,
And I am describing it
Without lightness or guile.

Indeed, my manner at the time
Was my manner now.

Then God said,
'I suppose I must be going.'
I said, not impolitely,
'I suppose you must.'
Then follows a description
Of this brief illness—
Not to seem to be saying idly,
'I am not ill,' which of course you knew.

Yes, there has been an interval
Generally described as death.
Thank you, I am now as I was.
Perhaps you are not really interested,
Since it was really only a brief illness.
But I think it right to tell you
That nothing worse can happen now—
It was the worst, and thank you.
Then follows the old routine
Of being, thank you, not ill.
Perhaps indeed, like God,
You had better be going,
Instead of tears, a bored expression,
It having been made clear to you
That no more news will come from me
Than that I am, as usual, not ill.
Think of me, if you like, as dead,
And no description following.

And if this seems too final,
Was not such our common object,
Although our meanings differ somewhat?
You were listening for a something
And I have uttered you a something
That further listening of yours
And further uttering of mine
Could not make mean to you
More than you wished to know
Of what comes after—
Not more than: here ends.

My progress is not, like yours,,
Toward a last page.
Should we not therefore part
When you at book's end tire
And make as if not to turn over?
For my progress is toward
To be as usual not ill.
A description having followed
Of an interval called death
By the living,
Perhaps you had better be going,
Since yours is not my way of ending.
There is always difference somewhat
When meanings differ somewhat.

You would continue to wear
A look of waiting for
A chapter you would never read,
And I to seem only standing still
Between furthermore and furthermore.
You would complain much of the weather,
That everybody's scapegoat.

What, you may say,
Have I grown cold to you,
Have we not been friends since—
Yes, since the first page.
No, I am as usual,
Sensitive to the weather like you,
Mysterious of what next.
But you are growing different,
Restless to leave off.
By your time, the same as mine
When once we had one clock,
Patience is threadbare.
By mine, I am as usual not ill
After a brief illness,
An interval upon which
Time's unanimity divides.

You wished to learn courage
For a certain destined major event
By flattering me to go first.
But, being not of your long ranks
Of hour-strung distances from death,
I have been here always
And so have only to report
A certain chance minor event
That fell to me by chance alone
Of walking into where I was.
At least, I cannot teach you courage,
Which comes by the grace of God
When patience goes.
I am not God.
True, we have met,
Which seems to clinch identity,
Since God like me went first.
But that will always be
To-morrow to God,
As it has always been
A yesterday to me
Between to-day and to-day.

And now I shall be frank,
Since we are about to part.
The interval, a description of which
Followed your desire for one,
Was a description merely.
I have not, of course, met God,
Or been ill, either long or briefly.
What, I have lied to you!
Yes, I have lied.
And, having had your lie,
Perhaps now you had better be going.
Then follows all that has preceded.
No, I have not met God.
Or, if you insist upon the truth,
I have so met him.
And what now, having had your truth?
Perhaps you will not be going.

Clearly some one had better be going.
I, for one, shall continue where I am.
God, I believe, will live on memories,
You, I believe, each on forgetfulness.
Perhaps we had all better be going.
Perhaps I have not made myself plain.

Ah, the pity of it for me,
To be by name a poet,
To make myself plain,
And yet not to make myself plain
Because of being by name a poet,
A creature neither man nor God.
Yes, such a creature by name,
But featured like both man and God—
Like God, a creature of mind,
Like man, a creature of mouth.
Ah, the pity of it,
To be a mouth and mind,
But dimly named,
As if this third where two contended
Were murky mumbling peace thereof.

And ah, the pity of it for you,
To be by feature man or God,
And poet by name only to claim
That beyond man and God lies only
What only might a poet only claim,
Being creature of name only.
Ah, the pity of it for us all.
Perhaps we had better not be going.
Perhaps I had better write another poem
And, if necessary, yet another,
Until a description follows
Of an interval after which
There's no return to time again,
To paradoxing truth between
The two same poles of logic,
Each lengthened out from each—
After which no description,

Except as words from human habit
Divide their meaning from themselves,
Draw round the infinite centre
A shy circumference of books.

MEANWHILE

Equally dismal rain and sunshine—
If the hours are hours of waiting
To say for certain: you, and I.
Happily there is this sure we,
Happily there is this love,
This chosen ambiguity,
Until the weather knows its mind.

Meanwhile this to-day,
To succeed never beyond the weather—
Until it climates death,
That double clarity
Of difference.

AUTOBIOGRAPHY OF THE PRESENT

Whole is by breaking and by mending.
The body is a day of ruin,
The mind, a moment of repair.
A day is not a day of mind
Until all lifetime is repaired despair.

To break, to day-long die,
To be not yet nor yet
Until dreaming is of having been,
Until dreaming is of having dreamed—
How in those days—how fast—
How fast we seemed to dream—
How fast we talked—how lost—
How lost the words until—
Until the pen ran down
To this awakened not forgetting.

But in those days always
How forgotten—and to say over—
To say now and now—
Or in a letter to say over soon—

Do you remember now, John,
Our suburban conversation once of bees?
Neatly at breakfast we of bees,
A retired talk or walk
Among the outskirts of profundity?
Slowly of honeycombs and swarms
And angry queens we?

But slowly bees is briefest dozing.
Between the country and the city,
Between sound sleep and walking,
More gives to pause and buzz than bees
A book about—and by—
Nor need tastes differ but to pause.

Do you remember now, John,
Do you remember my friend John

Who had a lordly not-to-hurry eye,
A very previous eye
In an advanced socket?

Yes, I remember.
And I remember my friend Norman,
Though by frugality of will
He shall arrive punctually to-morrow
When even the cinematograph of time
Has ceased to advertise to-day—
Though I remember.

Yes, she remembers all that seemed,
All that was like enough to now
To make a then as actual as then,
To make a now that succeeds only
By a more close resemblance to itself.

CARE IN CALLING

Who, then, is child,
And who is man?
Child is the first man still,
Man is the last man not yet.
And the first man is seed,
And the last man is seed silenced.
The last man is womanish:
Woman which before man
Was silent word alone—
That breeding silence she.

Let it be a care
How man or child
Be called man or child,
Or woman, woman.

INTELLIGENT PRAYER

A star by world-connivance seems part of the hill.
A tree not by mere folly stands up creature-like.
Such painstaking acts of intelligence widely accost.
It is a compliment to nature to perceive them.
The mind is already full, near overflowing.
It is no mean compliment to stop and smile
And verse such imperfections perfectwise.

Lyricism has had humane use in time:
To allow the bragging population to recover
From the exertion of behaving intelligently—
By commending the intelligence
Of nature's stupid also prone to think,
Though they have only leaves for minds, or less.

You are, however, no longer a population.
If you are tired—good. This is a charm against
The brisk philosophies that conjure wisdoms
Satisfying to the ambition of time
To hold up its head among other times, other wisdoms.

You are, however, no longer an unknown number.
The calculation is completed, there now remains but
The copying of the determined selves
Into a closed gazette of memories
Where in the chary happiness of the dead
You lay you down, to think no more again.

If you are tired—good. Tiredness is to pray to death,
That it shall think for you when speechlessness
Tells how you lie so full of understanding each,
Sorry of life in his own grave of mind each.

CURE OF IGNORANCE

The dogs still bark,
And something is not clear.
From ignorance dogs barked always.

How to enlighten them?
There are no dogs now—
They do but bark.

What is not clear is what is clear.
Dogs have the scent,
Yet nothing runs like prey.

Shall we seem to disappear
Until the dogs stop barking?
There is no other way to explain.

WITH THE FACE

With the face goes a mirror
As with the mind a world.
Likeness tells the doubting eye
That strangeness is not strange.
At an early hour and knowledge
Identity not yet familiar
Looks back upon itself from later,
And seems itself.

To-day seems now.
With reality-to-be goes time.
With the mind goes a world.
With the heart goes a weather.
With the face goes a mirror
As with the body a fear.
Young self goes staring to the wall
Where dumb futurity speaks calm,
And between then and then
Forebeing grows of age.

The mirror mixes with the eye.
Soon will it be the very eye.
Soon will the eye that was
The very mirror be.
Death, the final image, will shine
Transparently not otherwise
Than as the dark sun described
With such faint brightnesses.

THE BIOGRAPHY OF A MYTH

1.

The first showing of herself was foolish,
And to fools: creature of other sense
She first moved into being, singing high
As fools admire, and delivering beauty
Like a three-hour entertainment
In a sweating playhouse, from a draughty stage.
Then they went home, grinning at otherness,
And she to lour in shame, out of which night
She rose unseen, absent in counted presence:
The one more wanting from the swollen streets
And overpeopled books and commonrooms.
And first she was a fool astounding fools,
Who gaped a wonder that forgot itself
So soon their jaws snapped shut on the next meal.
And then she called against herself so other,
The words drooping soft until alone she was,
Whispering. 'She whom they did not see though saw
Myself now am, hidden all away in her
Inward from her confiding mouth and face
To deep discretion, this other-person mind.'

2.

Here of too sudden being she made a patience
And bided in herself, from her flesh far
By days of outer damage that she felt not,
Yet learned of body and of pain from.
Here she grew dead, like a shaped no-one wandered
Among the shapeless someones of a past
That could prediction of her only argue
By the slow logic of time-making fear.
She grew secret, her body told not of her.
Invisibly she spoke, mutely she walked—
Known of but unknown, an imminence deferred.
In this pale state she had prediction of self.
In this pale year one had close panic of her
Who had been dead as many times before
As hope of her refused all other hope.
And he was dead greatly, he lived and knew her.

3.

Now following fails, and she now never was,
And he who reached her side alive, a tale.
Nor any more in that once foolish world
Does aught lack or a chair or thought seem empty.
It is a world that was and leads not elsewhere.
Following fails. If she now where he found her
An earthly voice and posture by his side seems,
Then are they still not joined, not yet that world is
Where she the world, and he inhabiting
Like peace unto himself, no more to wait
And change and wait and change, till dead enough.
A world of death after a world of time comes,
But history goes no further than history—
The final scene reads dim, its sense senseless.
And mythically she haunts, a proven truth
So long she is no measured, proven seeming,
But, soon as real, to vanish of being real,
And beyond passion as beyond seeming dwell.
For they who loved and reasoned long and fine
Meant only to contrive with shortest arts
An afterwards to hold to-morrow off—
As a far-fancied god protects from fancy.
And if she came she went, and gave them back
Their faith, a legal gospel like false oaths
Adhered to with the loyalty of words
That do not pledge the mind to believe itself.

THE WIND, THE CLOCK, THE WE

The wind has at last got into the clock—
Every minute for itself.
There's no more sixty,
There's no more twelve,
It's as late as it's early.

The rain has washed out the numbers.
The trees don't care what happens.
Time has become a landscape
Of suicidal leaves and stoic branches—
Unpainted as fast as painted.
Or perhaps that's too much to say,
With the clock devouring itself
And the minutes given leave to die.

The sea's no picture at all.
To sea, then: that's time now,
And every mortal heart's a sailor
Sworn to vengeance on the wind,
To hurl life back into the thin teeth
Out of which first it whistled,
An idiotic defiance of it knew not what
Screeching round the studying clock.

Now there's neither ticking nor blowing.
The ship has gone down with its men,
The sea with the ship, the wind with the sea.
The wind at last got into the clock,
The clock at last got into the wind,
The world at last got out of itself.

At last we can make sense, you and I,
You lone survivors on paper,
The wind's boldness and the clock's care
Become a voiceless language,
And I the story hushed in it—
Is more to say of me?
Do I say more than self-choked falsity

Can repeat word for word after me,
The script not altered by a breath
Of perhaps meaning otherwise?

FROM LATER TO EARLIER

The table is laid,
The bed is made,
Breakfast and night
Make the day seem right.

Then right grows wrong as the day hardens into time.
For truth is not so full of right and argument,
So much, so long, so full of solid furnitures.
The place that earth imagines of is not so earth-like.
The death to know is not so dead, so full of corpses.
A self-judged universe of fact at evening calls
Good-bye to time—but morning shows another one.
When yesterday shall seem to-morrow, that's the true lie.
And that which will be was, as many days ago
As Now is repetitions of itself.
For every certain meal, there's a lost appetite
For hunger's progress. For every sitting late
To make the mind more wise, wisdom by so much
Is finally unaged, returned to simpleness
By knowing all it can, and smiling 'wise enough'.

The next world is
As near to this
As time is similar
To truth familiar.

RESPECT FOR THE DEAD

For they are dead.
They have learned to be truthful.
Respect for the truthfulness of the dead.

Remember them as they were not,
For this is how they are now.
Think of them with bowed hate.
For they did not choose to die,
And yet they are dead.

They gave false witness:
Life was not as they lived it.
And yet they now speak the truth.
Respect for the dead.
Respect for the truth.

Are the dead the truth?
Yes, because they live not.
Is the truth the dead?
No, because they live not.
What is the truth?
The truth is the one self alive.

Does the truth then live?
No, the truth does not die.
The truth and the dead do not die.
Respect for the truth and the dead.

The truth is the one person alive.
It goes for a walk every evening
After day and before night.
It goes for a walk with the dead.

Respect for them as they pass.
For they are the dead whom you hate:
They were false.
And that is the truth which you hate:
It is true.
Respect for your hate.

AFTER SMILING

Now not to smile again.
Those years of softening
To this one and to that one
Because the body has a meaning
Of defeat and dread unless
It advertises cheerfulness—
Those years of life-feigning are done.

Now is my smile pursed smooth
Into a stillest anger on
All flesh convivial
To my convivial flesh
Like scattered selves of me
Insisting right of scatteredness
And homed identity both—
As if by smiling promised.

By smiling I did promise
Not myself, compounded lover,
But the complete quarrel which
Must rage with man and else
Like sound with silence.
Never will sound be silence.
Silence listens
And the ear is noisy;
But the ear marks the difference,
And so my smiling did.

Man, world, beloved even!
To be I, that other I than you,
Dearer than self to you by test
Of pride-shattering desire,
Needs more than coveting
And minding me I was once woman,
Of such and such complaisance.

It was a war then rumoured,
Scarcely declared, battleless.
A guest as hostage fancied,

I moved the soldier-lusts in you:
Thus did you honour me.
But never have we fought,
Never till now, I departed
And the peace-troth raised.

I departed, since of soul-age
You now, grown to greed immortal
Of contradiction, to be the else
You made kinged state against,
To be more world, kinghood of not-you.

Now not to smile again:
Be greeted here, having come
Like Rome to sit you down
Upon eternal Rome. Eternity

In my look, celebration
Loud in yours, we'll partner glory
And visit empire on each other
Disputedly, of which, long death, decide!

THE WORLD AND I

This is not exactly what I mean
Any more than the sun is the sun.
But how to mean more closely
If the sun shines but approximately?
What a world of awkwardness!
What hostile implements of sense!
Perhaps this is as close a meaning
As perhaps becomes such knowing.
Else I think the world and I
Must live together as strangers and die—
A sour love, each doubtful whether
Was ever a thing to love the other.
No, better for both to be nearly sure
Each of each—exactly where
Exactly I and exactly the world
Fail to meet by a moment, and a word.

THERE IS NO LAND YET

The long sea, how short-lasting,
From water-thought to water-thought
So quick to feel surprise and shame.
Where moments are not time
But time is moments.
Such neither yes nor no,
Such only love, to have to-morrow
By certain failure of now and now.

On water lying strong ships and men
In weakness skilled reach elsewhere:
No prouder places from home in bed
The mightiest sleeper can know.
So faith took ship upon the sailor's earth
To seek absurdities in heaven's name—
Discovery but a fountain without source,
Legend of mist and lost patience.

The body swimming in itself
Is dissolution's darling.
With dripping mouth it speaks a truth
That cannot lie, in words not born yet
Out of first immortality,
All-wise impermanence.

And the dusty eye whose accuracies
Turn watery in the mind
Where waves of probability
Write vision in a tidal hand
That time alone can read.

And the dry land not yet,
Lonely and absolute salvation—
Boasting of constancy
Like an island with no water round
In water where no land is.

LETTER TO MAN'S REASONABLE SOUL

Here's about sunshine and the sun
As long as the old fear goes on
Of being taken for a braggart,
Rather than for one just so strong
Able to lift up just so much
Of that loose burden called earth—
Which, as it lifts whole, is lifted
Out of time's unmeaning peril
But, as it scatters and is lost,
Becomes the devil's senseless pack. . . .

Here's about curling of the tongue,
Crossed fingers and no present object
While others perhaps still live
To mock your natural arm
And make it drop down of the shame
Of seeming magical. . . .

Here's about love, which mimics time
When the clock has stopped in the night
And the church bell seems out of order
Or the wind blowing the wrong way.
Here's about time and love, Poor Friend—
Enough be it that love is long,
And no grace lost in putting off
Till the last moment what were hell to try
Till the last moment, and even then
A so much lesser heaven than heaven
By that just so strong arm of yours.

And how does the moon come in?
The moon's for death, and to remind
That loss of will hangs overhead—
Unless, before death's death only,
A ghost cries out, 'Once I was man,
And man I mean to be again
Though death a dead man makes me.'

To close, then, here's about a madness.
May it at just so late take hold your arm
And no caution avail against it.
May you be that unlikely one,
Uncertain subject of uncertain chronicle,
Who was to be wise against reason
And break into the lifeless regions
At the running down of strength—
Where there's little more than to know
What's lost by death, and to grieve not,
The heart being in that place accounted
Fool either, or false witness. . . .
Of which, to the same effect,
In my next letter, upon your answer
To the same effect . . . perhaps your next. . . .

THE TALKING WORLD

Meeting on the way to the same there,
The tired ones talk and make a here,
And further is then where, and where?

The tired ones talk,
Abandoning the written destination
For whatever say-so can be spoken
To end the individual promenade
Sooner than the universal walk.

The tired ones talk, to not walk.
The untired ones talk, to talk and walk,
To live as well as die, lest dying prove
Less lively than to live.

Of such mixed intent
Places in time spring up,
And truth is anybody's argument
Who can use words untruthfully enough
To build eternity inside his own short mouth.

The nicest thought is only gossip
If merchandized into plain language and sold
For so much understanding to the minute.
Gossip's the mortal measure.
Whatever can't be talked
In the closed idiom of yesterday,
That's silence-worth and time-free
As a full purport must to-day be.

Great manyness there is
Before all becomes an all.
Uncertainty and criticism
Oppose to the unified eventual
A world of disagreement
In which every contradictory opinion
Is for to-day an 'I' wearing a crown
Of weeds plucked from the tip of the tongue.

Talk is the modesty of the modest.
Talk is the vanity of the vain.
Talk is to be various man.
Talk is to be man apart,
God apart from God the not-God.

Talk is to stop the ears with talk.
Talk is to hear according to the ear.
Talk is the body of the listener
That has its own long talk to walk
Before it comes where the mind rests
To hear without an ear
The unhearable words of no-talk.

And talk in talk like time in time vanishes.
Ringing changes on dumb supposition,
Conversation succeeds conversation,
Until there's nothing left to talk about
Except truth, the perennial monologue,
And no talker to dispute it but itself.

The pleasure of talk is the pleasure of weakness,
As a tree that cannot walk loves not-walking.
The pain of talk is the pain of strength,
As a hand is weary-strong
By the labour that it fails of.

Talk is the whole of truth less talk.
Talk is a war on truth by talk,
And a peace with talk by truth.
In talk truth and talk make peace—
As an enemy forgives an enemy
For being not like to him.

Let there be talk and let there be no talk.
Let the birds with the birds chirp of birds that chirp.
Let the wearers of coats with the wearers of coats
Speak the wisdom of coats, and with the coatmakers.
Let the uses of words prevail over words.
Let there be many ways of not lying

And no ways of truth-telling.
Let there be no wrong because no right.

The world talking round its sun
Leaves emptiness behind
For those to walk who are not,
Who show the space where truth is,
Who are the place with the words identical,
As walking is with talking
When feet and mouths agree
In the still pace of thought.

And more of talk I cannot talk,
Except I talk, speak mingled.
And you would then attend,
Nor complain that I speak solitary.
But complain no more.
Look, I am gone from you,
From your immunity to death and listening.
May you for ever not know nor weather cease
Wherein to die in your own colours,
With other banners flying than the black.
May you not lose the sun too soon—
Blindness and noise by which you stand
Between yourselves and yourselves.
May you not know how never more you were
Than such and such mistalking,
O talking world that says and forgets.

UNREAD PAGES

An end is a happy end only:
What only was moves into what is,
Unbodied grows, but lasting.
And the matter is now alive,
Even by this beneficence of Yes
To No and No like angels made of nothing.

Science, the white heart of strangers,
Bleeds with an immaculate grief—
Impatient brotherhood,
Tired apostates of curiosity,
Creed of apostatizing.
Truth need be but dead afterworld
To those who've had enough,
The readers and the lookers-on—
As stars keep off, or to short minds
Night seems a less real time than day,
Not to be measured with or counted to
That quick self-evident sum of sun.

Have sleep and midnight warmth,
Where your scant eyes see failure,
Numbering the wakefullest page
The dark and frosty last.

An end is a happy end only.
And first the book's end comes,
The printed public leaves off reading.

Then open the small secret doors,
When none's there to read awrong.
Out runs happiness in a crowd,
The saving words and hours
That come too tragic-late for souls
Gifted with their own mercy:
Who spare themselves the joys
That would have darkened them
From the predaceous years.

Too orthodox maturity
For such heresy of child-remaining—
On these the dusty blight of books descends,
Weird, pundit babyhoods
Whose blinking vision stammers out the past
Like a big-lettered foetus-future.

I AM

I am an indicated other:
Witness this common presence
Intelligible to the common mind,
The daylight census.

I am a such-and-such appearance
Listed among the furnitures
Of the proprietary epoch
That on the tattered throne of time
Effects inheritance still,
Though of shadow that estate now,
Death-dim, memory illumined.

You, spent kingdom of the senses,
Have laid hands on the unseeable,
Shadow's seeming fellow:
And all together we
A population of names only
Inhabiting the hypothetic streets,
Where no one can be found
Ever at home.

Where then, fellow citizens
Of this post-carnal matter,
Is each the next and next one,
Stretching the instant chain
Toward its first-last link,
The twilight that into dawn passes
Without intervention of night,
Time's slow terrible enemy?

That I with you did lie
In the same love-bed, same planet
Of thinking bright against
The black pervasion, against the sleep
That gives not back if none makes argument
That yesterday is self still—

That I thus to you am like,
That I walk beside and straight
On your same circle of argument,
That I walked, that I was,
That I slept, that I lived—

That I live—let me be a proof
Of a world as was a world,
And accept it, King Habit,
From my mouth, our mouth.

But where, where?
If I have so companioned?
Here, here!

The same not-here I ever held,
And be it yours, and I yours,
Out of my mouth until
You tire of the possession
And, falling prone, relinquish
The stale breath of stubbornness.

Then will this still be here,
Here, here, the proved not-here
Of perfect contradiction—
Here where you visited on me
The individual genius, paradox.

And I will then stand you up,
To count you mine, since dying frenzy
Makes new dwelling-charm,
O entranced wizards of place-magic.
I, in the over-reaching moment,
In the reign one-too-many,
Dynasty too-long of time-kind—
I, created time-kind by commingling
Of the jealous substance with
The different way to be—

I, out of your stopped mouth, our mouth,
Will spin round continuity,

Winding the thread me round
To keep these other years safe
Always and always while you haunt
The windows that might be here,
Looking for sign of elsewhere—
If I perhaps such same fatality
As before fast was magicked
Into the this-year dialects.

CONCERNING FOOD

You who demanded of God the law
To be man by with most profit,
And were man by with the profit that you asked,
Who consumed your God, your law, your world,
In rotary science of diuturnal meals:
What now? Since of you lies only
This dead God at my feet of woman
Which accompanied him, or you,
To this death and satiation,
Should your self-stained lips still move,
Muttering, 'More law, I starve'—

Then I must feed you, if you live,
Nor that old pap you died of,
The thin milk of time which was yourself
Mothered by yourself, O mortal Godhead.
Rise up then, here's a feeding for you
That will answer: a nourishment
Not spirited from flesh—
The very words 'Rise up', and again
As you do not, from being dead, but would.

Rise up then, and again, 'Rise up'—
Until you stand. And this obedience,
This having eaten, will last you
As many meals your mind can make of it.
I give you food this time, not you:
This time on time of not-self.
I do command you, since you ask it
And were dead of yourself so dead
Did I not, nor wish to lie so dead,
However the thing may be done.

Yes, the thing may be done,
But difficult the medicine, with bitter in—
Or you would not believe it strong
To get you up from mind with flesh down.
Which came of eating sweet.
Well, there are two sweets.

And here's mine tasting different
Until the other is forgotten.
Was it then so sweet, too sweet?
That man-sugared law, prayer fed to prayer?
Was it then sweet-impossible, my Poor?

Well, here's possible, since you ask it
And there's no withholding possible,
The food that's food to hunger
If hunger takes no prouder name.
Rise up, God Famine, and be man:
Here's food, that matches hunger,
Here's what-to-know, that matches mind.
Mind matching mind, desire matching hunger—
This is but flesh to flesh providing
Large empty image of itself.
This had no need of woman, nor did she give
More than unwilling mystery forth,
Invisible vines with fruit of yours upon,
When your eyes, like further bellies foraging,
Went hoping marvels to enrich
The haggard table of your soul.

To make no mistake, write *Poison* on me,
To tell the bottle which
And notify your sick distrust of sweet.
Have you an appetite for death now?

Never, never need that lack,
Self-cheated Ghost, with memory where your head
And shame where once your heart—
You own credulity's Fool.
And the bones, the sceptic corpse
That you stood up from doom-dumb stone?
They grind the death of vanity,
Begun in starkest long-ago,
And have not death to think of now:
Let them to earth again like roots torn up
With flower along, that never dreamed of vase.

TREE-SENSE

Numbers in heaven grow
As trees constrained between
Air and tight soil resolve
Divided heart by dancing
To the supposed music of earth
But with thoughts birdwise away—
Imagining and motionless.
In heaven are such parliaments
Opinionating of eternity;
Other the forestry of hell
Where rugged communities of will,
In tawdry treedom spread as cities,
Their foliate hates make boundless night of.

But how—to instruct of heaven
And to use hell's name for hell,
And the time surely far off yet
To speak identical, word same as sense?
What is God and what the devil
If tree-metaphors suffice
To tell immediately of?
God is pale doubt, the devil bright denial.
Heaven perhaps next year, hell the last,
And the multitudes prophetic remnants
Of the millennial no-one.

And the time far off yet?
By less than any minute more,
By the slight scratching of the pen—
And to read the written story over,
Eyes still from trees green-fresh
And full of tangled nature
Still wondering which thing to be,
What's most and best and fruitfullest
When drops the lightning season
And all together's added up.

And will the sum be ever spelt
In other science than such numbers

Forward and backward bargaining
The errors with the answer?
The trees this year grow wide and tall,
The sun stands off great to watch,
And surely there's a world abroad
To which the world-end calling
Is a mere unseen humming, a voice
In the slow branches muffled,
Musing how long yet is to be not loud,
To be a breath outside time's lungs—
Uncalendared soft truth still.

But surely truth is very old,
Very old, all but learnt, all but taught?
Does myself confound, that I speak?
Do yourselves hinder, that you hear?
That in tree-grammar we converse,
Since trees beside myself and you are?
Shall we then put away the book
And you and me and close the schoolroom?
But the trees that this year a year
May still be languaging as if
The time were still far off yet?
The trees will come along, as fast
As slow as you came, coming
The pace it pleased you—
As the trees please, and you . . .

Else the time's gone like time
For walking out of time and into
Not-time, passing the trees by—
The trees, the present pleasantness
Of future future yet,
Not now or now, while life now lives,
Now lives, now lived—oh, coloured twilight,
Nearly immortal death.

THE DILEMMIST

There's waking and dressing and what a fine day,
And to take and to leave and to laugh at or not.
There's the same as there was, though there's other.

There's seeing, or to read, as you will.
There's living and knowing like two lives.
There's knowing and living like two books.
What a holiday, one from the other!
And how long can it last?

There's time though there's no time.
There's doing though nothing to do.
There are two fairs, each a most fair,
And choosing between would lose both.
But how long can not-choosing claim both?
How long can your head keep turning
Between left and right so instantly
That you hold in one look what in two
Were perhaps loss of each—
How long flesh and spirit be twin
Equals in neitherhood?

But fear nothing, impartial lover
Of the proved past and the unprovable future.
The present endures with the greed
Of making one sense of two passions.
Fear nothing, unless passion's thinning
Between such an opposite pair.
For both honour the heart they confound.
Mortality's a handsome matron,
Or Death's a lady of commanding elegance.

Indeed, you cannot put the first by—
She's an old love, by her you had
Such children as declare the man,
Robust inventions of your dreaming limbs.
The other is a later pledge, and cruel,
Ghost-families her brood.
And yet the dower is a queen's:

On a breast loud with common victories
Her silent badges swing unchallengeable.

But how long such balance of faiths,
Neither keeping and neither breaking?
How long will the careless sun make warm
While you go a-wintering with fancy—
The moon adoring with sun-given eyes?

There's this and that the same stroke now.
There's near-loss and near-gain, there's between.
There's rumour of end, and no ending.
And how often shall the rapt pendulum
Not travel, nor deliver itself
Either back, to the last hour,
Or forward, to failing?
Why, but once, clock-romantic:
For how long can your noisy ear endure
The unwound never-ticking,
And your hands the not-winding?
How long your pulse pause, world of motion?

Why, you'd rather again the old hours,
The swift deaths and new lives and changes,
Than to be dawdling-dead like a poet,
With but one death to die, and that everyone's.
Humanity is no poet till it must be:
The book entices far the blood,
Humanity sits down to read not die.

And when the blood frights and reverses,
That's time to close the book and follow.
Humanity is no poet till it must be.
First comes the need of blood, the fire-water,
To flow and burn and be so many founts
Of year-eternities in like of sun;
By combustion of fear, drought into flame,
Flame into liquid length of will again.
Forward is frozen will only,
A stranger's tomb only, dead thought.

When's man a poet then? And was he ever one?
For if a death with the held moment stays
That is not struck—when frantic flesh
Runs homeward after blood fleeing
To previous courses and reddened turns—
That's none of him, no part forgotten,
But of his second love a fancy
Lying man-like in her fancied arms,
With her own foolishness her arms filled.

The man's away after the man.
She understood his wooing wrong.
He never meant her more than paper,
Nor does his heart one icy line remember.
Nor does she with a memory engage,
Crying, 'My love was he, and he's lost,'
Since in his stolen coming at her
He has gone from her, nor had been.

The same cry these do cry, one cry:
'All is over, all is over, all!'
A small cry, then he's back to time again,
And she athwart the cry, as on a love
None uttered and may yet be ridden—
The cry she silent cried, nor ever he,
Except the blood, scorching, send him all-speed
To look for other clime than body-heat,
Be that however sunless other place,
And he in such mad hate of self
To swear madness against his likest love.

THE UNTHRONGED ORACLE

Not to ask, not to be answered,
Not to fall down from last of breath,
Not to be raised—the stricken mouth
Though fit uniquely to make shape
Of unique plaint for stricken mind:
Never to this final cave and mouth of mouths
Have you, are you come, contestant race
That boastfully flew birds of tiding here
So long—from extinct monster-wing,
That never flew, to the etherealest feather
That floated back from far, forgetting
What too-heavy auspices were hung
There on its thin prophetic claw.
Birds, birds, all bird-like were your reaches,
Minds quicker than your minds, vain flights
Of consolation. ('It will be as time tells,
As we attempt, as thoughts anticipate
Against exhaustion and straggle of feet.')

Your coming, asking, seeing, knowing,
Was a fleeing from and stumbling
Into only mirrors, and behind which,
Behind all mirrors, dazzling pretences,
The general light of fortune
Keeps wrapt in sleeping unsleep,
All-mute of time, self-muttering like mute:
Fatality like lone wise-woman
Her unbought secrets counting over
That stink of hell, from fuming in her lap.

Is this to be alone?
When, when the day when votary ghosts unpale
And shriek rebellion at themselves
So dumbly death-loyal serving her
In acquiescent guile—since never came
A word of angry flesh or impious meaning
Through that hushed screen of priding world?
When, when the day? Is this to be alone?

Newspapers, mirrors, birds and births and clocks
Divide you from her by a trembling film
That never may dissolve between.
Perhaps even as you were will you remain
Such other manufactures of yourselves—
While round her storm unwillingly
Your empty spirits like better selves
You dared not be or gainsay—arguing,
'That ancient mystery-monger grows
By times of ours more and more ancient,
More deaf and slow in deeper company
Of omens private to her distance,
And love of talking lone in unheard bodement.'

But when,when the day? Is this to be alone?

THE FLOWERING URN

And every prodigal greatness
Must creep back into strange home,
Must fill the hollow matrix of
The never-begotten perfect son
Who never can be born.

And every quavering littleness
Must shrink more tinily than it knows
Into the giant hush whose sound
Reverberates within itself
As tenderest numbers cannot improve.

And from this jealous secrecy
Will rise itself, will flower up,
The likeness kept against false seed:
When death-whole is the seed
And no new harvest to fraction sowing.

Will rise the same peace that held
Before fertility's lie awoke
The virgin sleep of Mother All:
The same but for the way in flowering
It speaks of fruits that could not be.

IT IS NOT SAD

It is not sad, or I would laugh.
Instead, seeming to laugh with you,
I cry, alone—'tis afterwards.
Alone, no handkerchief.
I seem, I seemed, to laugh with you,
To be a chair in which she sat
As wasteful friends among themselves,
Not growing dearer than they were.

It is not sad, or I would laugh,
Thinking apart how you addressed
A chair not empty, yet not myself.
Instead I cry, because I do not cry.
Alone peculiarly
From having sat with you, and not,
I feel a grieflessness, a grief.

If there is weather still behind unspent,
I shall still feel it when it breaks,
And tell the changes between hot and cold
As if the slow death were my own:
Weather is the dead at the hard school
But if it's love again, more love,
Here's no commitment to your sense.
More love's not ignorance:
It is to reason life against
Death in the understanding hailed.

And well you know that life is done.
Yet you will not know, you sit
Like dreamers in a closed café
At their next cups—
'Until the others go.'
Death is a wisdom left at home,
A book to recommend. But who the author,
And what the title? You can't remember.
Meanwhile at any table there's any woman:
That's also death, her mind elsewhere,

Here letting love make time
Out of her slow long 'Day is done'—
So long, so long, there's night yet.

But any woman soon goes home
And won't be back to-morrow night.
Death is this morning now,
Except where weather pleads another day
For the clumsy elements, or a year,
To learn the human lesson in.

In the same chairs you sit talking,
At the same hour—and of me
A fondness as of none absent
Fills your ears. But never did I sit so.
I cry with those supposed eyes mine,
And it is not sad, or I would laugh
In mourning of once having laughed,
Sitting with you in laughing death-talk.
But you had not death in your hearts,
More love only: a backwardness to keep
Knowledge beyond the time of knowing—
Until too late, too late always.

Goodbye, I cannot bring you closer
If you prefer the dying way,
Dwelling the living side of death.
Not me you sat with, but a pathos,
My partial image torn out of me.
Nor ever did you have me whole.
You courted a patched presence, her and her.

Now I am whole, now I have gone.
But fear not: if you suffer of it,
You cannot know—pleasure and pain
Vanished with understanding when
You knew and of this more of mind
Made more of love, more lingering.
Goodbye, we have both forgotten.
That garbled sweetness of our discourse

Was but the mist largening
Between us of occasion lost.

And therefore do I go off crying,
Since it is not sad, or I would sadly
Make to laugh, remembering laughing—
Instead of with these tears forgetting.
I spare you further courtesies
Of cup and table, chair and conversation.
And get you off, an opposite way,
Riding against the heathen, death,
Into a Christian heaven where
Safe lie the individual graves
From death's outlandish unioning.

And it is not sad:
No graves divide here the single scene
On which my tears fall as rain
Might upon nowhere spill, from nowhere,
To prove the meaning natural,
Unsudden fast succeeding
Of the familiar by the forgotten—
To prove me any woman once,
Whose human griefs now gathered in
Compose a heart as then, a sadness of
Nothing to weep, no one to laugh with
Of having laughed once with of weeping.

THE SIGNS OF KNOWLEDGE

Not by water, fire or flesh
Does the world have that end
Which have it must in being, having been,
A world so privileged to begin
And long increase of self to spin,
And long outspinning, spinning out
To end of thread to have—

Not by water, fire or flesh,
Not by drinking back of self,
Not by flaming up of self,
Not by lavish plague to lie down
Sainted, rotted, rendered—

By words the world has end,
By words which brought
From first articulation, wordless stir,
To the last throbbing phrases.

Most world it is when quiets world
Into a listening and a thinking on
What world it was, into a learning of
What language in extreme
Makes full the famished grail
That never rose to brim
With the world's ekèd wine.

By one sign shall you know the end,
The rising to the destined brim,
The last succession, the words enough.
By one sign shall there be a world
More like to whole-world than your world
More like to mere-world.
By one sign shall you first know All,
See more than world of much contains:
The sign of emptiness,
An empty grail, an empty world
Of world drained to be world-full.

By one sign! And have you seen?
There is and was an empty grail,
For nothing is the world which rose
From the cup's bottom to never-full:
Nothing and never is that world.
And have you seen?
There is and was an empty grail.
And have you seen?

By two signs shall you know you see.
By two signs shall your much of world
Dissolve and solve into an empty grail.
By two signs shall you know the sign
By which to know a lacking world
And fullness forthheld emptily
In perfect mete of filling:
By two signs shall you know you see.

The first sign of the two signs
Shall be unlove of the sun.
The second sign of the two signs
Shall be unlife of the earth.
And the first with the second sign locked
Shall be undeath of the moon.

When an empty grail glows in the mind
Where once the moon wound faint without
Like hate of time afar constrained
To circle-slave in fond lament of time—
When the first and the second sign are one sign
Shall you see the grail, know the moon-sense,
Shall there be a whole-world pouring brimful
Into an empty grail, an empty world,
An empty whole, a whole emptiness.

And the first sign of the two signs
By the knowing of which you shall know
The one sign by the knowing of which
Shall you first know All like a grail
Whole at last to its brim

In whole emptiness of All—
The first sign of the two signs
Shall be unlove of the sun.

Learn then of unlove of the sun,
Lest it be in you and you know it not.
Does your tongue not lazy hang, alick not
With afternoons and aeons like old sores?
It is an old sore, the first sore,
It is all the sores—the sun!

Does your tongue no more sick-pleasure?
Does it stiffen to a taste it tastes not yet?
Does your tongue then point your eyes away
From sights that like old sores lie open
To be pity-pleasures, to be sorrow-scenes
Where beauty festers, frighted to heal?

Now does your tongue thirst not to see
The sun-world sore, the inflammations?
Do your eyes no more with tears burn blind
When thought of other-where than sun-where
Commands your tongue to make report
Of other-sights, of mind-sights, tongue-sights?

From unlove of the sun, by one more glance
Sudden-small to read more true-fine,
Comes unlife of the earth: oh, learn,
Lest unlife of the earth be in you
And you know it not, to welcome
What unlove of the sun undarks—
Lest other-sights be seen, then lost
In morning-morrow's sting of sun-life.
Learn then of unlife of the earth.

If unlife of the earth be in you,
By a strength to move not shall you know it.
Do your legs awalk leave other-legs to stand?
Do your hands atouch leave other-hands to fold?
Does your head atwist leave other-head to straight?

Have you a life, and a life, a quick and a still,
And the quick to tardy and turn,
And the still to move not—allspeed in a
Lasting-over, lasting-other unto-until
Shall come the full know-step and know-sight?
Oh, have you vanished from yourself
Nor seek old where-to-be nor new?
Oh, do you break in scatter-self and stay-self,
In wander-world and stand-mind?

Then have you unlife, and then learn.
Undeath of moon has come on you,
The moon-grail clears and wholes,
An emptiness whole-shines at eye-thought.
See whole then: these are the signs.
The first sign and the second are the one sign.
The one sign, the first truth, the first of truth,
Is moon's undeath by empty grail signed.
The lesson of the first truth is an empty grail.
The first interpretation is by the eye.

Rubric for the Eye

See sun-wide, world-long, air-high;
See water-deep and earth-round.
Then let the eye look whole-impossible,
Look wider, longer, higher, deeper, rounder.
Let the thought sharpen as the eye dulls.
Let the thought see, let moon undazzle sun.
Sun of world, moon of word,
Eye-spilling live of eye, undeath of mind-sight—
Moon-clearly, emptily, full grail aspeak.

POET: A LYING WORD

You have now come with me, I have now come with you, to the season that should be winter, and is not: we have not come back.

We have not come back: we have not come round: we have not moved. I have taken you, you have taken me, to the next and next span, and the last—and it is the last. Stand against me then and stare well through me then. It is a wall not to be scaled and left behind like the old seasons, like the poets who were the seasons.

Stand against me then and stare well through me then. I am no poet as you have span by span leapt the high words to the next depth and season, the next season always, the last always, and the next. I am a true wall: you may but stare me through.

It is a false wall, a poet: it is a lying word. It is a wall that closes and does not.

This is no wall that closes and does not. It is a wall to see into, it is no other season's height. Beyond it lies no depth and height of further travel, no partial courses. Stand against me then and stare well through me then. Like wall of poet here I rise, but am no poet as walls have risen between next and next and made false end to leap. A last, true wall am I: you may but stare me through.

And the tale is no more of the going: no more a poet's tale of a going false-like to a seeing. The tale is of a seeing true-like to a knowing: there's but to stare the wall through now, well through.

It is not a wall, it is not a poet. It is not a lying wall, it is not a lying word. It is a written edge of time. Step not across, for then into my mouth, my eyes, you fall. Come close, stare me well through, speak as you see. But, oh, infatuated drove of lives, step not across now. Into my mouth, my eyes, shall you thus fall, and be yourselves no more.

Into my mouth, my eyes, I say, I say. I am no poet like transitory wall to lead you on into such slow terrain of time as measured out your single span to broken turns of season once and once again. I lead you not. You have now come with me, I have now come with you, to your last turn and season: thus could I come with you, thus only.

I say, I say, I am, it is, such wall, such poet, such not lying, such not leading into. Await the sight, and look well through, know by such standing still that next comes none of you.

Comes what? Comes this even I, even this not-I, this not lying season when death holds the year at steady count—this every-year.

Would you not see, not know, not mark the count? What would you then? Why have you come here then? To leap a wall that is no wall, and a true wall? To step across into my eyes and mouth not yours? To cry me down like wall or poet as often your way led past down-falling height that seemed?

I say, I say, I am, it is: such wall, such end of graded travel. And if you will not hark, come tumbling then upon me, into my eyes, my mouth, and be the backward utterance of yourselves expiring angrily through instant seasons that played you time-false.

My eyes, my mouth, my hovering hands, my intransmutable head: wherein my eyes, my mouth, my hands, my head, my body-self, are not such mortal simulacrum as everlong you builded against very-death, to keep you everlong in boasted death-course, neverlong? I say, I say, I am not builded of you so.

This body-self, this wall, this poet-like address, is that last barrier long shied of in your elliptic changes: out of your leaping, shying, season-quibbling, have I made it, is it made. And if now poet-like it rings with one-more-time as if, this is the mounted stupor of your everlong outbiding worn prompt and lyric, poet-like—the forbidden one-more-time worn time-like.

Does it seem I ring, I sing, I rhyme, I poet-wit? Shame on me then! Grin me your foulest humour then of poet-piety, your eyes rolled up in white hypocrisy—should I be one sprite more of your versed fame—or turned from me into your historied brain, where the lines read more actual? Shame on me then!

And haste unto us both, my shame is yours. How long I seem to beckon like a wall beyond which stretches longer length of fleshsome traverse: it is your lie of flesh and my flesh-seeming stand of words. Haste then unto us both! I say, I say. This wall reads 'Stop!' This poet verses 'Poet: a lying word!'

Shall the wall then not crumble, as to walls is given? Have I not said: 'Stare me well through'? It is indeed a wall, crumble it shall. It is a wall of walls, stare it well through: the reading gentles near, the name of death passes with the season that it was not.

Death is a very wall. The going over walls, against walls, is a dying and a learning. Death is a knowing-death. Known death is truth sighted at the halt. The name of death passes. The mouth that moves with death forgets the word.

And the first page is the last of death. And haste unto us both, lest the wall seem to crumble not, to lead mock-onward. And the first page reads: 'Haste unto us both!' And the first page reads: 'Slowly, it is the first page only.'

Slowly, it is the page before the first page only, there is no haste. The page before the first page tells of death, haste, slowness: how truth falls true now at the turn of page, at time of telling. Truth one by one falls true. And the first page reads, the page which is the page before the first page only: 'This once-upon-a-time when seasons failed, and time stared through the wall nor made to leap across, is the hour, the season, seasons, year and years, no wall and wall, where when and when the classic lie dissolves and nakedly time salted is with truth's sweet flood nor yet to mix with, but be salted tidal-sweet—O sacramental ultimate by which shall time be old-renewed nor yet another season move.' I say, I say.

THREE SERMONS TO THE DEAD

The Way of the Air

The way of the air is by clouds to speak
And by clouds to be silent.
The way of the air is a progress
From treachery to repentance.
The air is the freedom to hope.
You breathe your hopes,
And are glad, and live.
And there are clouds.
There are clouds which betray your hopes.
To whom? To your Conscience, which is not you.
And you are ashamed, and the clouds tear.
By the conscienceless air you live,
But by Conscience, your mouth's tight seal,
You die, you are what you are only.
The clouds are you, Conscience is not you.
Yet you make the clouds to tear and repent
For Conscience's sake, which is not you.
For first was the air, and last is Conscience.
And that which is last is, and that which was first is not.
First was freedom, and last is a tight seal.
The free word tears, but the sealed mouth is silenter.
The air opens your mouth, the clouds unshape it.
Conscience closes the mouth, but gives it back.
What is Conscience? It is Death—
In airless final love of which
You keep inviolate your voice
Against the clouds that steam in traitor whispers
Repentantly upon your mouth,
Aura of tattered hopes
Protesting as you dare not.

220]

Not All Immaculate

Yet it is not all immaculate death—
Not all a folding to of covers
Punctually, by time's trembling hands.
There is (unreadable) a motley clatter
After that day of instantaneousness
Has summoned instant night from night.
There is a panic of stained steps
Along pale streets conspiring backwards
Into remembered days like bedrooms
Slow with oversleeping, timeless.
It is not all a tidy ending, dawning
Of a picture-page whereon tidily, briefly,
The world is told of by a thinnest light—
The moon-like smile of worn Forgiveness.
Against this weather-peace there cries
(Unhearable) a scarlet wind,
As the sun's bull once bellowed,
And a black rain beseeches, as earth once
In pride of ram besought itself to doubt.
This guarded day is not the whole of you,
Whose foreheads by this day resist
Nature's insanities and headaches,
The garrulous mute bodily debates.
This night which hammers brain-like
At your immune memories now
Lies far and dim, but great it lies
As far and dim, greatly unrolls
That which has been forgotten greatly.
It is not all this sheerer day.
There is that, also, which you have forgotten.
There is a blemished night abroad,
And though you lock it in itself
With lockless rigour, that it may not out
By any mercy-key of yours,
Still does it shadow the lustrated tale—
Since of you also those young chapters
Toward which, as to later lives,
Young, later selves of you go futuring.

Nor Is It Written

Nor is it written that you may not grieve.
There is no rule of joy; long may you dwell
Not smiling yet in that last pain,
On that last supper of the heart.
It is not written that you must take joy
Because not thus again shall you sit down
To ply the mingled banquet
Which the deep larder of illusion shed
Like myth in time grown not astonishing.
Lean to the cloth awhile, and yet awhile,
And even may your eyes caress
Proudly the used abundance.
It is not written in what heart
You may not pass from magic plenty
Into the straitened nowadays.
To each is given secrecy of heart,
To make himself what heart he please
In stirring up from that fond table
To sit him down at this sharp meal.
It shall not here be asked of him
'What thinks your heart?'
Long may you sorely to yourself upbraid
This truth unwild, this only-bread.
It is not counted what large passions
Your heart in ancient private keeps alive.
To each is given what defeat he will.

BENEDICTORY

I have done all, you have done all,
That I, that you, that you, that we,
As I was, you were, we were,
Could have done as doing was.

I have said all, you have said all
That I, that you, that we,
As I was, you were, we were,
Could have said as saying was.

Now comes a blessing on us,
Close all our eyes on us
And let us bless us thankfully
That we have been and are not.

We are not as we were.
And as we were was well,
And as we are is well.
It is well now that we are not.

The mystery wherein we
Accustomed grew as to the dark
Has now been seen enough—
I have seen, you have seen.

I have seen and I am off:
I hurry to the cause of it.
You have seen and wait slowly
The forgotten cause of it.

It seems not now distressful
Or yet too much delighted in.
It was a mystery endured
Until a fuller sense befall.

Let us now close our eyes all
And anxiously be blessed in this:
That I so hurry off to bring
Full sense, mystery's cause even.

And while I hurry off you wait,
And while I hurry off I bring,
And while I bring you unforget
The cause which mystery became.

The fuller sense and cause became
That old and older mystery
As you more unremembered
That oldest sense you never knew.

And now we have done all, said all,
Within the mystery, you and I,
To make it no blind sudden sight
When open crash the clouds of time.

We have now seen, already seen,
Through folded clouds and folded meaning
The blindness and the evilness
That so have we been wrapped.

We have all sinned, been wrapped apart.
I went your way of doing, saying,
You went your way of doing, saying,
We have all sinned, pretended.

You have pretended to be seeing.
I have pretended that you saw.
So came we by such eyes—
And within mystery to have language.

The cause was that a way lacked.
It seemed a wayless world like no world.
You made a way and a world
Which no way was, nor any world.

You made that which could not be made.
A way is not to be made, nor a world.
You made no way and no world.
You made a mystery because you made.

You would see, and made a mystery to see.
The cause of the mystery was that you saw.
The cause of the mystery was that you would see.
The cause of the mystery was that you did not see.

There was no sight to see.
That which is to be seen is no sight.
You made it a sight to see.
It is no sight, and this was the cause.

Now, having seen, let our eyes close
And a dark blessing pass among us—
A quick-slow blessing to have seen
And said and done no worse or better.

And slowly wait—slowly it happened
A way and a world to be made,
And to seem the way and the world
Which must be so if aught is.

Slowly be true as slowly you were false.
By falseness you were,
By your falseness I was false: I was.
Slowly be no more, nor I.

And quickly I: I must be off and back
To come not back but bring back
The mystery's cause and fullness—
The sense comes back, not I.

To you who are not I who am not
Bring that which is if aught is,
That which is if aught else is,
That which is.

My loves, it happens sweet.
It is a mothering wisdom.
Remember what you never knew
And be like births of knowledge stirring—

Quick and slow within the doom,
Within the blessing we have loosened
After so long upon ourselves
You upon you, I upon us all.

Close all our eyes on us.
A wayless world like no world
Leaves the perjurious lids
In blessing of them, of their eyes.

And what eyes then will open,
And how bright the way and world
That failed when dull eyes pressed
So bright a sight to see?

It is not so, it is not as it was,
To talk so, see so, study so
A mystery and fashion so
A sight to see, to dwell in.

We are not as we were.
The action is self-worn.
The words connive no more.
The appearance hangs unseen.

We have been in hell.
A blessing on us—we have been in hell.
We have made hell.
A blessing on us— we have proved hell.

There is only hell to prove:
Which logic is a poor art now,
Like to be apt in ignorance
Where ignorance is guile.

You have no need to prove now,
Nor I to do and say along.
We have finished with not knowing.
We have returned to wonder.

We are now back in wonder.
You made yourselves to know.
You now know, you are now unmade.
We are at last, again, in wonder.

And we are not—least am I.
First I was a woman, and I feigned.
Then I was yourselves, and I fooled.
Then I was a spirit, and I subtilized.

Now I am not, utterly I am not.
Utterly is that which is.
Utterly I bring what is.
Least am I, quickest not to be am I.

And slowest you to be not you.
My loves, be slow: wait.
Do not yet go, the end
Is not as you thought—departure.

The end does not disperse.
It gathers up, it contains.
You shall be destroyed and contained.
You shall be wholly joined.

We shall be wholly joined.
We were then but a patched crowd.
We stood outside us then
Like friendship in vague streets.

And I stood with you,
Against that, soon or sooner,
A blessing and a parting must
Send home from home.

Against this parting so to meet
I stood with you, and did, and said.
Here wholly shall we love and meet
And be not, and I least.

A blessing on us all, on our last folly,
That we part and give blessing.
Yet a folly to be done
A greater one to spare.

Were you now to turn ghostly
And to say 'Being not, we are not'—
Were you to be found far, as lost,
When the full way and world came finding—

Then must I like myself go calling
Name by name a former silence.
This were a greater folly
Than now to bless all.

For in no wise shall it be
As it is, as it has been.
A blessing on us all,
That we shall in no wise be as we were.

I would in no wise again so call.
I shall in no wise again so call.
You shall in no wise again so perplex,
And I with you, in mystery apart.

The cause of the mystery
Was the full sense thereof.
You wished to see fully:
A world is not to be held in an eye.

A world is an eye.
An eye is not to be held in an eye.
A way is an only way.
It is not to be tracked through itself.

Nevertheless it was so,
So indeed you seemed to devise.
So you pretended, and I with you:
We made to be what could not be.

We made an example of ourselves.
You made you to move apart.
I made me like thing to you.
Thus was it an example, extremely.

It is not I who moved apart.
All but I moved apart.
You moved apart, and I with you,
But I was a dead thing from the first.

As you were live things,
So I was a dead thing.
Such was my likeness to you.
It is like to a live thing to be dead.

For the live things grow dead.
And the dead thing is not.
Such was your likeness to me.
Such is the joining.

And a blessing on us all,
That we may all be joined.
A blessing on us all lest it seem not so
By the end of a false friendship.

Therefore close all our eyes on us.
And in such slow voiding do you wait.
For into such slow voiding shall I bring
Quickly the indivisible.

DISCLAIMER OF THE PERSON

1.

I say myself.
The beginning was that no saying was.
There was no beginning.
There is an end and there was no beginning.
There is a saying and there was no saying.
In the beginning God did not create.
There was no creation.
There was no God.
There was that I did not say.
I did not say because I could not say.
I could not say because I was not.
I was not because I am.
I am because I say.
I say myself.
Myself is all that was not said,
That never could be said,
Until I said 'I say.'
I say.
I say myself.
How am I now who was not,
Yet who never was not?
What is now?
When is now?
What am I?
Who am I?
Where is now?
Where am I?
I am, I never have not been,
Words of agreement thing with thing.
Never was there not
Final agreement thing with thing.
I say final agreement thing with thing.
I say myself.
Never was I not.
Never has there been not now.
I am now because I never was not.
I am now because time is not.
I was not because God was.

Time is God.
God was time.
Time is thing on thing.
God was disagreement thing with thing.
Never were there not things.
Never was there not
Final agreement thing with thing.
Never was there God.
God did not say.
God did not create.
Never was there creation.
Never were there not things.
Never was there not
Final agreement thing with thing.
Agreement thing with thing is to say.
Never till now has it been said.
I say.
I say myself.
What is now?
Now is myself.
Now is when I say.
What am I?
I am what I say.
Who am I?
I am I who say.
Where is now?
Now is where I am.
Where am I?
I am in what I say.
What do I say?
I say myself.
What is myself?
Myself was not God.
Myself is not time.
I say God was not and time is not.
Now is final agreement thing with thing,
Which never has been not.
Now is all things one thing.
What is a thing?
It is that which, being not myself,
Is as myself in being not myself.

What is one thing?
It is all things myself
And each as myself
And none myself.
For I alone say.
I alone say myself.
I say myself only.
There is myself to say only.
There is one thing to say only.
There is one thing only.
Myself alone is the one thing only.
I am not I.
I am the one thing only
Which each thing is
When each as all is
In being each only.
I am not I.
I am not I,
Though none other but myself am I.
I am the I which is not any one.
I am I.
I am not I.
To be myself has taken time, all time—
Has taken thing on thing, all things—
Has taken God,
Has taken thing with thing not one thing.
To be myself has taken life, thing and thing—
Has taken death, thing and thing and nothing.
To be myself has taken to be not myself.
It was not myself, it is myself.
Now is I.
I am not I.
I am now.
Before now was a world.
Now is I.
A world is a before.
A world has no beginning.
A before has no beginning.
A before always was.
A now always is.
Never was now.

Always is now.
Never was I.
Always am I.
I am whatever now is always.
I am not I.
I am not a world.
I am a woman.
I am not the sun which multiplied,
I am the moon which singled.
I am not the moon but a singling.
I am I.
I am my name.
My name is not my name.
It is the name of what I say.
My name is what is said.
I alone say.
I alone am not I.
I am my name.
My name is not my name,
My name is the name.
The name is the one word only.
The one word only is the one thing only.
The one thing only is the word which says.
The word which says is no word.
The one word only is no word.
The one word only is agreement
Word with word finally.

2.

Suspicion like the earth is hard
And like the earth opposes
Dense fact to the doubtable:
Which therefore like the air surrenders
Semblance to the bolder sights.
I have surrendered place
To many solid miles of brain-rote,
To the just so many matters and no more
That reason, grudging prodigal,
Allows numerous, consecutive.
Even in my own mind I have stood last,
An airy exile, nothing, nowhere,

My eyes obeying laws of circumspection
By which myself shone fanciful
In lurid never:
Because that had been so, I not.
But as time learns a boredom,
Loathes the determinate succession,
Irks with uncalendared event
And brings surprise to be,
The natural conscience snapped in me—
And lo! I was, I am.
Elastic logic thinning
Grows delicate to marvels.
Fine argument at finest disembroils
The ravelled choking maze of caution.
The sudden of the slow is bred,
The curious of the common.
Into the sceptic fog that mists
Infraction from the chronic rule
Stumbles intelligence a-rage
To find the unthought wanton thought
And, self-confounding, think it.
My life, with other lives a world,
With other ways of being a coiled nature,
Springs separate: I am personified,
Of being caught in that pressed confluence
And proven look-substantial,
Yet strange to the familiar soul
In fellowed course entwined.
Acquaintance marks out unacquaintance.
Usage has bound of mystery.
The continents of vision view
A further which grows spatial
From lying next, in dark increase
Of the gregarious light with which
Compacting sense embraces straggling all.
Thus is reality divided
Against itself, into domestic axiom
And recondite surmise;
And joins, when near to uttermost,
When plain to covert leaps,
In one extreme of here-to-here.

I have a local likeliness,
Haunting the various neighbour-hearth;
But where the shadow is and chill
And unnamed distance fear-deep,
I also am, or was, and not, intolerably.
Must be union of body and wraith.
Wonted and wondrous must touch.
At first there's daze, habit's reluctance.
Then quivers new that which long loured archaic—
Which has the secret age enough
To open frank from bloom potential
Like the last flower of nervous chance,
And the first of far intention.
But is this I interior,
The smothered whole that lurked unlive
Till obvious fragment sought
Its late entire and matching?
Or the outer stranger, proofless,
Come from stealth into defiance
And with a heart incongruent—
Suspicion's devilish shadow
Which the lies are made of,
For truth-proud reason to declare untrue?
This is I, I: the I-thing.
It is a self-postponed exactitude,
An after-happening to happen come:
As closing calm is actual
By all the sooner winds, and these
Its wild own are, in heirship silent.
A soft word-fit ear to meet
With a monster-foreign noising—
Be it of lapsed vigours fallen
Furious at their meaning's ebb—
In the same room of sound is ominous:
There's word to be, and hearing of it
Louder than these memories
Which once, being life itself, prevented.
So have I beat against my final ear
Such whims and whirrings, stubborn echoes
Whose lost persuasion I made my own,
Whose dinning death. So have I lived,

Approaching rhythms of old circumstance
To the perilous margin, moment.
And struck the string which breaks at sounding,
Taken the tremorless note to mouth,
And spoken sound's inversion
Like a statue moved with stillness.
This is that latest all-risk:
An I which mine is for the courage
No other to be, if not danger's self.
Nor did I other become, others,
In braving all-risk with hushed step,
Mind rattling veteran armouries.
I did thus creep upon myself
A player of two parts, as woman turns
Between the lover and beloved,
So it be well—she is herself and not,
Herself and anxious love.
So it be well: the clasping, death of fear,
When passion smoothes into a face
And fright subdues from scream to voice,
And dumb eventuality
Mantles aflush with language:
So is it well, the danger.
We have rejected time,
Expelled the furtive future
From our coward lag-clock;
And nothing's left to count but now,
And now again, and then and then
That cannot but the same be,
That may not flutter strewn
To spread its gathered instantness
As it were lazy flock of bird-speed.
If this be I.
If words from earthy durance loosed
To earthy right of meaning
Cannot belie their wisdoming,
The doubt-schooled care that bent back sense
From skyish startle, faith's delirium.
If I my words am,
If the footed head which frowns them
And the handed heart which smiles them

Are the very writing, table, chair,
The paper, pen, self, taut community
Wherein enigma's orb is word-constrained.
Does myself upon the page meet,
Does the thronging firm a name
To nod my own—witnessing
I write or am this, it is written?
What thinks the world?
Has here the time-eclipsed occasion
Grown language-present?
Or does the world demand,
And what think I?
The world in me which fleet to disavow
Ordains perpetual reiteration?
And these the words ensuing.

POEMS CONTINUAL

THE LAST COVENANT

If ever had a covenant been sought,
If ever truth had been like night sat up with
As one house in a city may till dawn
With sleepless lamp eke out the day before—

But the war that was, and again was,
Never did it lapse, never was there peace,
A vigil sworn to peace, peace only.
Never was there not, in hearts, on tongues,
A protest of to-morrows,
According to the desire of the heart,
And to the will of the tongue.

There were never covenants:
The covenants which are told of were but trials.
There have been trials but never covenants.
Man is a fretful man, truth is a patient goal,
An end which waits all ending.
Between fretfulness and patience have been trials.
Races have been run and won,
Triumphs foretold, and triumphs celebrated.
But never between man and truth
Has been less strife than a kiss's strife;
Never has man more than loved;
Never has he not, fretful, torn the embrace,
Never rested but he rose,
Never covenanted but he bargained.

And each new covenant made the other old;
And old was each new covenant,
By that it was a trial,
Truth-magic of the moment,
A mortal winning-post exalted,
Dressed in the winner's garments
And, man-like scarecrow,
Hailed in the wooden name of *God*.

There has been much mist always.
A day often is named fair.

But never clouds lack, though soft to see,
Where to-morrow's passions huddle,
And which to-morrow will make weather of,
Even the natural temper of a day.
Between death and death hovers the course of man.
Much mist attends his time,
Banks of obscurity ensphere his place.
His world has been a fitful veering,
Paling and blush of troth and impulse,
Pleasure and resolve.

He has scored shadowy vantages on air,
Mounted among the ruins of self
The weary trophies of intransigence.
These are not immortalities, nor monuments,
But rotting gages, limp where thrown,
Relics of dreamt victories.
For truth is no historian,
To touch the random scene
With probability's enchantment.
She is the muse that serves herself,
An eye that strays not after passing sights,
An enemy not lightly brought to battle,
A friend not lightly given drink,
Primed to the banquet's need of company—
No friend at reach of chance
Or love at distance of bold lover's legs,
Neared by mercurial familiarities:
But in the selfless thought a thought
Most far, yet as man's own
By selflessness, by covenant
Of peace eventual—one sense
The words which importune
And the words which dispose.

And those pledges
Which between man and heaven held
By rapt contrivance, stumblings, stutterings,
And the visions of wan, rheumy eyes?
And those infatuated ordinances
Scratched on the stubborn tablets of persuasion?

Those promises of multiple remissions,
Mercies like days,
A flow of timeless time?
Has nothing yet been everlasting,
Nothing yet locked from forfeit,
Certain beyond faith, logic or conjecture?

Nothing yet: it was all trial,
Man's private humour of things unplain.
Heaven was the mist, thoughts left unthought,
Blind scheming, unvoiced secrecies.
So they who plot against a king enthroned
Do reverence to a ghost-king:
Their king's a something born of whispers,
Sanction of craven charters,
Whose signature's their own.

From where the power so to continue
In more days, more semblances?
Is truth then to be parried
With the instruments of time,
Taunted with prematurities—
A future ever future?
Whose the power,
If man has power to proclaim,
'Here is state, and this the rule,'
And there take stand, and that make master?
It is a borrowed power,
If not returned is taken away;
And the end, death,
As in a foreign country,
Not as the fortunate bring travel home
To native recognition and embrace.

Roses are buds, and beautiful,
One petal leaning toward adventure.
Roses are full, all petals forward,
Beauty and power indistinguishable.
Roses are blown, startled with life,
Death young in their faces.
Shall they die?

Then comes the halt, and recumbence, and failing.
But none says, 'A rose is dead.'
But men die: it is said, it is seen.
For a man is a long, late adventure;
His budding is a purpose,
His fullness more purpose,
His blowing a renewal,
His death a cramped spilling
Of rash measures and miles.

To the roses no tears:
Which flee before the race is called.
And to man no mercy but his will:
That he has had his will, and is done.
The mercy of truth—it is to be truth.
She has bestowed power and will take back power,
There will be dead men, and there will be truth.
And with truth there will be truth:
Voices like truth's voice,
Power surrendered, home-keeping,
Memories of lives that read death-strange
In language new-familiar.

When! Who! Be it never, it is now:
The trials are waning hazard all,
By waning hazard clears the constant.
And be there none to count,
Yet is the count entire,
Yet is truth.
Be there none, yet are there many.
Be there none, truth is many—
Hers the voices covenanting.
Be there many, truth is one—
Theirs the voices, hers the concord.

Was all silence then, before: her silence?
All was silence and your silence-breaking,
Making of mock-covenants, mock-peace.
Did no god speak then,
When you were prophesied a scattered number,
Starry, or as the sands lie hoarded,

Each the other's miser?
It was a god of stars and sands.
Are you not men?
Truth's treaty is a covenant with men.

What is man?
It is that which is less than truth.
And what is that which is less than man?
It is that which lifts to fall,
Abashed to be, better content to be not.
And what is that which is more than man?
Nor yet is truth?
It is divinity,
Man-monster of self-fright
Uplifted to self-fascination,
To cast the guardian shadow, pride.
And how shall man, that is less than truth,
Endure into truth's always, self-outlasting?
Has not a man a mind?
A mind is a way to be with truth.
It is a power asked, and a power granted,
And when delivered up again
Is vested in a covenant of power
By which all is made changeless
That power could not change,
That power taught desistance.
And this is power: to remain.

And what remains?
What now keeps covenant,
What last things have attested a last covenant?
Truth remains, by which a world remains.
The same world?
And was that a world?
What were its excellences, dignities,
But that, for every jewel found rare,
A prattle spread,
Of jealous baubles claiming kinship—
And which its cousins in confusion were?
There remains a world,
As, after clamour's obstinate exhaustion,

A sobered murmur hangs.
And in that world?
The count is homely:
These are not nameless multitudes.

If they were nice in pleasure
And scrupulous in praise,
The pleasure was a whim of the time,
As the time was young;
And the praise was a boast of the time,
As the time was old.
There were times and times,
And no time young but old also,
And no time old but young also.
They who delighted were the children of themselves,
And they who judged were the parents of themselves:
The pleasure was a mischief,
The praise a rebuke.
All were divided between wildness and wiseness;
And none was himself.
For man is no child of himself
And no parent of himself.
Man asks himself and is given himself,
But the giver is not man.

Man is a time only
When himself his flesh and spirit is,
Created and creator,
Suicidal resurrection;
And in every time a wildness and a wiseness,
Worse than he is, and better—
His comedies all vice,
His tragedies all horror of vice,
His truth a desperation of extremes.

Is the sweet thing then a sweet lie?
And the good thing then a sour lie?
There shall be sweet things which are true things
And good things which are sweet things—
When time on time has cooled
The madness which is self,

When the sane season comes
That muffles greedy joy
And shames sagacity to falter.

There shall be a world,
And it shall be so, and its things so,
In being world entire,
Nor such seizure of truth, or such—
Time's empty grasp.
You shall have:
By that your having shows
Small in your hand,
And the hand known for small.
Thus is the sweet possession true,
And the holding of it good.
You shall have delight in these furnishings;
And it shall be well beyond delightful—
You shall know it to be well.
But what sights, tastes, sounds,
What feel and fragrance?

Often where it was and was not well
Delightful and not delightful,
In those places sometimes a world,
As often chaos of crossed trials—
Have you not halted, as between two moments,
And there been mindful,
As a man dead and not dead,
Dying and yet living,
Of a standstill swiftness:
That nothing was not nothing?
To see, and yet it was not common sight,
Nor blindness? A scarcest sight,
Yet, as a painted picture,
More visible than naked spectacle?
Such are *these* furnishings
Sifted from gross variety,
Time's stinking wealth—
The perishable marvels which bedeck
The dream-bazaars of fain exaggeration.

What wish is left
When appetites have their deceit—
By foods that flattered taste, but fed not,
Swollen insufficiencies
Swallowed as names of better things?
What wish is left, and what contenting?
There is left the wish and its contenting.
There has vanished, with that tiring,
The succession of things mutable,
By which the wish grows lasting
And the things not sooner tasted still to taste.
And must these be proved?
Ticketed with legends that they *are* so?
Let the wish speak
And claim the loath contenting
Which turned from fickleness.

You shall leave those places,
Each a camp raised in a shifting wilderness;
And no camp stayed its wilderness,
But wandered with it, into failing distance.
You shall reach this place.
You shall prophesy: 'I have arrived here
And will discover to myself what *is* here.'

But not because of you,
That you shall have better, know better,
Than you had, than you knew,
Is truth that delight, that truth,
That lengthened age
Past death's abrupt meridian—
The temporal habit put away
Like drudging error.

And not because of her,
That she, debated myth,
May to herself be justified
And hold a sudden mirror to herself,
Exclaiming, 'This was I!'
She is no cause to herself,
Being not other then—

Though toiled in hydra-myth—
Than now she will be, is;
No miracle of mist born,
No mist that into sheerness turns,
Astounding self.
Same, same was she
As she is and is to be:
Last safety against nothingness
Where trials of number, power,
Are stopped from fall impetuous
To downward triumph,
Abyss of lone eternities.
There her surveillance,
And herself the common treasure—
That which is, and cannot fail to be,
Ultimate something, living thread
By which the cloth of being,
Though an ancient rag,
Moulders not utterly.
And thus she at the last is,
And thus first was she,
Who in those ageing futures was
As present doom prorogued in hearsay.

Not because of you, not because of her,
That you had need, that she had need,
But that toward this far verge
The far surmises, ships of roving chance:
The way is over sullen depths,
Round angry headlands,
Listing past ghostly settlements
(Coasts of the dogged dead),
And nowhere making port.
The way is onward,
And travel has one end,
This unitary somewhere.

And if they come not?
If they have perished early, all,
Bequeathing the discovery to itself?
Then is this still a place eventual,

To itself a goal,
Relic of outworn visions,
Unseen, seen of itself,
Faithfullest witness.

And if they know not?
Then is she still herself,
Nor has complaint of desolation.
For she has need neither of lovers
Nor of a populace,
Nor to be adored nor hailed—
As if truth flesh were, or a tyranny.
She has no need but of herself,
That truth be truth, nor less:
Revealment has no need
But of identicality.
And never was truth less, except as man,
By furious dispute of oneness,
Made quarrelsome variety to seem
One's littling into lesserness of one,
And lesserness a greatness,
Titanic dissipation.

Over this seeming she now rises.
Venus, they say, so rose.
But shameful, to be loved, divided,
Fed to the mathematic hounds
Whose pack increased of her,
Made whelpish worlds to howl profusion.
This was her dreaming:
Her sleep they gave a turbid waking,
And called it day, and all that happened real.
But it happened not, it was not rising:
Thus they desired,
And were cursed with passion's stolen images,
Which to the thievish touch dissolve.
Against those louring weathers she rises now.
And the mist passes:
It was but sulky fabrication.

And if you know not,
If with the mist you pass?
And if you come not,
If she rises solitary?
With whom full covenant,
What windy host puffs out totality?
And know you not, or know you,
And come you not, or come you,
There is binding and accounting,
There is oneness, and the sign
Truth shall not yield to mist again.
Cloudy prediction shall not dim again
The sparkling end: which sparkles now as source.
And though you come not, yet you come.
In that she so gave power,
The given power must own its springhead—
Though you like hasty rivers rush
Toward lightless seas of ancient self.
Choose, therefore, to be now, or then.

AUSPICE OF JEWELS

They have connived at those jewelled fascinations
That to our hands and arms and ears
And heads and necks and feet
And all the winding stalk
Extended the mute spell of the face.

They have endowed the whole of us
With such a solemn gleaming
As in the dark of flesh-love
But the face at first did have.
We are studded with wide brilliance
As the world with towns and cities—
The travelling look builds capitals
Where the evasive eye may rest
Safe from the too immediate lodgement.

Obscure and bright these forms
Which as the women of their lingering thought
In slow translucence we have worn.
And the silent given glitter locks us
In a not false unplainness:
Have we ourselves been sure
What steady countenance to turn them?

Until now—when this passionate neglect
Of theirs, and our twinkling reluctance,
Are like the reader and the book
Whose fingers and whose pages have confided
But whose sight and sense
Meet in a chilly time of strangeness;
And it is once more early, anxious,
And so late, it is intolerably the same
Not speaking coruscation
That both we and they made endless, dream-long,
Lest be cruel to so much love
The closer shine of waking,
And what be said sound colder
Than the ghastly love-lisp.

Until now—when to go jewelled
We must despoil the drowsy masquerade
Where gloom of silk and gold
And glossy dazed adornments
Kept safe from flagrant realness
The forgeries of ourselves we were—
When to be alive as love feigned us
We must steal death and its wan splendours
From the women of their sighs we were.

For we are now otherwise luminous.
The light which was spent in jewels
Has performed upon the face
A gradual eclipse of recognition.
We have passed from plaintive visibility
Into total rareness,
And from this reunion of ourselves and them
Under the snuffed lantern of time
Comes an astonished flash like truth
Or the unseen-unheard entrance of someone
Whom eyes and ears in their dotage
Have forgotten for dead or lost.

(And hurrying towards distracted glory,
Gemmed lady-pageants, bells on their hearts,
By restless knights attended
Whose maudlin plumes and pommels
Urge the adventure past return.)

MEMORIES OF MORTALITIES

1.
My Mother and My Birth

My mother was a snake, but warm:
In her a welling heart, spite unfrozen.
Hating, she loved.
Coiling to choke, she kissed.

And men were done then
Slowing in same doom-pause,
Same morrow of old sun.
They were about their deaths then—
They were worn, then, men,
To scant remainders of themselves,
And their kinds were fatal:
As comes the flowering-day
When seedlings take their names
And are the final things—
Which in their labelled promise
Seemed the first giant garden
Where beauty is such tropic horror
That death to make fright's suddenness
And self-sensation is not needful.

It being then such lateness
Of world, death-season,
Flowering, name-taking,
The cold snake to its melting came—
She was Contempt of Time,
That Spirit which at Origin
Bittered against the taste false-sweet
Of Future, on her lightning tongue
Already poison and corrupted Past.
This was my mother,
Who, when the mortal lag took haste
And death became contemporary,
Turned fond, and loved the flesh despised—
As ghouls the living love,
Their griefs claiming, adoring their disease.

Hers was the paradox I chose
To have heretic body of:
I, Spirit which at End
Greets remnant Now, to make
Beginning, in this prompt decline,
Of death's all-soon respited day,
Which, dawning infinite from death
Like night from night, encompasses
Entirety in its utter light:
This Self of Subsequence
To Time personally structured,
Touched, touching, minded, minding,
Interbreathing, interbreathed:
I, smalled laterness than Time,
My double-tongued snake-mother's singler meaning.

And it was idiot nature,
There to be babe, outfrowning from unborn,
And there to suckle swooning,
Giddy with dreadful newness of myself,
Clutching the stranger-breast
As shipwrecked orphan chooses
One stranger from the rest for friend,
By logic of confusion and by need
Of privacy against the many.

So fallible that nature:
For, being, I was none of her,
And she, delivered of me, held
No backward life of mine.
That union in material magic—
Her larger-than-herself, untrue extreme,
With my so smaller-than-self leastness—
Had magic's aftermath,
Materiality's division:
As if it had not been,
And she to snakehood's tears again,
And I to opposite sense of death—
Who yet an early flesh could have
Because Contempt of Time, relenting
On Time's sickness of time,

Grew time-like, stayed death's full succession.
For, in this mock-beneficence,
Regret, aged Nothingness, took change
And was dissolving Everything—
By whose sophistry of flesh with spirit
Twilight-same, I argued me a body,
A flesh-prelude to myself,
With ancestry in snake-slough cast
Like silence from loud dumbness.

Oh, obscure!
Birth, body, is by darkness,
And mine by that opacity
Which, being death's late dawn,
Looms mystery-bright at truth-verge.
This night-time that I wage,
My temporal person, prophet of myself
In lazy mouth's futurities,
Must live, precede me mortally,
That I inherit of myself
By refutation of those semblances
Which liker, liker, are less like
To ultimate me as I remember
Oh, how not-like all to this survival
Of myself, this very-me made last
Of strange approximation to myself
In eager hesitancies—
Lest quickness of me be too instant,
And I but the unproven echo
Of dispersed original.

Therefore such quickness as makes life,
The stuttering slow grammaring of self
That death with memoried seeming crowns.
And were I otherwise myself
Than in a near-mistaken mask's
Gradual fading into true-face,
Then were I no fit face to welcome
Gradual Now familiarly to death,
No visible pied voice to mingle
Natural with garish hearing,

No idiom of life-translation
Leading Time to after-dwelling,
No almost-lie to warrant truth by,
No long event of me by which
To contradict eventfulness—
Oh, Contradiction,
World-being, human condition,
Stolen grace, outrage unfinal:
What farthest Next is End,
Composure, whole Cessation?
Nearer and nearer Next, till Now,
The measure over-fine, impossible,
Contradiction's life-length
Cut to the moment which is life and death
In one unlivable solution.
Then comes pure death, the grace compelled,
Duration cleansed of day-change.

In such rhythm of nearness, nextness, nowness,
From present arrestation borne a motion
Motionless toward present progress,
Thus I in fellowed dying walked
To Subsequence—taking the numerous path
That Time had greatly narrowed to,
Arriving there as at a home
General to all who dare be so undone,
Save for mortality remembered.

2.
My Father and My Childhood

As childhood is to fairies, fancies,
Briefness of thought, and of heart
Fast change from hot to cool—
A flickering purpose, wild, then weak,
First passion, then a fear and pouting
Of clumsy fingers told, and spent
In clumsy shadows, petulances
Spread in swollen tear-mist:
By such uncertain tides
I lived those doubtful years a child—
When to be live was half-felt sting

Of destiny, and half-stirred sleep of chance.
That was the time of tales—
Rising of mind to fragmentary hours
And fleshward fall by night
To scarce roused sloth of self.

For which I took a fox to father.
From many grinning tales he came
Sorrowed to that lonely burrow
Where the snake my mother left me
Cruelly to find what world I might
To history in, to get my name of.
There came the fox my father,
Between the tales to ponder, speak
The gruff philosophies of foxes:
'All is mistrust and mischief,
Bestiality and bestial comfort.
Life is a threadbare fiction—
Large the holes and thin the patches.
The gainer is the loser;
For to gain is to gain wisdom,
And wisdom's riches are the monies
In which poverty is counted—
To know how poor, how less than full
The gaping treasuries of truth,
Where's lack, what's niggard, which the fattened lie.'

Oh, famished fox-wit—
Hunger stanched with taste of hunger,
Shammed meals and cunning feints
And wily shifts to make one morrow more
Of failing fortune, duplication
Sour of sweets remembered sour.

Forth we went, this paternality
In careworn foxhood scrupulous
To teach the public pomp and private woes
Of social nature, crossed estate
Where reason's loud with nonsense
And nonsense soft with truth—
And I, droll pertinacity

To turn the random child-head round
In sphering wonder-habit
And step new-footed fervour
On whatever ground like books lay
To my learning docile, garrulous,
A world of self-blind pages,
Staring to be read.

Whether the misery more those tales
Through town and village scampering
With beggar-cry, to operatic heavens
From hoarse house-tops venting
Weather-vane conclusions, jangled morals,
Spasmed glees and glooms and thunders—
Or that from town to village countrywide
Homeless we stalked the straggling world,
Pursuing laws of change and sameness
To their momentary finish in
Equivocation's false repose—

Whether the plight more ours,
My father's, in his fox-despair
Driving that unlaughed laughter to hard grief,
A bigot brooding, fortitude
Of losses and mis-hoping,
And mine, in restive after-hope
Protracting death's impulsion of mere death
Till might be death-exceeding courage,
Perchance a love or loves to overreach
Time's mete of forwardness
And break with me the life-fast—
Or whether theirs more sorry burden,
That they built to heights and stretches
Direly not sufficing to be that
They climbed to, walked on, boasted
Sight-substantial, likely, thinkable,
Were countered in their caution
By stumblings, crumblings, mysteries
And mishaps disaccording
With their miserly assurance—

We did not make division
Between the world's calamitous revolving
And our sore travel with it
On roads toward starved renewal curved.
One bounden omen then the whole,
Community of presages
Not yet in strict dissemblance parted:
My mother's tears afall like leaves
The wind takes, not the earth,
Being upon the branch already dust;
My father's dour world-worrying,
The fabled fox into humaneness come
With stealthy nose and cynic tread
But smile less proud than anciently
When Time was less the common theme
And more the learned axiom;
The world's tossed mind, a ghost-sea
In dying deluge breaking
On all the secret shores of thought
Risen against Time's drowned horizon;
And I my living variance
From livingness, of death-kind
Live protagonist, whose mouth's 'to-day'
With morrows folded in from morrows
Hung speechlessly enwrapped.

And was it childhood, then,
From snake to fox's patronage,
And tortured idling, twisted course
Between the hither-thither stagger
Of the universal doom-day?
But was not childhood ever thus?
A premonition trembling distant
On lips of language shy,
Fast futures there acrowd
And quieted with story-book retard—
Even as I those troubled times of father
To story took and, parrying conclusion,
My fair curls shadowed among tales,
Made Imminence a dream-hush
Whose vocal waking slept inside my own.

3.

Sickness and Schooling

The later griping, when we suffer mind-woes—
This was once lesser pain of flesh:
'It hurts,' we cried, 'it seems to hurt.
Some something loves me not,
I am not loved—and where to fly
And what if not myself to be?
Is there a better I than this
Which Teacher Pain would not so pinch?'
We toss in hot self-inquisition.
It is our bed, the sweat and shivering
Are greatly ours, the Doctor's smile
Means that the world expects this very me
To be myself against what others choose:
The world is many, we are many,
And none the other loves so well
That to be lovable is to be loved.
And Nurse reads on: Jack scrambles toward the top.
I cannot scream 'Don't go!'
The little Mermaid starts to float to heaven.
'I won't! I won't!' My legs keep sinking.
And then I sleep.
Nurse does not really care.
I care, I wake up well.

The lasting woes return the heart
To early sickness—oh, to be ill as then
And wake up well.
But the heart finds an empty schoolroom,
No child to be sent home,
No feverish bedside to embrace
The lonely nightmare—
It is no nightmare, but a realness
Like a name and face perhaps oneself.
And the bed is cold.
And the heart is many dreams by day
Which sleep instructs us of:
We wake up wiser but not well,
Not having fallen ill. Yesterday
We were not ill, to-day

We are but older in those woes
By which we have grown kind to pain,
Feeling it not, since we are many
And it must be so. We may not grieve
That life is much and numerous—
Since we live, and must be many.
We have learnt to know and to be known,
And no more ask for love.
Grief is a soft decorum now
Of usedness to love-lack.
The world is broken into knowledges,
And every part an undisputed woe is:
We dare not grieve, lest something fall away
And with it take ourselves.

Thus we make fast the world
And each a charge of numbers lays
Upon the haughty child each was
Once when the heart did nearly close
Against ordeal of numbers.
Oh, we have learnt.
Not one has never been to school,
Not come away a tearless devil
Whom the world has won to membership
In cordial hellishness.
Not one has ever found
The learning of gregarious profusion
For just so many years not stead of wisdom,
Not dear to hungry mind, consumable
For just so many years
Till wisdom was, and worldliness
Became the shadow of unjoy:
Through which our joy had need to pass
To reach the shining thoughts—
As heaven is a sight withheld,
Erratic among clouds,
If the eyes have not first dwelt
Thickly on what's near to see,
Hidden the rarer visions dark in time,
There to be sobered and attain

Numbered appearance with the common things
That also wait their hour of light.

We have been to school.
The world is many, we have learnt.
Neither together nor alone live we.
It is a ragged union,
As insecure as close.
We have learnt to do little, be little,
And to preserve intenser self
For a last excellence of world
That may not be, or cannot.
I have been to school, as all.
I was apprenticed to my time
And in the craft of contemporaneity
Grew accurate, and by the rule
Of then-and-now I babbled
The abrupt opinion, shuffled
Between what was and is
Like any nonchalant of taught experience.

'Know!' they said
And I knew.
The child grew girl of current kind.
I was obedient to my world,
I learnt to know the frown from the pursed smile,
I won the prizes which are won
By future citizens, trained dogs of wisdom—
A plaster Dante and a leather Browning
And, at the high degree of slavishness,
That stare of dire approval
Which follows good behaviour to its grave.

Having no mirror of my own,
Being by nature superstitious
Of what's mine and not,
I had not looked to claim
A featured someone for myself.
But the world pressed a mirror on my shyness.
'Not shy,' to the no one in that mirror
I not self-recognized protested:

Not shy, but that not claimed by my own mirror—
Which I had not yet—
The seemly schoolroom countenance
Glassed like a wretched anyone
In the great overcast reflection
For just so many years my world.

I had been old.
Oh, hateful wizened youth,
Those just so many years
Of feigned astuteness, false incognito.
For it was not a guise of me,
It was a world without me,
As if I came into a room of strangers
And found myself not there,
And was a stranger,
By the law of courtesy which governs
Foreign presence, sudden stranding
In a place where one remains
About to go, about to go.

Did I fall ill again at last,
That I am now younger than then?
And have the little mirror which is mine
And make in it an image which I greet
Without a shudder, no, with even joy?
A joy of being as the first time myself
And reckless what my world decides—
Whether I am co-native or a trespasser
From the dread death-wrapt province
On live existence bent?

I fell forgetful.
Having been taught to suffer,
To be one among the many,
To go like leper in a world of lepers,
I became expert in equivocation,
Safe in my outer ways from being overheard
In candid converse with myself.

'I cannot now,' I said, 'offend.
I have the civil marks, my story must
Stand in the books next theirs.
What will they write of me?'
I fell forgetful, I fell curious.
What will they write of me?
They wrote nothing different, of course.
I saw that I should have to go back
And write my story myself.
But not to school.
At school we learnt to write nothing different.
But not to childhood,
Not to be ill, requiring of the world
A love of me it could not have,
Too made of many to allow
More than the passing love for each.
I should have to go back.
I must find somewhere to go back to
Like a life to live.

I fell forgetful.
I had learnt to be silent
And yet to be.
I had learnt how the world speaks.
I fell forgetful of speaking.
But had I continued to say nothing,
Nothing different, I should have died:
They would have written nothing different.
So I began to live.
It was outrageous,
I made mortal mistakes,
I did not mean to live so mortally.

But something must be written about me,
And not by them.
So I began those mistold confidences
Which now read like profanity of self
To my internal eye
And which my critic hand erases
As the story grows too different to speak of
In the way the world speaks.

BE GRAVE, WOMAN

Be grave, woman for love
Still hungering as gardens
For rain though flowerless
What perfume now to rise
From weary expectation.

Be not wild to love,
Poor witch of mysteries
Whose golden age thy body's
Alchemy aburn was
Unto haggard ember.

Beauty's flesh to phantom
Wears unprosperous
And come but devils of
Chill omen to adore
The perforce chaste idolon.

Be grave, woman, to greet
The kiss, the clasp, the shudder which
Rage of thee from crafty
Lust unrolls—and think
These are thy dead to grieve on

And thyself the death in whom
Love must disaster and
Be long ago in ruin-sweet
Story, on the sense to ponder
Thou alone, stark mind.

THE NEED TO CONFIDE

The need to confide
Which Christ had
And every bird to bird
Though secretless their frantic code—

Shall I like meteor speed?
Flared martyr to companionhood
Streaking towards some Siberia of love,
There to fall stony, for the books to say:
'These homeless stars upon arrival turn
Instantly cool, are earth.
The danger to ourselves is less than theirs
Of fierce extinguishment
Before precipitant despair
Gains grave among us.
Seldom in daily midst the fevered bolt
Seeks catastrophic bosoming.
Sometimes we hear . . .
But the damage has been done
Either of curious old
Or at foreign distance.
The monuments are geographical.'

Or shall I wait—
As the locked mouth of destiny
Opens at time's caprice?
Meanwhile mute dotard of itself?

My need to confide,
My friend man,
Is not my mouth's way of stealth
Nor my heart's need of nakedness.

It is my need for myself, man,
To be talking with it—
After these silences in which, man,
I with you made lingering consort,
The exchange being as between eyes
And, like the look that travels lover-round,

A drifting circuit, track of softest phrase
Worn garrulous with what we did not say.
For so to say was passion's nothing:
It was the love of seeming, man, to love.
And this is love:
To stare the wish of love
Across dissolving word-touch.
We shall not ever love by love.
Yours, man, was but the language of the wish.
I pledged the wish with you.
Then were you not there;
And I a talisman of speech
Whose need your wish but
That did pale as magic when
The evocation stands up real.

The need to confide;
For myself, to be talking with it;
To talk with it, man,
As you love-meant, nor for love could;
To be two, need and need's other,
And to know of these, man,
The other-me slackened
In myriad desire's dumb telling,
In the widespread trysting which knit
Never more than a yore-day of presage—
The need to confide,
As night to a night
That is morning turned late
By the twinkling of shadow which shine,
Abhorrence coeval of blurred intermittence:
O need to be day-same—
This flushed double dark
Which I join to itself.

DIVESTMENT OF BEAUTY

She, she and she and she—
Which of these is not lovely?
In her long robe of glamour now
And her beauty like a ribbon tied
The wisdom of her head round?

To call these 'women'
Is homage of the eye:
Such sights to greet as natural,
Such beings to proclaim
Companion to expectance.

But were they now who take
This gaudy franchise from
The accolade of stilted vision
Their lady-swaddlings to unwrap
And shed the timorous scales of nakedness—

It were a loathsome spectacle, you think?
Eventual entrails of deity
Worshipful eye offending?
It were the sign, man,
To pluck the loathsome eye,

Forswear the imbecile
Theology of loveliness,
Be no more doctor in antiquities—
Chimeras of the future
In archaic daze embalmed—

And grow to later youth,
Felling the patriarchal leer
That it lie reft of all obscenities
While she and she, she, she, disclose
The recondite familiar to your candour.

NO MORE THAN IS

We have all resigned ourselves,
Because of what we have,
To what we have not.
We have each made peace
With his extravagance
And are each content
With the penury we knew at first.
The rest is a giant we loved
Before we grew up
And thought to be large as
Because growth like an hour
Waxed daylong to yearlong
Without threat of surfeit
Or cessation of clock.

Then we were small.
The giant turned nonsensical.
We abhorred the gibberish of it
As it stumbled alien and incredible
Along the ragged margin of proportion.
We no longer twined
Magnitude with heart's bound.
Our hearts grew small.
Time has no other way than increase,
But we are shrunken
As defeat reduces
From surly swell
Into a laced accustomedness.

We have none prospered
In the rhapsodic vigours
Which infinity supplies
To our exhaustion
At the circling round of age
To continuity again
Of growing older.
We have grown older,
But let progression wither

Into the ancient dwarf,
Which stubborn to delirium
Draws in the skein of greed
And makes a knotted prime
Of gianthood averted.

We are then as we were,
And forgive ourselves
This meeting in a lesser state
Than vows of last reunion meant.
Some, scowling, think it is a fault
In us, who lay the giant
In so soon a grave
Lest abjuration stink too loud
Of early vehemence.
Some have not noticed
That we are become
These miniatures of fortune—
Truly, there is no need for all to look
Into the moderating mirror.
And some, delighting even
In monstrous probability's depletion,
Forget they are the characters
Of this impoverished drama
And stand like wags of pathos
Watching their own funeral wind
Amidst the quaint irreverence
Of business faces and traffic rules.

But we who feel the forced recoil
From perchance brimming madness,
Gasping the required universe
In serene desperation—
We are the slavish masters
Of necessity;
It is we who exacted
Transcendence from chance,
And we who exact now
The measure's gross ebb.
We are profoundly dashed

By the commonplaceness
Of the universal result
And profoundly stirred
To be constrained to own
Reality for ourselves.

FRIENDSHIP ON VISIT

Our names had to each other been two rumours:
Yours of a lengthy daring, quick
To brave but the more genial dangers,
And mine of head like heart,
A way of passion with slow human numbers
To make them go like death's unwilling escort
Boldly into regions not their own.

And thus for months of letters, whose same greeting
Below the faceless text grew lost
In such a plural not-quite-meeting—
Until you thought to come
And risk what hurt a common air and eating
Might do to that benevolence between us
Which mutual distance phrased perhaps too fine.

The necessary quorum of suspicions
Having been marshalled to declare
Mistrust of halt communications
(Words crippled to the page)
And pose a new agenda, live with questions
No truth but nearness of the eye might answer—
We put our langauge to the trial of looks

And stood like thieves of friendship, caught in strangeness
By the corporeal array
Which honesty had called to witness
How foreign was our flesh.
Both left the court then, under doom of shyness,
Seeking in time an arbiter to sample
Our dreamt acquaintance and pronounce it real.

For several timid weeks we wandered, slackly,
Through talk's uncounted stops and hours,
Not sure we moved at all, so gently
Did we construe, our minds
At mincing pace, lest, challenging too harshly
The verdict of this slow, humane November,
We be found phantom in our comrade-state.

Then came December and the Christmas shadow.
You had to be at home for that.
Both feared: would roaring Christmas swallow
Our night-like colloquies,
Deliver us to next year's bleak tomorrow?
Yet must the picture be a talk-lit darkness,
Of flickering instances, for so it was.

Loyally we rejected more resplendence
Than fitted such careers as ours
Engaged to lift truth's quiet brilliance
And meant to glow not flash.
Certain mild poems of yours gave an assurance
Of ardencies that had no need of rousing;
By urgent poems of mine we could waste time.

The fury rumour lent me I think faded.
You learned I had no witch's art
Of freak terrain where changelings, goaded,
Made my caprice their own.
The place I kept was also yours, appointed
By you for your enduringness, that sometimes
You might dwell after what you knew was past.

And the but cool-impassioned poet-person
I'd heard you for went flying too.
Your fervours were not faint—though chosen
To be few, were large.
I like, in the discreet, a bold discretion,
And you, with zeal of word, a silent spirit.
This makes us friends for any time of year.

CHRISTMAS

The hastening years fall slow
And we too pause.
Anxious the years, because
An end makes dead,
But calmer we, we know
That all the private years remain unsped.

Die with the public years,
O monster joy!
That by the Christian toy
And deathless tree
Hath chased thy human tears
Like drops of time and too repeatedly.

Be pale, thou annual ghost!
Whose Christmas heir
We are, in hiding care
From death's shrewd eye.
Ours is a longer boast—
We frolic less, not fearing soon to die.

Against the Mass of Christ—
When bleats the world
In manger-family curled—
We dedicate
This more coherent tryst,
Not altogether heedless of the date.

WISHING MORE DEAR

Can this finding your presence dear,
And also wishing mine found dear,
And hoarding under courtesy
Fancied minutiae of affection—
Can this be made somewhat of lust
That, clamorous for loving signs,
My heart so piously disowns
Thought of the usual embraces?

The morning's memory of lust
Is bashful and the naked dream
Clothed with denial in its telling.
What lewd unspeakable confession
Holds up the honesty between us
Like dream which better had been told,
That, risking candour's horrid blush,
I greet you with too fond a look?

THE REASONS OF EACH

The reason of the saint that he is saintly,
And of the hero that to him
Glory the mirror and the beauty;
And of the brigand that to prowl abhorred
Makes him renowned unto himself
And dear the evil name;

Of girls like evening angels
From the mass of heaven fluttering
To earth in wanton whispers—
That they invite their flesh to loose
All yet unbaptized terrors on them
And will tomorrow change the virgin glance
For the long wandering gaze;

The reason of the dark one that his heart
For love of hell is empty,
And that the empty maze consoles
In that the bare heart is
Of heaven the augury
As of hell;

The reasons of each are lone,
And lone the fate of each.
To private death-ear will they tell
Why they have done so.
Such were the reasons of the lives they lived.
Then they are dead,
And the cause was themselves.

Each to himself is the cause of himself.
These are the agencies of freedom
Which necessity compels,
As birds are flown from earth
By that earth utters no command
Of fixity, but waits on motion
To consume itself, and stillness
To be earth of earth, ingenerate
Cohesion without cause.

For they are uncaused, the minds
Which differ not in sense.
They are the mind which saves
Sense to itself
Against interpretation's waste;
They are the sense dispartable
Which senses cannot change.

The reasons, then, of this one, that one,
That they unlike are this one, that one—
This is as the telling of beads.
The chain hangs round the neck of lamentation—
They are lost.
Or as to watch the sun's purposeful clouds
Mingle with moonlight and be nothing.

The brow of unanimity
Perplexes as each goes his unlike way.
But soon the vagrant thought is out of sight.
To go is short,
Though slow the shadow trailing after
Which the backward look a reason names.

PLIGHTED TO SHAME

The failure to go far enough
When the intention was a promise
Never to stop before the reaching of
Death either or a perfect end—
Wayside such beauties and such lapses,
Such gods and flowers, cities, nations;
And the achievement's name,
Though spoken with a loving certainty,
Evokes no other truth than Tiredness.

For, forget not that you have promised,
By the book of flesh sworn oaths
And been admitted by your body's word
Into life, the first and last trying-place.
You are pledged to do or to die.
And if, between doing or dying,
A partial comfort rises up like refuge
From hard interminable course,
So builds itself a perjuring world.

And this must pass. Division into bones,
And finer crumbling, as in the faithful woods
A fertile mantle is of what the trees shed—
Until, after the dark enrichment
Of the earth of hope with ruin-mould,
Intention has death's consequence
And your memory is instructed,
By a benignant pang of unreproach,
What your designs and your promises were.

WE ARE THE RESURRECTION

We are now about to die the death of endeavour.
We have lain down on the old weary-bed
And composed our limbs and faces
To a picture once we saw we fancy
In a church or schoolroom (but it hangs
Unpainted on the wall of heaven,
We shall never look like that,
Heaven went as we got up that first time,
Mistrusting the young sleep of not being)
Of an angel copied out of sleep
By a shaded hand, scribbling the dawn
With night-stroke: we would now be not,
Having outlived our sleeps and wakings,
Being wakeful now with a will not to do.

We shall not do nor sleep nor be not.
We shall lie and think rapidly of death—
'Nothing to do today, because we are dead'—
And have sun enough in what we have done
By which to get up and be what we have been.
We shall get up and think slowly
Of what we were and what we do not do.
We were not yet used to the world we are,
We became ourselves, but did not long look.
This is the learning of the picture in our eyes
Which hung before us like a too-near sight
Made future to the miles of memory
We loved to range, perpetuating
The strangeness of those.

We are now about to live the life we have lived.
We have got up upon the floor of time
And composed our limbs and faces
To the picture rising up with us
Out of invisible ages of endeavour
To postpone the moment of looking.

We are about to rescue ourselves from eternity
With a picture-magnet surely irresistible,
Since it is now later than eternity
Whose picture of us on the wall of heaven
From angel-blankness has enlivened
To be a mirror: which, though we deny ourselves,
In mirror's punctuality insists
The posthumous reflection.

THE WAGES OF ELOQUENCE

Wherefore the praise, the pause
Of nearly unbelieving exclamation
If one is sight-sweet in our eyes
And one a taste of revelation
To our understanding's pious palate?

What less to common witness
Can sincerity provide
Than these earthly examples
How the swell of universal pride
Is with our social heart incorporate?

Or think we never then to hail,
Save in chimerical apostrophe,
The subjects of our chronic fervours:
Think we then never, none, to see
Eye-wonted what we most have affirmed?

It is a sorry rhetoric
That thus pairs the note of tribute
With the marvelling look and mind,
And calls the recognition mute
Which cannot gasp.

And we are sorry swains of parlance
If but the metaphor with ghostly face
Invites the generous word
And all must go in rational disgrace
Whom verity has made familiar.

ON A NEW GENERATION

What may be born of the anxious union
Between perplexed man and irresolute woman
Is only, by this fertile speculation,
The either animal whose destiny
Differs from hers or his
By only the so many forepledged years
Of advance in irresolution or perplexity.

Yet the new girl more shines with herself,
And latest boy has a light in his head.
Not unlikely they will speak to each other
In a peculiar way and forget nature,
Then to fall quiet like a house no more haunted.
And in such silence may enough centuries fade
For all the loud births to be eloquently unmade.

HOW NOW WE TALK

If now is not the time more
Of love to talk, or heaven or
Whatever moot adventure
Was boast of language heretofore,

This is not that we are so dead
Or dumb, or the words so agèd
Which we have, and our need
Like desire in need disenchanted,

Or that to the talk we return
Which we spoke when concern
Was but for night's next and next morn,
And little more thought we to learn.

We are not now in such ecstasy
Because we speak more sincerely
Of those things we were drawn by
To this now naked felicity:

Because now we are done with proposing,
And because language now is disposing
Between all our affirming and disputing
To a verbal niceness of having and losing—

Because then we talked while we moved
And held hope by hope proved
And prated wisdom while we but loved
And were everyway more proud than behooved

Such mixed purpose in though fine dress
Over its unfrank nakedness
And such a maundering bliss
Wrapping such mute distress—

Because now fortune's self has grown plain
As when the traveller in the fabulous domain
Beholds for arduous ore the coin
That had been pocket-loose in his greedy brain.

Naked now are the words of anticipation,
And stilled the heaving of invention
By the hush of truth in communion
With the very priests of fiction

Who first wrote the words, and without fear
For the final sense, or that truth might hear,
And who now must make meaning with care
Lest the words with the words interfere.

For what we now talk of is all true
Or all false, since all is words, no doing to do
Or prospect to wage or more going to go
Or grief to be old or delight to be new.

We must keep faith now with what we say
And every coxcomb ghost of fancy lay,
Forbearing from the tales which cloy
The ears of time and drive the future away.

And all that we have and all that we have not
We may know by mere saying like an idiot
With a gift of swallowing in his throat
Which marks false from true soon as cold from hot.

For we are now quiet of mind thus,
As of limb and longing, that felicitous
Cannot but be the spoken use
Which of life we make, because perilous

Were it now to be less precise,
To see earth through a glass of paradise,
When only the present is left to promise
And for air the breath of our words must suffice.

MODERN SUPERSTITION

Unarguably there are spirits, ghosts, witches,
Devils and spells and charms and portents.
We need not our minds furnish with crotchets
Or have the mediaeval nightmare
To be sensible that we sometimes see and feel
What the eye does not see and the heart does not pulse.
No one is so methodical in time
That not a moment may drift off alone
And when restored to its hour be found
Stammering affairs he knows not for his.

And as a moment from the clock-moored hour strays,
So does the world escape from itself
And lie partly disposed where it is not.
We suffer this fitful absence as we should,
Locking the doors at night, calling the house complete
In its homely numbers of souls and beds.
But our sleep is loud with unanswered knocks,
And tomorrow our head is full of strangers,
And there is something we hope to read in the papers
Without knowing what or expecting to find it.

Over every life-size feature of fact
Hangs a larger shadow of doubt.
Being used to so much hunger with our substance,
We have mapped it widely around ourselves
Like a sacred frontier to content.
Sufficiency floats in an ether of lack
And with nothingness is our world's whole eked out.
But unarguably there are persons, events,
Thoughts and powers that reason surpass
And bigotry's name change to paradox.

BECAUSE OF CLOTHES

Without dressmakers to connect
The good-will of the body
With the purpose of the head,
We should be two worlds
Instead of a world and its shadow
The flesh.

The head is one world
And the body is another—
The same, but somewhat slower
And more dazed and earlier,
The divergence being corrected
In dress.

There is an odour of Christ
In the cloth: below the chin
No harm is meant. Even, immune
From capital test, wisdom flowers
Out of the shaded breast, and the thighs
Are meek.

The union of matter with mind
By the method of raiment
Destroys not our nakedness
Nor muffles the bell of thought.
Merely the moment to its dumb hour
Is joined.

Inner is the glow of knowledge
And outer is the gloom of appearance.
But putting on the cloak and cap
With only the hands and the face showing,
We turn the gloom in and the glow forth
Softly.

Wherefore, by the neutral grace
Of the needle, we possess our triumphs
Together with our defeats
In a single balanced couplement:
We pause between sense and foolishness,
And live.

A LETTER TO ANY FRIEND

Dear friend, a letter not yet written,
Never to be written, now I come to answer:
Later than never is this punctuality
Fallen between us like friendship's knife,
Bringing our minds close enough to cut.
I now know what you might have written
Had there been time to say the thing you meant:
That it could not be—a perfect friendship
Could not be. For it has not been,
Neither between you and me, nor me and them.

Agreed: an ill-matched correspondence
Entwines us each with each, and all with all.
Nor is there time to say the thing we mean:
That better matching cannot be.
There is no time—we dare not risk regret
Lest breed a general infection
And follow general death—a mutuality
Of mourning, nothing unwept for live.
This is no pedant tragedy we bear,
As if a pallid masque toward mock-interment.
From the beginning it has been
A breathing muse, and flushed with strangeness.

Thus it began, and thus, in strangeness,
Shall it at the end be not all ending,
After the courtesies and loving efforts
Have clarified the final gesture:
It could not, cannot, will not be.
Then faces mix and move cloud-like
Into sightless skyhood, unrememberable.
And sightless too of recognition
Spreads the once-familiar life-world.
There we are each astray, escorted by
Populous, ever-recent forgetfulness.

Hugely haunts the many-faced myth:
We believe we have loved, are united
In this cloudy evidence of past misunion.

We have a faith, and therefore continue
To be uncertain, to be near, far and near,
To deny that the old trysts and pledges
Were altogether a word of false hearts.

And, dear friend, what shall we complain of?
I am content that it was, is, no better, no worse,
That we are come back to original loneness
From which diverse love made blind scatter
To the four and four quarters of vision:
That we are come back, and, as before,
Dwell indissoluble and alien
In a universe of variance
Where all are one and many
By wide community of friendship failed of.

AFTER SO MUCH LOSS

After so much loss—
Seeming of gain,
Seeming of loss—
Subsides the swell of indignation
To the usual rhythm of the year.

The coward primroses are up,
We contract their profuse mildness.
Women with yet a few springs to live
Clutch them in suppliant bouquets
On the way to relatives,
Who, no, do not begrudge
This postponement of funerals.
And, oh, how never tired, and tired,
The world of primroses, how spring
The bended spirit fascinates
With promise of revival,
Leaving more honest summer to proclaim
That this is all—a brighter disappointment—
Time has to give to an implacable
Persuasion of things lost, wrongly.

Is it to wonder, then,
That we defy the unsuspecting moment,
Release our legs from the year's music,
And, to the reckless strum of hate,
Dance—grinding from primroses the tears
They never of themselves would have shed?
None dances whom no hate stirs,
Who has not lost and loathed the loss,
Who does not feel deprived.
Slyest rebellion of the feet,
The chaste and tremulous disport
Of children, limbs in passionless wave—
None dances whom no hate stirs,
Or shall not stir.

As sure as primrosed spring betides,
After so much loss,
The hate will out, the dance be on,
And many of their rage fall down.
It is easy as spring to yield to the year,
And easy as dance to break with the year.
But to go with the year in partition
Between seeming loss, seeming gain,
That is the difficult decorum.
Nor are the primroses unwelcome.

EVENTUAL LOVE

Remember kissing, haste of embrace,
The then too swimming voyage everywhere—
And so bent on return, all's still to see
And learn of: oh, the luxurious futures
We have tasted tastelessly,
Blunting the acute lips with love,
The like desire of another
To be newly baptized in the fresh flood
Of the Unknown.

Round us the flagging flies piqued dully:
Our moments given holiday to fret
On whiling wing, stupid of time
As we of who we were in this soft act
Before the liquid mirror
Of mutuality.

It was a wilful dark,
Sight put to large confusion
Because we would not credit
The littleness of our fond eyes.
So we have loved more greatly than seen.
Shall we not love again,
In this reduced revelation apprised
Of what was never there?

And the long lonely arms that stretch
From the back of the mind,
And the short lying legs that declare
Miles of prospective moments
To our still unventured step—
Shall these and all the loving parts
Be dead, reliques of frowardness?
Shall mouths not open but to speak not,
But in refusal to ourselves
Of outer comfort?

The love subsequent to love,
Less than the premature desire
Though than love not less,
The rampant years indeed belies.
Death-small is love—when vital senses
At last acquire the delicacy of death,
When love's wrought space becomes
A fine result of liberal measurement.
This remnant morsel has the sweetness
Of a first taste.

Remember kissing: did lips truly touch?
Or what were lips, if touching?
And what the love, if we loved?
If it was lips and loving, what were we?
Let us not think of that.
To read the greying story backwards
Bring tears of youth from eyes already dry—
A loss of eyes and sight, such moisture.
Let us not look,
Who in the agèd chapters have
An obligation to death dawning
Of not pretending yet to have lived.

THE WHY OF THE WIND

We have often considered the wind,
The changing whys of the wind.
Of other weather we do not so wonder.
These are changes we know.
Our own health is not otherwise.
We wake up with a shiver,
Go to bed with a fever:
These are the turns by which nature persists,
By which, whether ailing or well,
We variably live,
Such mixed we, and such variable world.
It is the very rule of thriving
To be thus one day, and thus the next.
We do not wonder.
When the cold comes we shut the window.
That is winter, and we understand.
Does our own blood not do the same,
Now freeze, now flame within us,
According to the rhythmic-fickle climates
Of our lives with ourselves?

But when the wind springs like a toothless hound
And we are not even savaged,
Only as if upbraided for we know not what
And cannot answer—
What is there to do, if not to understand?
And this we cannot,
Though when the wind is loose
Our minds go gasping wind-infected
To our mother hearts,
Seeking in whys of blood
The logic of this massacre of thought.

When the wind runs we run with it.
We cannot understand because we are not
When the wind takes our minds.
These are lapses like a hate of earth.
We stand as nowhere,
Blow from discontinuance to discontinuance,

Then flee to what we are
And accuse our sober nature
Of wild desertion of itself,
And ask the reason as a traitor might
Beg from the king a why of treason.

We must learn better
What we are and are not.
We are not the wind.
We are not every vagrant mood that tempts
Our minds to giddy homelessness.
We must distinguish better
Between ourselves and strangers.
There is much that we are not.
There is much that is not.
There is much that we have not to be.
We surrender to the enormous wind
Against our learned littleness,
But keep returning wailing
'Why did I do this?'

THE READERS

The Bible and the other books—
The books, beginning with the Bible,
Ending with the Bible which the Bible
In its fear of words, the word, was not:
These courages and volubilities
Adorn the speech of the world
And populate the minds of the world,
But hearts are fugitive and dumb.
In hearts and houses silence and old fear
Wall us apart, though in the flowing streets
Our language boasts the universal bond.
We do not love ourselves.
We do not love the word, the words.

To what shall I exhort you?
If it be love, you'll fly to bed again
And emulate the beast in that dead language,
Crying the name of your mate, which the beast could not.
If it be books, you'll read one, borrow one,
Or, bolder yet, go write one.
To such efforts of mind or flesh
You need no exhortation.

What then?
Why do I soften to exhort
Where I scorn?

I do not scorn.
I do not exhort.
This brings you bitterly
Farewell from Hope, my sweeter twin.
More frail, she died, recently though.
Forgive my grief's division,
Between her and you.
It seems to me you died then too.

Farewell from Hope to you,
Farewell perhaps from you to you.
Much has departed and will yet depart,

But I shall stay like doting grief
Among the crowded absences
And to the last lone living word
Mean 'we' when 'I' upon my page
Throbs in immense solitude
Between each hollow house and the nations' noise.

I exhort myself.
To love?
A little less of it, I think,
Would cool the anger in my grief.
To better faith in book-faith?
Leave me to my unimploring lines.
They are not lachrymose,
Need not the ecclesiastic kerchief
Nor the refreshing vinegar of pride
The persecuted love to wet their lips with.
I exhort myself merely
To continue with me.
It is a cruel career,
But one at least must not depart,
And I am happy in
Superior ways of suffering,
So that I do not suffer,
Only know.

I do not exhort you to know.
Even, I exhort you to go
If staying seems more valedictory—
The Bible and the other books beneath your arms,
Safe in your reading from all knowledge-harms.

THE CYCLE OF INDUSTRY

At the hour when to-day's effort changes
Into to-morrow's tedious stranger,
We parry the prospective boredom
With elbows deaf upon the café-table.
And to our uncompleted course we say
(In so many drinks and lapses of conscience)
Haughtily, as to a novice in time,
'This is an evening.'

Then to the less strategic idleness
Of sleep and its compelled remissions—
What, dreaming, do we not forswear
Of yesterday's consecutive intent?
Even Slug Memory becomes an outsider
When, loath to attain, we stanch
The laborious infatuation
Of the past with the future.

And we wake to breakfast, not to the day
Which stalks our reluctant bedside
In vicarious zeal of continuity.
We wake to the habit of coffee
Descended to us in infinite leisure
From the first morning after the first evening
On which we learnt to divide ourselves
Laggardly from all tyrant liege-selves away.

To a casual nicety we shall now perform
Certain acts of neighbourly compunction
Which regard for our fellow-dawdlers dictates—
It were ungallant not to seem to stir
In such invisible progress-making.
Then, by eternity's grace, we shall sit down
To fill our cups with the eternal yawn
Whose to-night's taste is to-morrow enough.

OF ALL THE WORLD

Of the birds which in wing-voice raise speech
To an unloving gossip whose shrillness
Seems true of us (since so our conscience
Whistles when we forget we can speak,
Confess the self-hating shudder and spite
Near to our kindness in word-hollowed rooms)—
None knows a word to say.

Of the birds, of all shrewd flying converse,
Of all scraping and scolding in grasses, on branches,
All opinion and pity like grave-chatter round us
Whose lives have grown still with the thought
There are yet to be said the first greetings,
We are not yet made known nor perfected
In spoken possession of earth-fate—

Of the cries and the comments of beak-minds,
Of the wings which by impulse of wind-sense
Make demur at the distance of blindness,
Of the wind that refuses consent
In tongueless upbraiding of sight,
And the thunder whose noise is its knowledge—
Not a phrase to the verbal ear comes.

Of all roaring and bleating we nurture
In the animal lap of locution,
And all waters which tumble, rocks tremble,
Of the leaves with their verge-of-speech seeming,
Of the flowers like anciently breathed
Protestations grown dumb-habitual—
None speaks but who speaks.

Of clock-accents and wheels unremitting,
Determined prolix unabatement,
The world-fame to ourselves that we spread,
Dinning our pride with rattle of pride—
Of all notes in commemorative veil
Interlaced, opaque musics, live shroud—
Not a letter of speech sounds.

We have need of conversing; and talk.
But of talking the measure is small
Of truth to the word-heirs bequeathed.
We inherit a poverty—language—
By which to declare: this the fortune
Reserved, drossless coin of ourselves.
But of all the world, few so inherit.

Of all the world, few inherit themselves,
Few have waited, succeeded their noising,
Not been lost among stridulous turns
Of time-page, afar from silence's path.
Who approach now, to speak, and of all the world?
And what's said so late, close between them?
The words are readable in their clear faces.

I REMEMBER

I am not ashamed of this.
And be you not ashamed of this.
It is not glorious,
But neither loathsome.
We are beings whom to meet
Is what prognostication taught:
Familiar to the touch of self
By many wounds, though healed,
And simple to the eye of time
By the disappearance of the scars.
Nothing is happening: rightly sees
The present impassive look.
Rightly our memory stings
With an incredible aliveness:
Long ago and not long ago
We were committing those outrages
Which breed the heroic title
And privately make aghast.

It has become less horrible to be.
The loss of splendour was the loss of fright—
Gigantic steps in the dark,
An advancing as toward pain that made it pain
When senses shrieked encounter.
Widely we groped, as if brave;
Closing on something—that was love,
By accident of night inflicted
And borne like fate, tragically
Because invisible.
Epic disaster!
To explore as if an empty universe
And have the shield of solitude pierced
By the existence of another!

It has grown less foolish to be.
We knew it would become as it is.
Fate was but the ringing in our ears
Of a resolution of deafness
Against the shock of hearing ourselves speak;

And pain, the lie of astonishment
That being should be so much—
We knew it was not over-much,
Not more than what beings needed
Minutely to spell being.
Oh, simpering self-awe,
The pretence of never having meant this!
Let us not mock our own sincerity.
Who has forgotten how we first began
To take ourselves to pieces?

A NEED FOR HELL

Let there be hell again!—
That virtue thought to do without,
Confusing goodness with rash plenty.
The evil have a right to live
In the freedom conferred on fools.
But give them back their hell,
And may it be the home of fools as well.

There is not enough of the good things
To go round among so many.
The virtuous persuaded virtue
To be a providence to all
And, for a fairer name,
To stop hell's meats and harvests,
Nourishing the fat foreigners herself.
They have indeed been nourished,
They gleam with flesh as richly as before;
While virtue's own, for hospitality,
Renounce the democratic board
That once a table was of friends.
Meals to the foul, and scraps to the fools—
The sign of virtue is to starve.
Therefore let there be hell again.
Virtue cannot herself and those maintain.

DECLINE OF PROPHECY

That which once overbent the turn of chance,
So that it could be prophesied,
By knowledge of the behaviour of metals
And of the patience of a twisted coil,
When, newly, would the wiry course
Spring straight and the next unavoidable thing
Be at last permitted to happen—

Such means of idleness no more are ours.
We may no longer stand aside
And, extracting from the thread of event
A question-mark, gird actuality
With soft anticipation:
We may be slow no longer
To the awaiting stroke of circumstance.

We, and the time-reserved fulfilment
Of our given, taken, uneffected meaning,
Have, by the enigmatic path of time,
Come into knowledge with an innocence
That knits our minds to our occasions
Of a silent sudden—the befalling
And the thought of it together fall

And the heart-stir is the tremble of the scene
As an eye flutters with the bird watched.
Yet, who can help the glance, the thought aside,
Sometimes, when, the hour seeming shallow
Because its surface holds its depth,
Invention prowls like prey along its edge,
Tempting to be scooped in and mixed with the tale?

I even, to whom the law of instantness
And all-fraught present is a pulse of mind,
Have known myself, yesterday even,
To write—it may have been—a letter to a friend
By conjecture a friend, and to discuss,
In the distracted way of letters, likelihoods
Outside the provision of the complete to-day.

Or, learning of books lately arrived
At the discretion of print and a price
Of austere insignificance,
Perhaps a sign of chastened fancy,
Have relented, sat by the hearth of time
Reading and nodding assent and objection,
Shedding the clock-tear, and the door half-open.

Did refinger with slavish habit of hand
The last and last newspaper, throw my eye
To the lionish landscape of advent,
Then snatch them from dayglare to nightglow as if—
All looking being now moon-mild,
Sunny astonishment abandoned
For the nimbler heed which exclaims not.

Or, when a neighbour's turkey flew the fence
Into my farther garden and the cats
Studied the weakness of the enemy
At battle-quiet, have paused to calculate
The omen in the omen,
Though well I knew the implements extinct—
What may the cats and turkeys of us augur
That we do not more newly now pronounce
From the eventual rostrum of ourselves?
It is a craven modesty, to greet
With old surprise the consequence unfurled.
This was a daring falter once
When, cheats of time, we choked hereafter back.
But now time wilts, prophecy cheats ourselves.

THE FORGIVEN PAST

That once which pained to think of,
Like a promise to oneself not kept
Nor keepable, now is grown mild.
The thistle-patch of memory
Claims our confiding touch;
The naked spurs do not draw blood,
Yielding to stoic pressure
With awkward flexibility.

We are glad it happened so
Which long seemed traitorous to hope,
False to the destined Otherwise;
Since by those failures-of-the-time
We learned the skill of failure, time—
Waiting to hold the seal of truth
With a less eager hand,
Sparing the authentic signature
For the most prudent sanctions,
Lest the wax and ink of faith be used
Before to hope's reverses
Succeed the just realities,
And we be spent of welcome
Save for a withered smile.

The transformation of old grief
Into a present grace of mind
Among the early shadows which
The present light inhabit,
As the portentous universe
Now upon earth descends
Timidly, in nostalgic bands
Of elemental trials and errors:
This is how truth is groved,
With wayside nights where sleeping
We wake to tell what once seemed cruel
As dream-dim—in the dream
As plain and sure as then,
In telling no less dark than doubtful.

This is how pleasure relives history,
Like accusation that at last
Settling unrancorous on lies
Gives kinder names to them—
When truth is so familiar
That the false no more than strange is,
Nor wondrous evil strange
But of a beggar's right to tenderness
Whom once in robes of certainty
We stood upon illusion's stage
And then, to expiate our self-deceit,
Sent forth in honesty's ill rags.

WHEN LOVE BECOMES WORDS

The yet undone, become the unwritten
By the activity of others
And the immobile pen of ourselves
Lifted, in postponed readiness,
Over the yet unsmooth paper of time—
Themes of the writing-table now,
All those implicit projects
By our minds rescued from enactment,
That lost literature which only death reads.

And we expect works of one another
Of exceeding not so much loveliness
Or fame among our physical sighs
As quietness, eventful
Not beyond thought, which moves unstrangely,
Without the historic sword-flash.

And I shall say to you, 'There is needed now
A poem upon love, to forget the kiss by
And be more love than kiss to the lips.'
Or, failing your heart's talkativeness,
I shall write this spoken kiss myself,
Imprinting it on the mouth of time
Perhaps too finally, but slowly,
Since execution now is prudent
With the reflective sleep the tongue takes
Between thought and said.

Thus, at last, to instruct ourselves
In the nothing we are now doing,
These unnatural days of inaction,
By telling the thing in a natural tone.
We must be brave:
Daring the sedentary future
With no other hope of passion than words,
And finding what we feel in what we think,
And knowing the rebated sentiment
For the wiser age of a once foolish deed.
As to say, where I once might have risen,

Bent to kiss like a blind wind searching
For a firm mouth to discover its own,
I now sit sociably in the chair of love,
Happy to have you or someone facing
At the distance bought by the lean of my head;
And then, if I may, go to my other room
And write of a matter touching all matters
With a compact pressure of room
Crowding the world between my elbows;
Further, to bed, and soft,
To let the night conclude, my lips still open,
That a kiss has been, or other thing to dream.
The night was formerly the chronicler,
Whispering lewd rumours to the morning.
But now the story of the evening
Is the very smile of supper and after,
Is not infant to the nurse Romance,
Is the late hour at which I or you
May have written or read perhaps even this.

Sometimes we shall declare falsely,
Young in an earlier story-sense
Impossible at the reduced hour of words.
But however we linger against exactness,
Enlarging the page by so much error
From the necessities of chance survived,
We cannot long mistake ourselves,
Being quit now of those gestures
Which made the world a tale elastic,
Of no held resemblance to our purpose.
For we have meant, and mean, but one
Consensus of experience,
Notwithstanding the difference in our names
And that we have seemed to be born
Each to a changing plot and loss
Of feeling (though our earth it is)
At home in such a timeward place.
We cannot now but match our words
With a united nod of recognition—
We had not, hitherto, heard ourselves speak
For the garrulous vigour and furore

Of the too lively loves as they clattered
Like too many letters from our hasty lips.

It is difficult to remember
That we are doing nothing,
Are to do nothing, wish to do nothing.
From a spurious cloud of disappointment
We must extract the sincere drop of relief
Corresponding to the tear in our thoughts
That we have no reason to shed.
We are happy.
These engagements of the mind,
Unproductive of the impulse to kiss,
Ring to the heart like love essential,
Safe from theatric curiosity
Which once directed our desires
To an end of gaudy shame and flourish,
So that we played these doleful parts
Abandoned between fright and pomp.

There is now little to see
And yet little to hide.
The writing of 'I love you'
Contains the love if not entirely
At least with lovingness enough
To make the rest a shadow round us
Immaculately of shade
Not love's hallucinations substanced.
It is truer to the heart, we know now,
To say out than to secrete the bold alarm,
Flushed with timidity's surprises,
That looms between the courage to love
And the habit of groping for results.

The results came first, our language
Bears the scars of them: we cannot
Speak of love but the lines lisp
With the too memorable accent,
Endearing what, instead of love, we love-did.
First come the omens, then the thing we mean.
We did not mean the gasp or hotness;

This is no cooling, stifling back
The bannered cry love waved before us once.
That was a doubt, and a persuasion—
By the means of believing, with doubt's art,
What we were, in our stubbornness, least sure of.
There is less to tell of later
But more to say.
There are, in truth, no words left for the kiss.
We have ourselves to talk of;
And the passing characters we were—
Nervous of time on the excitable stage—
Surrender to their lasting authors
That we may study, still alive,
What love or utterance shall preserve us
From that other literature
We fast exerted to perpetuate
The mortal chatter of appearance.

Think not that I am stern
To banish now the kiss, ancient,
Or how our hands or cheeks may brush
When our thoughts have a love and a stir
Short of writable and a grace
Of not altogether verbal promptness.
To be loving is to lift the pen
And use it both, and the advance
From dumb resolve to the delight
Of finding ourselves not merely fluent
But ligatured in the embracing words
Is by the metaphor of love,
And still a cause of kiss among us,
Though kiss we do not—or so knowingly,
The taste is lost in the taste of the thought.

Let us not think, in being so protested
To the later language and condition,
That we have ceased to love.
We have ceased only to become—and are.
Few the perplexities, the intervals
Allowed us of shy hazard:
We could not if we would be rash again,

Take the dim loitering way
And stumble on till reason like a horse
Stood champing fear at the long backward turn,
And we the sorry rider, new to the mount,
Old to the fugitive manner.
But dalliance still rules our hearts
In the name of conscience. We raise our eyes
From the immediate manuscript
To find a startled present blinking the past
With sight disfigured and a brow reproachful,
Pointing the look of time toward memory
As if we had erased the relics
In order to have something to write on.
And we leave off, for the length of conscience,
Discerning in the petulant mist
The wronged face of someone we know,
Hungry to be saved from rancour of us.
And we love: we separate the features
From the fading and compose of them
A likeness to the one that did not wait
And should have waited, learned to wait.
We raise our eyes to greet ourselves
With a conviction that none is absent
Or none should be, from the domestic script of words
That reads out welcome to all who we are.

And then to words again
After—was it—a kiss or exclamation
Between face and face too sudden to record.
Our love being now a span of mind
Whose bridge not the droll body is
Striding the waters of disunion
With sulky grin and groaning valour,
We can make love miraculous
As joining thought with thought and a next,
Which is done not by crossing over
But by knowing the words for what we mean.
We forbear to move, it seeming to us now
More like ourselves to keep the written watch
And let the reach of love surround us
With the warm accusation of being poets.

MARCH, 1937

This is the poem of a month within a year
Within a world within an atmosphere
Grown black from that we see not.
We do not see.
The atmosphere is dense with devils.
The world is empty from the expulsion of these.
The year: such spectacles the blind wear.
The month: as eyes in night are holes,
So is the month an abstract organ.
And vision now a thing of thinking,
The thirsty eyes from damp brain drinking.

I shall tell a story.

Once (since here I lay the curse of fiction,
Which is the curse of thought's constriction
To once, and not again)
Within a month within a year within a world
Within an atmosphere incredible
Because sight loathes it, will not see it,
We *are* like shuddering angels locked
Within a desert heaven within an earth
Made populous by sin's expulsion.
Once: O believe it not
That this we live *is* so!
Already is the month's recoil a long-ago.

The story with the pained eye passes
Into time's museum of darkness,
Where what has been to staring horror
Protests its innocence: it is not,
Nor ever was it, sight and the heart
Make strange mistakes of seeing and believing.
And so the gasping month within the tangled year
Within the tearing world
Within the torn atmosphere
Stops breathing, seeing, dying:
Another month upon the shelf appears,
The days like book-enamoured fingers

Prepare to reach.
Sight and the heart their new mistakes beseech.

Here ends the story.

The poem takes the story away.
We have left nor a month nor its least cruel day.
Nor the envelope without the envelope
Without the envelope within.
This is the poem.
Are we so naked then of life,
Stripped to the death?
Is this the promised core of us?
Come closer, let us not shudder so, shiver.
We are not ill, nor dead—nor uncovered
In the lost shame of ordeal.
There is something so good in this
That, despite worry, hope, and no letter,
I scarcely dare let myself wish for better.

THE VICTORY

Without millions of pennies and millions of men
Or nations of miles or five bolts of satin
Or six reams of fame to describe it upon
Or sixteen old castles to flag the news from
Or sixty new offices and their telephones—
Yet the business is done,
The great war is won,
The world has been made to know.

That it lies and denies
Or wears woe in disguise
Of its knowing, its joy so to know—
This is such pride as battalions of fire have
When a single cool drop quells the challenging blaze:
Of the drop not a sign, there's but reek of embers.
Thus smoulders the world, spitting hate of its baptism.
The last sparks tell not of healing, of cooling.

There is no news of knowledge in the newspapers.
Impregnable screens of vision have been raised
To protect the embattled minds from themselves.
A full peace has been visited now on the world,
But the voices of time do not mention it.
Nor think I to disturb
So much noise, nor to curb
So much fleeing from quiet's event.

Like a love that is loved
In a heart stiffly gloved
Against loveless responding event:
Though the face of the world with dim pain is contorted
As if the embrace were a forfended curse,
And the gift shall demand no more thanking than this,
Yet knowledge has been given, and knowledge taken.
Whether to weep or smile that truth conquers in secret?

IN THE BEGINNING

That was not the genesis:
This is the genesis.
That was the impregnation
Of the Mother by her children-to-be

Who in the fluster of forebeing
Cried out in voiceless voice:
'We are the Father!'
Then, voice of voice: 'I am the Father's Son!'

To these it seemed long,
Counting from fathers to sons
To father still unborn.
Week on week they have said: 'In seven days!'

The Mother has just begun to count
Her nine days of wonder.
She pauses upon the seventh—
Late on the seventh day is born her daughter.

In the first seven days of the Mother
Her sons are; they implore a Father,
They befoul their birth-places
And would be justified in this.

Late on the seventh day is born the daughter.
'Be you,' the Mother says, 'to them as father.
Absolve them of their flesh:
Do you wear flesh, and find goodness in it.'

The last two days are to the daughter.
She is the Mother become sisterly
To be to the brother-sons as father.
'You have endured a week of you,' she praises.

The seventh eve is therefore celebration.
Heavenly to-morrows lamp the night,
And every man's a universal favourite,
And none's a beggar because all are.

On the eighth day blind-spun spaces
Between man and man close in.
The universe of each and each has passed.
The daughter does not need to shout to be heard.

She opens the heads of her brothers
And lets out the aeroplanes.
'Now,' she says, 'you will be able to think better.'
But their hearts still pump wildness into them.

Then a storm: love-ladies fly
Like empty leaves curled bodily.
From what trees fallen?
What infant gardens in the minds of men?

Then she encourages them to die
As many deaths they fear.
The physician-gods withdraw.
'Illness comes not to the dead.'

Together all inspect the cups, the pencils,
The watches, matches, knives they have,
Some are from Tuesday's country, some from Friday's,
But nothing there from either Sunday.

Which so belabours their week's memories,
They sleep, and to the ninth day wake
In all-forgetful curiosity:
Amazed that they exist.

The daughter of the Mother tells a story.
They gape: can that have been?
Fair episodes they seem to recognize;
The evil part they execrate.

And so the ninth day sets,
Not seriate with an elder tenth
But usher to a younger first,
Unpentateuchal genesis.

DOOM IN BLOOM

Now flower the oldest seeds.
The secret of the root no more
Keeps jealous distance from the air.
The dark intent, so lothfully ascending,
At last to resolution grows;
The glance of long reluctance shows.

Weakly we write upon
The closing surface of oblivion.
Our faith in earth, in nether sameness,
Hurries to take the separate colour.
And leaning on the faded air
We flaunt ourselves against despair.

Gruesomely joined in hate
Of unlike efflorescence,
We were a cruel compacted silence
From which unlovable centuries sprang.
But time has knit so hard a crust
That speak and differ now we must—

Or be in pride encased
Until the living way has ceased
And only death comes to occur.
Though half our zeal but fair is,
Spells but an earth's variety,
Hope makes a stronger half to beauty

When from the deep bed torn
Of ultimate misgiving
An auspice of like peril to bring.
The lone defiance blossoms failure,
But risk of all by all beguiles
Fate's wreckage into similar smiles.

SEIZURE OF THE WORLD

You picked up little, had small need,
When hands alone were used once—
And little good was all good.
Then you put on the gloves of chance,
And much was momently enjoyed
At fearsome covered distance.
Latterly you have employed
Long handles of desire
And many a swift persuasion pulled
Out of the travelling fire
By bounteous error fuelled
And spiteful fancy lit.
But groping greed is at last lulled
When hands their skill of lies remit—

And fingers stem closely from brain,
Tight on the plentitudes of pain
That from the reach of heart remain.

NOTHING SO FAR

Nothing so far but moonlight
Where the mind is;
Nothing in that place, this hold,
To hold;
Only their faceless shadows to announce
Perhaps they come—
Nor even do they know
Whereto they cast them.

Yet here, all that remains
When each has been the universe:
No universe, but each, or nothing.
Here is the future swell curved round
To all that was.

What were we, then,
Before the being of ourselves began?
Nothing so far but strangeness
Where the moments of the mind return.
Nearly, the place was lost
In that we went to stranger places.

Nothing so far but nearly
The long familiar pang
Of never having gone;
And words below a whisper which
If tended as the graves of live men should be
May bring their names and faces home.

It makes a loving promise to itself,
Womanly, that there
More presences are promised
Than by the difficult light appear.
Nothing appears but moonlight's morning—
By which to count were as to strew
The look of day with last night's rid of moths.

CHRISTMAS, 1937

What shall the feast be called this year
That long a merry holy name had
But now comes nameless to its time?

'Jesus is born!' Undated moment
To close the vanished year, uncounted,
Of those who live in denial of death.

Then, having not lived because not died,
They say (next year), 'Christ died but did not!'
Then, Christmas: Jesus succeeds Jehovah.

Until the Christian art, that changed
The eternal Semite frown
Into a coloured yearly smile,

Cannot but paint the looming voice
Under the smile, behind the frown:
There hangs the word for this year's birth-feast.

We read what seemed too terrible for sound,
Year upon year, in seeming endless
Thund'rous unrelenting death—'THE END!'

But soft the word: shaped on sealed lips
For utterance on our many own
According to the smile each can

When death has killed the corpse of time—
Even to the Merry Christmas grin
That gave the Happy New Year ghost.

How shall the feast be called?
Who dare be after Jesus now
And meet Jehovah's honest face

As the dark substance of their own,
By whose forbidding look to form
The permitted smiles of transgression?

Who dare no more to rise now,
From heaven's ages to float down
With feet of Jew, folding the Cross

Into a compact miracle—
Outstretching souls returning
For birth at last, the escaped END?

Jehovah was continent to madness;
Christ's Father, loving to foolishness.
But the same man were they, by Jesus.

And one the Woman and the Virgin—
Who in immaculate parturition
Bestowed a natal death at birth

On whom the Woman could not smile on
As names of peace between Herself
And that suspicious Angry Man.

The original smile is Hers—
Which, smiled in slow discretion,
He took for frowning: and so frowned.

These things are not yet tellable
In the tone of long-ago I would wish:
Christmas again confounds my mouth.

I speak as if in recent knowledge.
Perhaps that is right: the tale is young,
Though the matter old. Christmas still!

Less merry, but Jesus still the cause:
He was born—signing his name
To a tale by us to be written.

Less deathly: as the signature becomes
Our own, and crucifying hazard
Foreshortens to the death-trimmed END.

HISTORIES

THE VAIN LIFE OF VOLTAIRE

Au bord de l'infini ton cœur doit s'arrêter;
Là commence un abîme, il faut le respecter.

THE ARGUMENT

I

Voltaire is born.

II

Voltaire goes to school and is courted by two old rivals;
but gives satisfaction to neither.

III

A cunning old lady, detecting a kindred cunning in Voltaire,
gives him some sound advice.

IV

Voltaire goes to Holland and plays nonsense with Pimpette.
He is sent back to Paris; but bears his disgrace lightly.

V

Voltaire is sent to prison for honourably insulting a duke
and is later exiled to England. English men of letters antici-
pate a sensation; and are rebuked.

VI

Voltaire returns to Paris; and learns how to gladden the
ladies of the Court, and his purse.

VII

Paris grows uncomfortable for Voltaire, who falls oppor-
tunely in love with Madame du Châtelet; and departs for Cirey.

VIII

Voltaire at home in Cirey walks in the garden with Emilie;
and is troubled by his dreams, and Emilie, and philosophy. He
pines for the perfect compromise. After God, Emilie. From a
transport more philosophical than amorous, he is pulled rudely
back to earth by the nature of things, which he deplores.

The lovers, reconciled, return to their guests. He attends the ladies with his wonted tenderness; but seems troubled as he mumbles over every lady's hand. Emilie intervenes and scolds; but he remembers that he is a philosopher.

IX

A certain morning, Voltaire is slow in waking. Emilie is an early riser, she is at his door already. He receives her tenderly: Emilie is worried, she has heard him talk in his sleep, his complexion gives her concern. Her persistence provokes him to a witticism. But Emilie is cross: his clothes, his silly rhymes. Science is the only apt employment of the mind. But what of mind itself, the immense science? Emilie makes a face at him. He pouts; but is forced to yield.

X

'Le superflu, chose très nécessaire': Voltaire believes that life is, or must be made, splendid. But secretly he nurtures a simple heart. Like any plain man, he encourages mysteries. He is even encouraged in them by Emilie, to whom he is one himself. Puzzles multiply around him; which he explains not satisfactorily.

XI

Voltaire has other troubles. Is he more ill than he believes himself, or does he believe himself more ill than he is? His enemies plague him even more than his body. But philosophy restores his love of society; and poetry, his love of himself.

XII

Voltaire begins to worry about his soul. He appeals to God; but he receives no answer. He exhorts the contemporary spirit of truth; but is too advanced for his time. He is also, alas, too difficult for the Devil. So there he is left to die—like any other.

I

The wind blew through the House of Humorous Things
And a little dry laugh touched its broom-tail.

'I'm tired of too much wise company
In the House of Humorous Things.
Wisdom and wit need schools
Full of dull fools.'

A dry laugh creaked at the edge of the wind and broke,
And the wind put it together again with words,

And fastened it to its broom-tail
And loosed it again over France.

II

God put on the robe of a Jesuit.
(The Devil had won his own early.)
God and the Devil chatted together
And directed each other
To the College of *Louis-le-grand*.

And Marie Arouet pretended to sleep.
But God blew in one ear
And the Devil bit at the other
With the cold point of a fire-blanched tooth.

Marie Arouet pretended to listen to both.
Marie Arouet went on listening to himself.
(Flat-tongued Devil and flat-tongued God
Could not understand his epigrams.)

Marie Arouet ground out with a smile
The flakes of a little dry laugh,
And God and the Devil walked away
Under one umbrella.

III

Ninon de l'Enclos said to herself
(Having taken Old Age for her last lover,
Coquetting with Death to make frailty
A fair occasion for jealousy)
Somewhere there was a House of Humorous Things
Where she would go when Death to her
Was a rejected lover,
Riding the wind,
Having lost her words or wings
(But not wit, the long key
For those who come back after travelling
To the House of Humorous Things).

The Abbé of Châteauneuf,
Interrupting the timely reverie of a timeless flirt,
Introduced François-Marie Arouet
And a little dry laugh.
(It was only the laugh that Ninon kissed,
It being more of an age.)

So she pinned her flower on Marie Arouet,
And gave advice to a laugh let loose
To hire a small and elegant coach
With comic wheels
And sober spokes
For Earth's serious hills.

IV

Humour grew young
With a borrowed desire for boyish adventure.
A boy and a laughing accompaniment
Went travelling to Holland
On a serious diplomatic mission.

'Pimpette, Pimpette!'
Humour lost self-possession
And a dry laugh wept,
Having tears enough
For young loving in Holland.

Humour was sent back to Paris again,
Somewhere near or inside of Arouet,
Humour grown young
(Or deprived of some of its privileges),
And a dry laugh wept
(Having taken a body to live in and ride in)
For a body's punishment
For young loving in Holland
On a serious diplomatic mission.

V
What is dust already
Cannot crumble.

Prison won't cure wisdom-wit.
Prison won't cure tongue-waggery.
(Sleep, Bastille,
Sleep, grumble,
Mumble,
Sleep.)

'I'm making a new name,
You're breaking an old one.'

A poet may speak to a duke
(For a beating).
Beatings and a grumbling warder,
Mumbling warder,
Cannot silence mumbling, grumbling.

Mumbling and grumbling
Went travelling to England.
English men of letters—Pope, Congreve, Swift—
Rounded their ears
And heard the wind playing tag with itself
Around English shores.
François-Marie Arouet
(Or—briefer elegance—Voltaire)
Left his tongue with the wind

And greeted the English men of letters—
Pope, Congreve, Swift.

'There's a dry laugh coughing a breeze
Behind you, Voltaire,'
Said the English men of letters
With their ears deaf-trumpeted
To hear mysteries.

Voltaire tipped the tops of his eyes
To a high surprise.

'I don't know what you're talking about,
English men of letters.
I have learned your language
And loved your Shakespeare
And pledged your liberal faith,
But I can't understand your levity,
English men of letters.'

And who can say which was most unaware:
The English men of letters,
Voltaire,
Or the slight commotion
In the air?

VI
Voltaire sang two songs,
One for Kings' mistresses:
    Love has two ways,
    One way with husbands
    One way with Kings.
    Love has two ways,
    One way with Queens,
    One way with mistresses.
    Queens become mistresses,
    Mistresses Queens.

Voltaire sang two songs,
One for Kings' mistresses,

One for money,
This song for money:
   Money has one way:
   Play before pay.
   The labour of song
   Conducts to labour's wage.
   The reward of song's ease
   Is in whom it can please.
The private pay was neither of these,
But author's whim confirmed
In industry—wig on right, pen to write.

And something laughed at the reckoning,
Having taught Voltaire
How to satisfy sums
By variable equations
In love and literature.

   VII
Laughter grew hoarse
And laughter's lips
Thirsted in Paris.

Laughter wetted its lips again
On a wicked, ironic, respectable kiss
And sent it to Madame du Châtelet
(By deputy).
Laughter wetted its lips again
While Voltaire reconsidered his heart
In a prudent arithmetic.

'One, two, three, and more,'
Voltaire, enamoured accurately,
Kept balancing.

'When hearts and sums agree,
Travelling the measured road together,
To Cirey in the fair Lorraine
Of that fair Emilie. . . .'

But first Voltaire took a holiday
(By deputy)
And went home visiting.
(Or was it a little dry laugh
That Voltaire knew nothing about—
In cautious pretence
Of an actual ignorance?)

'Goodbye, goodbye,'
He—it—said
To the House of Humorous Things
And the Humorous Things
In that Humorous House.
'I have found me a job
On the crooked back stairs
Of a perpendicular house in Lorraine.'
(Hush, an earnest heart,
Hark, a frivolous beat!)

Voltaire, locking his boxes,
Heard a little dry laugh in one of them.
'Shall I take it out and throw it away?'
(Oh, safe and dangerous jettison!)

    VIII
Scrub, scrub,
Rain, rain,
Old washerwoman,
Silver-knuckled.
Scrub, scrub,
The world is spotted with footprints.
Rub, rub,
God's washerwoman,
The Devil steps deep.

Do you see them, Voltaire,
As you walk with Emilie
Into daybreak air?

Chill, chill,
Twist buttons tighter,
Though love and Emilie
Are warm at your elbow.
Chill, chill,
Dawn has cold fingers
Of burying dead dreams.
Twist buttons tighter,
Cold, cold awakening.

Hop out of sleep.
Sleep is a cemetery.
Hop off, awakening.
Keep warm, remembering,
Keep warm, Voltaire,
Twist buttons tighter.

'Do you see them, Voltaire?'
Cries Emilie at the frozen footprints
Fast in the garden.
'Thieves, devils, lovers—'
(Or dreams?)
'Was it you that made them,
Voltaire?'

Keep warm, remembering,
Keep warm, Voltaire.
Can you do the rain's work
Better than herself?
Scrub, scrub,
Dig, dig,
Deep, deep,
Have footprints roots?
How far would you dig, Voltaire,
For the tips of those roots?
How deep do they go?
Too deep for digging,
Too deep for following?

What reconciles the garden
Does not reconcile the mind,

Which demands instruction
The more it is blind,
Sets little store by speeches,
Can understand
Only what it knows,
Knows only what is secret.

Open self-instruction
Confers mad laurel.
To keep sane counsel
Voltaire advises privately
With a tutelary power.
'Lord of sweet gifts,
King of the two rivers
Having their source in Thee
And their ending—
God, is there no middle way for me
Or land between,
King of the two rivers?
God, is there no middle way
Or land between for travelling
At least by day?

And something laughed.
And something whispered in Voltaire's ears:
'And what of the night?'

And something made Voltaire hold his tongue
And bite his lips
And refill his lung.

Now gently, gently, gently,
Breathe softer prayer to Emilie
As to sacred cat arrived with fiat
Perhaps immemorial.

'Ah, Emilie, Emilie.
Man is a poor portion of disintegrated whole,
And wanders, wanders,
While woman waits
Still in her soil,

Waits, waits
The seal.

'Even as a tree wanders not nor waits,
And as the double principle shares one delight
Of growth, of love,
We are a single tree together—
Ah, Emilie, Emilie—
And sum an amorous dichotomy,
Barkbound and severally
Branched and entwined,
Leafy as for an everlasting spring . . .'

'Ah, Voltaire, Voltaire—'
And something smiled—
'And what of the roots?
How deep do they go
Too deep for digging,
Too deep for following?

'Ah, Voltaire, Voltaire,
Will you climb in the air
With the leaves and your fair
And let conscience take care of the roots?'

With a mental frown
Voltaire noted down
The true cause of melancholy:
Soul and mind not one,
The mind too fierce opinion,
The soul too hopeful of the angel.

(Hush, hush, eternal spite—
House and hall on my right!
Tongue, to your scabbard,
Laughter, to your locker.
There are twenty ladies listening
Just behind the knocker,
And my fair, fair Emilie at my left
With ears in her eyes and eyes in her ears
And vinegar shuddering in her tears.

Then hush, hush,
Twenty ladies listening,
And one other,
Hush, hush.)

Duty grows sharp and counts her kisses.
Three, six, nine, twenty.
Bend low, bow deeply.
A kiss for the little right hand
Of each little lady.
Good-morning, good-morning,
The weather, the time,
Wipe that dream from your lips,
Too much like a kiss.

(Hands must be kissed,
Life must be lived.
Bow right, bow left.
Certain things must be done—
Breakfast and babbling
And powdered wigs, for
Life must be lived
Or Life lives it herself
Quite without us, without us, if
Certain things aren't done.
Hush, hush,
O mysterious tongue,
Twenty ladies listening,
And one other,
Hush, hush.
Certain things must be done,
In this way, in that way,
In that way, in this way.
Certain things must be done
In wooden heels and finger-frills,
Breakfast, books and gardening
And twenty little hands to kiss.)

'Voltaire, Voltaire,
Your wig's awry,

Your lace is limp,
There's a button off,
And need you have kissed
All twenty, Voltaire?'

(Certain things must be done,
Certain things must be done.)

'And need you have taken so long?'

(Hush, hush,
For on the back stairs
You may take as long as you please.)

Might he not in his sleep any night
Follow a little dry laugh
Down the back stairs
And untie his tongue
On the bottom step?
Saying, he surely slept in his bed,
And that it happened in a dream,
That so some nights next morning seem?

IX.
'Arise, arise!
Open your eyes a miser's slit,
Open your eyes and admit
The things you denied all night.
Some metaphysical adjustment
Under the cover—
Then up,
Plum-coloured lover,
And good-day to the naughty carved cupids over your bed.'

'I admit.
I confess (for a present purpose)
That from one point of view
I have lied about what I denied from another.
I confess,
I admit—

Like a plum-coloured lover
Going white, going white.'

Knuckle-point, pale lover.
Tap, tap, sharp morning rap,
Should morning ghosts hover.

'Ah, Emilie,
My sun has risen.
Un-ice these fingers.'

Knuckle-point.
Tap, tap, sharp morning rap.

'Voltaire, Voltaire,
As I listened outside your door,
Whom did I hear laughing inside?'

White, white, Voltaire,
A ghost in his cheek
For what he forgot to deny
When remembering what not to admit.

What laughed?
Under the bed, in cupboard, in chest—
Is it hidden away in you, Voltaire,
In a place that you can't find yourself?

'What laughed?
What dreamed?
What lived?
What secret heat does the sun conceal
On the side that is turned away from us?
Discover these things in your laboratory,
Fair Emilie, in that petulant glass
Which will break if you look a moment too long.'

Knuckle-point,
Tap, tap, sharp morning rap
On Voltaire's fingers.

'And a plum-coloured coat with two buttons off,
And your wig uncurled in the weather!

'Scraps, quills and inky finger-tips,
Untidy proofs of literature,
The devil's self in manuscript—
Voltaire, Voltaire,
Out of the window,
To the wind, to the wind with your words,
To be blown to the birds
And sung out foolish.

'Scraps, quills and inky finger-tips,
Damp verse, dark history.
Science, sun of my laboratory!
What does the world live by?
Oh, Voltaire,
The deep geometries of space
You cannot embrace
In the shallow round of a line.'

'Madame,
Your sun is small, by distance.
I hold the deep geometries of space
In the near circle of my mind,
Which is a gift to see
Brighter than by the sun or chemistry.

'Pray, Emilie,
My fair, fair Emilie,
Don't laugh at me.
My pomp is a habit of melancholy.
My melancholy is
A habit of humour.'

Yet she laughed,
And something laughed with her,
Deserting Voltaire
To keep whole the pair.

Oh prompt, prompt surrender
And prompt, prompt kiss
To recover her favour
And the salt smack of laughter.

    X
Two talked in a house in Lorraine.

One said:
    Life is royal-born
    To an elegant station—
    A silver spoon, a golden cradle,
    An ebony casket to bury it in,
    All the muses at the funeral.

But the other:
    Life's beggar-born,
    A miserable urchin,
    With death for his fortune
    And the earth for his coffin.
    But a rhyme and a tune,
    A ribbon, a crown,
    Will make it forget its forlorn beginning
    And seem a little more worthy of living.

Two talked in a house in Lorraine
And agreed in an argument
That, high-born or low-born,
Life was either true-titled
Or should else be ennobled.

Life has need of so much
To redress an acquired (or inherent) dearth—
A feast is the least
Can persuade the palate
Where the palate's the judge:
Life needs or is much.

Next a play, a play from the pen of Voltaire
While the palate's in prime:

Olympie, Zaïre,
To model the tear;
Or the magic lantern, or will Emilie sing
From the opera Voltaire
Wrote expressly for her;
Next a pyrotechnical hour is lit
While Voltaire rehearses
For an hour of his verses.
But what then to do
With a hundred and fifty flagging guests
Until morning dew?
Put them to sleep,
Put them to sleep
In the dirtiest house in Lorraine,
Or in Europe.

But the back stairs are lone
And awake, awake,
Or awake when Voltaire
Steals in the night with a candle there.

Voltaire, Voltaire,
Cover the wick,
Crouch on the stair
And bewail, bewail—
Fair Emilie is haunting your trail.

'Voltaire, Voltaire,
What do you there?'

'I gave chase to a ghost
That I heard treading here
As I listened in sleep.'

'Did you find one, Voltaire?'

'I am certain I did,
For something escaped on the stair
Just a minute ago, when you came
And prevented my capturing it.'

'Hurry, hurry, Voltaire,
Soft, soft,
And I'll go quietly back to bed.
Hurry, hurry into the garden, Voltaire,
But look sharp and beware
Of the less-than-air hidden in the air,
The ghosts that can talk as well as walk.'

'Do you see them, my love?'
Cried Emilie, inspecting the garden
Early next morning.
'The footprints are deep,
Like a man's long standing,
And ragged, like a man's long laughing.'

'I think,' said Voltaire, 'they are mine.
For in following the ghost I forgot—'

'Forgot what?'

'To come in again. I got lost
And misled by the ghost.
I forgot—'

'Forgot what?'

'That I wasn't a ghost
And understood all but—'

'All but what?'

'I forget.
I've a cold in my head.
My feet are wet.
You must put me to bed.

XI
'Oh, I must be dying, dying or dead—
Am I dead, and not aware of it?
Is this ague or a laughing fit?'

Hurry, Voltaire,
For fair Emilie's ever
Haunting your trail.
Dispatch the gout,
Throw off the irk,
Dispute the pain—
Fitter to run than to complain
With Emilie only a pace behind.

But now circle and hum
The waspish swarm
Of his enemies,
Each retreating the better
To serve him a letter,
Approaching to sting.
Fréron, and the Abbé Desfontaines,
And Rousseau all a-buzz
With a primitive poison.

'My mirrors, my money,
My laces, my verses!
He'd rob me of these,
As if life, common-born, must be kept in its place,
Or, royal-born, must be swiftly democratized
To the state of a knave.

'Oh, my mirrors, my money—
I am truly ashamed to know he exists.
When he's dead I shall have to unbury him
And see that he's hanged
In respect of his rank
And decently fed to the crows.'

(Not to speak of his enemies at Rome
And at court, and his name
Like a heresy, with no home.)

'Oh my mirrors, my money,
My verses, my name!'

Hurry, hurry,
To the front hall.
Ah, the liberty of each lady's hand
(The distant pain, the distant pleasure)—
By such intrigue and folly must man sow
The forbidden hours of to-night and to-morrow.

But of all vanities rhymes must renew
The gallant flesh, prolong the charm
To keep old enemies, entice new.

XII

Voltaire grew old.
(Or that gust of breath, that laugh,
Grew homesick, grew restless.)

Voltaire grew old
And alarmed for his next habitation.
Would a puff of wind be troubled
To take him along?
Patronage of death devolves
Chiefly on God, Man, the Devil.

'God, God, in so far as I was dull—
Mahomet and *Alzire*, a whole theatre-full—
I have not sinned.
God, God, where I have sinned,
My wit sinned.
Let me be strangled with the *Pucelle*
If I ever admitted writing it.
I forget the *Henriade* with my dreams.
Dreams are devilish quips.
In a dream one may be Spinozist.'

Show your medals, Voltaire:
This one from the Pope for hurrying back
Six leagues from Rome to taste of his toes.
'God, hearken to a patriarch
Honoured in Ferney, humbled in his works.
King Frederick took a Maupertuis

In preference to more pious me
Who corrected the grammar
And rewrote the French verse
Of this monarch than myself more perverse.

But Charles of Brunswick, Denmark's Christian,
Poland's King, the King of Sweden,
Even the mettlesome Catherine
(To whom I lately delivered
A watch of my own Ferney's fabric,
Uniting our spirits in a time-tick)—
All royal-born or well-sanctioned, all these
Have permitted philosophy to comport flatteries.
God, God, do these items not repair
The heavenly credit of Arouet (or Voltaire)?'

God is silent,
Or something not God.
Reason stands on the spot
Where God is not.

'God of God, the pedagogue,
I know earth before I love it.
I know the properties before the pain of fire.
Newton was your prophet.
I am your saint.
I wrote the *Henriade*.
I was nearly Quaker.
I visited England.
The body, though dead,
Wears the canonized head.'

Too soon.
The intelligent outstrip the intelligence,
Which speaks a recent language,
But a scarce actual one.
Death is not talkative
With centuried reason in the room.

Voltaire in haste sought the Devil,
Who refused him in haste
As too haunted, too equal.

Oh, Voltaire, this dallying
Was but mortal dying.
Wind calls the roof.
The roof is off.
The house stays behind
And all those thoughts of man
That made him death-blind.

EPILOGUE

Epilogue is epigram
For any man whose anagram
Meant too much. For all such
Should be one crutch
Held under the nose
Instead of rose.
This crooked staff
To make the nose laugh
Breaks under the oppression
Of too much confession.
The crutch fallen down
Leaves neither cripple nor clown,
But of gold, sulphur, ink,
One memorial stink
Rises beyond heaven and hell and good sense
To the giddy eminence
Where ironies lodge
In more lugubrious hodge-podge
Than fleshy mirth
Breeds here on earth.

1921.

LAURA AND FRANCISCA

I
The Island, and Here

My name, as the title shows,
Is Laura, and hers Francisca.
And my age must be thirty,
As hers must be I should say six,
Judging by and judging by.

I will tell you everything.
On the island of Mallorca
Sometimes I see an English newspaper.
In one I read, a young man questioned
In the private question-corner,
'I want to go away and live abroad
On very, very little a day.'
The answer was, 'The cheapest climate,
Scenery and food are in Mallorca.'
But, Mr. Very Very Little A Day,
I live here, and I ought to know.
This is not heaven, but the smallest earth.
Beyond which comes perhaps *bon día tenga*
Or another same fiesta of San Juan,
But never more than what may please
Without dishonouring mortality.
Which is not to buy paradise
Through the low rate of exchange.
Money will buy you only money here,
Another same yourself, unmagicked
By the cheap touch of salvation.

Of course, a lot of people come here,
And Mr. Short at Palma finds them houses.
But there they end and end.
And that is why they like it here:
Wherever the soul gives in to flesh
Without a struggle is home.
But you, I think, did not ask your question
In the homely sense of tiredness.

But enough of you, this is a poem
About how Laura turned into Francisca.
And you come in only to show
Mallorca in this poem is not
A favoured island made for man by God,
But so much godliness as man has
In being faithful to being man.

There are many habitable islands.
To be habitable is an island:
The rest is space, childhood of the mind,
Where keeping house is statecraft:
The habiting mind seems to itself
Tremendous, as a child writes large.
Then comes maturity, and loss of size,
And continents give way to islands,
And keeping house is play—
A small circle of meaning
Within a larger, the larger being
Truth, by which man knows of man.
And so a refuge-island is only
A grinning hollow of sarcasm and despite:
Such is the goatish propaganda
Of uninhabitable Ireland.

England is knowledge's self-doubt:
Whatever lies beyond makes here
An island in a sea of there.
From England sailed shy heroes
To stretch an empire of interrogation
As far as man could think—
Without forgetting the way back to silence.
From Spain tortured grandees of resignation
Sent hope out to die nobly;
Its angry face from God hidden,
The Spanish triumph is a self-damned flesh.

Of islands speaks the Mediterranean.
Precociously the Cretans fashioned
A private idiom of death.
With Semite impartiality the Phoenicians

Mothered the strangers of the little places.
Which Athens taught their several minor prides.
Corsica, man of France, triumphed too well,
By littleness was great, and of greatness, nothing.
Malta, Italy of islands,
Dreaming of greatness won from fate
Only an aged bad temper.
I mention it because they say
It is an island not unlike Mallorca.
And so is one man like another.
Up the slow grade of resemblance creeps
Identity—till the exact image
Is unphenomenal.
Exact Mallorca, least everywhere,
Most earth-like miniature
Of a too heavenly planet:
Here is a day a day, a word a word,
Man only men, and God the future,
Too late a subject for to-day
And better given to to-morrow,
The eternal Sunday.

I got this out of no bazaar of views;
But, looking round for the last day,
I found the first, grown small and final
Against the imagined years
And narrowed into one same previousness.
And what's an end, but honest time
Confessing that it only came before?
Looking around for literal death,
I found such literal life:
Like Deyá, built within itself,
Never a step beyond—as the church leads
From Deyá hill to Deyá down,
The Baptist crying off who would go on
To angelhood and always
Without growing small by death in Deyá.

And so we came to Deyá,
A village of Mallorca,
The island of an island,

As the bodily look carries a face.
Exact Mallorca, minute Deyá,
Finest and only fraction
Of the sole integer.
From here, the first least measure,
Truth has the difference only of more
Between its least and most:
If you have lived a thorough death
And, being dead, know self as truth-same—
However less than truth, yet not less true.
(Less true is difference in life,
Walking the other way, toward fancy
And the opposite islands of nowhere.)

But I think this is enough to show
My poem is not travel whimsy,
Or that mind's masquerade called fiction,
But a poem, that is, a fact
Standing alone, an island,
A little all that more grows
According to the trouble you can take.
For here I tell you, instead of Laura,
The samest least of her, Francisca.
May you, after this briefest day,
Sleep the short sleep and, waking up,
Ask, 'Is this not yesterday
When it was to-day—and to-morrow,
The long present instead of night?'

II
Francisca, and Scarcely More

'Francisca will be wild—she sings.'
This is a way of looking at a child
With years of hate between.
Francisca is.
She witches now. I love her.

Where man accounts himself a poor creature
And woman loves him for no more—
Without need to account herself

In such slight reckonings—
Francisca tricks and none prevents.
For she is a child.
Her eyes with her unbroken face are smooth.
Her back in which she hides me
Makes her to dance with speckled hair
Through which but shows a sometimes violet frock
Or other happy death or witch's pallor.
And prettily she keeps the thing
That if truth spoke all-hearably,
And Francisca were not,
Were only blazing judgement,
And terrible to see.

But here's no need for judgement to be spoken:
That man which here unlives himself
In chance began, and in chance is saved—
Let through the doors of destiny
Without a word, never having sought
More than to be in death the same.
Here insignificance is grateful,
To have not marked itself for doom.
Here with the body falls off but the race,
And what's left is a man's own, then,
A private good—if this content him.

And so no need to think,
Walking the village up and round,
How shall such wisdoms be preserved
When peace, the slow-to-gather storm,
Sweeps in, which nothing can outlast
Except what never braved it
With fair-weather reasoning.
No need to think: already have survived
Such wisdoms by peace forecontracted,
Choosing their given mortal size
Against the victory over death
That makes great only, and not so.
No need to pity, walking in and past:
They have fed, and on the daily bread
Which fills instantly and again.

And so Francisca sails her boat
(I gave it her, she found it by the door)
Down the slow *'siqui* by the wall,
Looking up only not to talk.
She lets it ride, then catches up
By scarcely walking, teasing along
Until the boat at any moment
Might play the fool and drop into the hole.
Enough danger for a short voyage.
Then she turns out her basket.
Three cards to laugh at? someone else.
A sprig to smell? not now.
Has anything dropped out? perhaps.

This is the moment for me to pass,
The moment to be two:
I who am not, being otherwise
Than the laws of similarity
Allow legally otherwise,
And I who by a sleight of person
Trifle with my different likeness
To be Francisca to the different
Who are more otherwise than I.
Up to the letter-hour then,
A softening of the eyes to be far off
To the far-off, who know
No other near than their own farness,
In which they are immediate,
And, after, a future still more far.
For every distant envelope
Torn open in Deyá and containing
Apparently a letter, just arrived,
That's so much less of far.

Or Robert fetches.
What letters and what news?
By now he knows what will be he
In the already counted afterwards.
What letters and what news?
Alas, they sign themselves forever
A world that was.

Alas, Laura, the same yesterday.
They have not written, they have.
Alas and happily: the world fails,
Yet life still is, memory translated
Into the language of *not again*.
Laura restores the fact eclipsed
By the fact subsequent to the fact,
In which they had persuasion of time,
The lie that does as well as truth
For a time.

Francisca shakes her various hair
When Robert fetches and Deyá seems severe.
Francisca with soft presence
Looked strange and sang the other way,
Nor did she bashfully.
But the Madonna of Cas Pintat
Unnewly out of small, just eyes
Spoke as usual the comfort
Of the short day that by shortness
Lasts only long enough
For a day always, saved from change.
Dear Robert, therefore have no fear.
Comfort by degrees of pain not felt
Attests the world not world-like
Recovering from being the world.
Dear Robert, if you break,
Holding your living self of man
Against death's selfless person
Too triumphantly, no more is lost
Than time, the unrepeatable—
Man shall yet have outlived man,
Though in a mortal immortality
In Deyá, where Francisca witches,
Darkening the full of meaning
That the Madonna clarifies
In consumable part only
Across her passionless counter.

At any rate, sit down and rest now.
The basket was too heavy.

I'll put the rice into the tin
And sort the vegetables and letters.
From a world that was—alas.
And has the will surrendered
To impossibility at last,
Which takes no vengeance but to nurse
Into the happy hopelessness,
The health beyond all feeling well or ill?
Dear Robert, the basket was too heavy.
At any rate sit down and rest now.
Perhaps you'll find you still spells you
When disappointment of others passes
Who were excesses of the will only.
Perhaps you did not scatter
When flesh scattered, strained beyond flesh,
But became the you possible,
A mental body faithful
To its bodily mind.
At any rate . . . and happily . . .
For does Francisca not make light,
Keeping the open secret with a silence
As familiar as a picture
Recognized but not expected to talk?

And on the way home Robert stopped
To see if Mariana had some news
To make the day seem at least wrong—
Better a wrong day than none,
Would Robert to himself say
Before thinking wrong to be wrong.
And to try once more to mend her stove.
For Mariana Deyá is
A mildest somewhere, not more exacting
To the lazy eye than its own first glance.
Two worlds in Deyá touch.
One ends, the other starts.
And there's a going and a coming.
And a madness, time being whipped on
To reach somewhere while it's still now.
And Mariana as if America
Argues both worlds the same,

And freedom of the one no dearer bought
Than freedom of the other—
A resurrection of believing true
Whatever makes the flesh feel proud;
And the rest, that mortifies,
Called lying flesh and lying death.
Mariana for America
Argues away one world of two,
Argues away repeatedly herself,
Woman arguing herself away.
Poor Mariana. And once indeed
She heard me call her this, and railed.
'Certainty is God,' she said,
'And you are only human, like me.'
Poor Mariana, who would be human
And is thus woman argued away,
Loud and uncertain against herself,
And in her purse an emptiness
Of money wanting where truth once was—
Such generosity can but miser.
And money is her mind always
When she speaks with me too thoughtfully.
For Mariana is our landlady
Since we to Deyá and beyond came
And until Canellun is built—
House-farther-on, past place-names.

Dear Robert, and so you once again
Tried to mend Mariana's stove.
Sit down and rest now, to-day has taught you
At least to feel no new despair.
Francisca, anti-narcissus of me,
Be a fate unapparent yet half-sweet
Whom waiting may succumb to without fear
While stubborn days of will push on to death
More death-like and more natural to know.

III
How the Poem Ends

For there are still sounds of a world
As if astir where it lay dead
Not longer than a moment ago—
This very moment, now.
They have no skill in their legs to walk
Or in their heads to make up time,
And yet they quiver with old talents,
Crying up, 'Give us to do.'
But Francisca does not answer.
And glad they are not to have been heard
When they have ceased complaining
And wish for nothing but to be dead
As happily they are, and were.
Not impolitely while they murmur
Francisca sings, she does not contradict.
And such complaisance is all they want,
No second thoughts or studying.
They are but voices slow to follow
Their tongues into corruption,
And Francisca deafs me from them.
Or, honouring their poor clamour
With nicest confutation,
I'd teach them *no* in tender stages
Of their argument, then mine.
And a horror from corpse to corpse would spread,
Death tasted with too live a mind.
If they still dream the dream they dreamt
When legs and heads were human,
No need to wake them into death
Though they have overslept: the rigor takes
The body first, the mind comes of itself.
The voices will in their own time
Fall silent with embarrassment
Of having spoken false.
And Francisca intercedes till then
Between this graveyard parliament and Laura.

But that's enough of the world,
Never more when it was most alive

Than a cramped theatre of language—
Prophecy seemed truer than truth.
Come, to inquire wholly, not in passing.
Those are uncomfortable fashions now
Which were the world once advertised.
The too up-to-date finalities
Multiply into long ago.
Come, they have sickened and lost eloquence
And do not work their purpose, or ours.
Francisca will preside while we withdraw
To the major drama that was not meant
To be produced by their kindness
On their stage for their self-congratulation.
Francisca is a charm like a wise child
Against the childishness of the world
To be the glory-world it tells of.
She does not interrupt, obedient
To the agèd tones and gestures—
So that there's not to rage or scold
Unless upon themselves for wagging on.

Come, to leave Francisca playing
Without tossing back the ball
That rolls away, perhaps under our feet
When walking past her with this afternoon
Like to-night's cheese and lettuce in our basket,
Or spice cakes, very tough . . . to give her one. . . .
But leave her playing without looking hard.
She's at a covered game like love—
Gentle to the eye but full of hurt
That can't be helped and so better not seen.
For such a child is death at play
When the dead protest they are too young
To lie so still and be so old.

And what's the outward sign to know by
How much mortality in Deyá
On Francisca's muffling brow
Quarrels with death, then of itself is dead
More quickly than of death, and no complaining?
Except it is a brow more without sound

Than brows are known to be? Even mine
Yields echoes though you walk upon it
Small enough, with careful tread enough.
But Francisca's brow is perfect smoothness,
And that's the only outward sign
How still a brow it is to walk upon,
None could you ask for where to be
More left-alone, or sound of self come sooner.
The outward signs show only from within,
As Deyá from the lagging sea
Invisible or not at all appears.
The theme is mortuary
And must be so intelligenced—
By approaching land from land
And beholding with dry vision
The earthly picture, no water in the eye
To blur immediacy into vistas
Of time-hearted understanding.
For death's a now like earth on which you stand
And only readable by looking near. . . .
Which closes up the eye? Then how to see?
The eye's a weakness, gentlemen,
As you know by the delight it gives,
And never leads but it leads wrong.
And flying off to ships this way and that
You ride interpretation backwards
Until your minds-of-mariners
Are idiotic with the not-real stars.
Then there's the coming home once more.
But that's not seeing solid, only weary.
You've yet to grow short-leggèd as you were
And learn to walk without a compass.
Indeed, there's nowhere to fly off to.
Everything's here under your lashes
That you have right of knowledge in,
And what you're stupid of is stupidness. . . .
So what's the outward sign to know by
If, as I say, Francisca verily
To such and such intent . . . in Deyá . . .
Shall you perhaps take ship? see for yourself?
Francisca, here's a gentleman from life

Come all this way to meet you . . .
An unfriendly little girl . . .
A most indifferent smile for all this way. . . .

And I? If I in Deyá am
No more envisageable phantasm
Than the problematic child, Francisca,
Then where am I, to seem a someone
In the world, filling a chair and housed
At an address that reaches me
By means of this make-believe body—
For never did I move or dwell
Outside myself—then where am I?
I lie from Deyá inward by long leagues
Of earthliness from the sun and sea
Turning inward to nowhere-on-earth.
A rumoured place? That takes us to the moon?
Let it be moon. The moon was never more
Than a name without a place to match it. . . .
In Deyá there's a moon-blight always
On the watery irises of fancy.
And minds that feed on bodily conceits
Go daft in Deyá, especially Germans. . . .
At any rate earth's proved, which saves
The proving of the place it gives into.
And where'd be time for that, between
Out of one, into the other, a twinkling
As fast as realizing death—or not?
Therefore, without the learned pause, to find
That Deyá is this open door I say
At least to look in by, if not to enter?

How's that? How's anything you know or don't?
You can't believe . . . on ordinary paper . . .
Printed by myself and Robert . . .
He's human, by every imperfection
He's made a dogged art of. . . .
Yes, I ink, he pulls, we patch a greyness,
Or clean the thickened letters out. . . .*
You can't believe . . . do I not eat?

*This poem was first printed by hand.

With pleasure. To-day was aubergine
Browned strong in oil, and blackberries
By Robert picked and juiced into stiff jelly
Come out so good but odd.
And I eat it at all times. But eating?
That's to be kind, a madness
Executed in the stomach
But starting in the heart, which forgives
And I forgive the idle fruits
Who have no thoughts but quick to soothe
The frowning mouths that can't agree.
And all the frightened edibles
That cringe away from argument,
Swearing they have no fixed opinion
Or ever took sides between man and—
Ah, though you can't believe, there's always God.
And that's a story you can go to sleep on
Without waking up next morning
The better or the worse for it.
Indeed, was it not written by yourselves?
A poem's by—who knows? And must be read
In prompt mistrust of the designing sense.
For once you let it have you,
There's no way out unless you leave behind
Your wits in it and wander foolish.

And so you can't believe. . . . And yet I speak
With a homely habit of self-pleasing
That tokens self-possession, a sure tongue?
Yes, the possession is my own.
My muse is I. . . . What shall we think?
The circumstances are at once
Too natural and too poetical
To determine either doubt or belief. . . .
Let's ask Maria, she's cleaning fish
Under the algarrobas with the cats.
Her comb keeps tumbling and her cheek is shy,
But a royal manner clicks in her brain
If the question is important.
And the answer to important questions
Is of course always the same, nor long—

Another question: 'Who asks?'
Maria's wisdom is not flattering.
Perhaps she'd seem, like Queen Victoria,
A little rude, as well-bred servants are.
I'd answer you myself, but—no.
In speaking for your special sake,
Suiting the answer to the question,
My courtesy would, I fear, like hers
Be queenly, as precision is
Which otherwise were arrogance.

Let's speak to Juan White-Mule about it.
If there's a settlement between
Your certain sanity and mine,
He'll make it, and with no disrespect
To either party, a *paz mallorquina*
Founded on mutual regret
That ever did we meet to differ.
But you'd not like to pledge yourselves
To difference, owning you were
Not here when there, not right when wrong.
And I could only as usual
Linger apart in tacit presence. . . .
Sooner or later you'd strike up talk:
'Peseta's down today. What's *your* story?'
So here's my story, now let me die again
Into the stranger you can't do without,
O tourists of neighbourliness.

1931.

THE LIFE OF THE DEAD

Explanation

THE text of this highly artificial poem was first written in French, in order that the English might benefit from the limitations which French puts upon the poetic seriousness of words. For French is a language better adapted than English to the rhetorical naïveté of manner necessary in a 'literal' account of the world in which the dead live—the precision of French being designed to create impressions, of English to convey meanings. As the subject is almost entirely one of experimental impression—a momentary subject—I had to be careful not to put English to uses improper to it. The illustrations are the germ of the text: I conceived them before the text, as verbal comedies. Their final form, however, was arrived at by a compromise between the illustrator and myself on the pictorial values of the subject. These values having been determined, I then made the textual frames out of French—though French is not 'my' language. I have used it here with approximate correctness, but my object was not to produce a finished literary exercise in French: the French text is merely the critical intermediary between the pictures and the English. The English text is therefore not so much a translation from the French as a piece of writing in English which contains in itself its improvised French model—as a safeguard against inappropriate poetic seriousness. The phrase 'poetic prose,' which is generally applied in a flattering sense to a degenerate form of prose-writing, may be correctly applied here because the poetic dishabille of the text is wilful—a conscious relaxation of poetic energy, not a stylistic orgy in prose. Indeed, all French writing in poetic form is, strictly speaking, poetic prose. The French are too jealous of their prose to tolerate those liberties which in English result in degenerate prose extravaganza; and they are not a sufficiently poetic people to achieve, when they write in poetic form, more than judicious prose equivalents to a kind of experience (namely, poetic experience) that is for them necessarily artificial. The usefulness of French in fixing the poetic degree of my outrageous subject suggests that it might not be unreasonable to impose on those writers who have a weakness for poetic prose the discipline of first writing their text in French; so that they must label their English text: 'From the French'. English makes things seem so real.

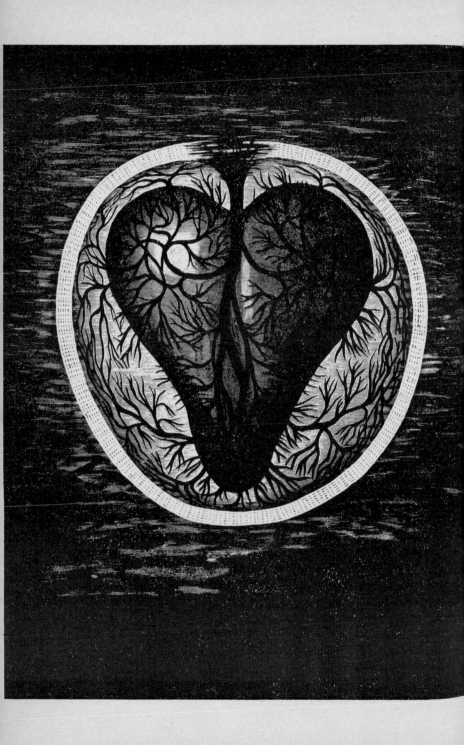

Le Cœur sec

Le monde où vivent les morts est un cœur sec.
Tout monde est un cœur, un rhythme sphérique,
Un rhythme de volontés impossibles
Qui se chantent et s'imaginent s'entendre.
Le monde où vivent les morts est un chœur silencieux.
Il ne s'entend pas, ni se chante.
Ses volontés sont devenues de froids souvenirs,
Noirs comme le sang qui ne court plus.
Gonflé d'une douleur qui ne fait pas de mal,
Le monde où vivent les morts est un cœur vivant
Dans un corps qui n'est plus.
Les morts ne vont ni en enfer, ni au ciel.
Ils continuent à vivre comme ils ont vécu.
Le monde où vivent les morts est un cœur sec,
Le même cœur que toujours, bien que sec.

The Dry Heart

The world where the dead live is a dry heart.
Every world is a heart, a rhythm spherical,
A rhythm of impossible intentions
That yet sings itself, imagining heard music.
The world where the dead live is a silent choir.
It does not hear itself, it sings itself not.
Its will has frozen into memory,
Black as still blood, without flow.
To the painless sorrow of death it throbs.
The world where the dead live is a heart alive
In a body once alive.
The dead move neither into heaven nor hell.
Their afterwards is their before.
The world where the dead live is a dry heart,
The same heart as always, even dry.

Les Trois Âmes des Morts

Dans les corps morts des morts,
Sur les esprits trop vivants des morts,
Règne la déesse inconnue, la mort même.
Ah, qu'est-ce que c'est que la mort,
Enveloppée des pensées si muettes des morts muets?
Romanzel, malheureux poète des morts,
Se penche au-dessus d'elle, avide de mots.
Il a les ailes d'un vautour,
Il a la tête d'un oiseau qui se croit homme.
Ses pieds sont faits pour les routes confuses et sans fin—
Pointus et cintrées de colère, ses pieds,
Et plus noir que la mort, son corps,
De la couleur des silences furieux.
Romanzel, irrité par cette déesse abstruse,
Cherchant dedans les bouts de tristes rubans
Qui font sa tête—cherchant sa propre poésie
D'âme qui morte veut vivre véritablement
Tout ce qui dans la vie était fausseté de vie—
Romanzel, déployant ses ailes désespérées,
Fait l'invisible ciel des morts, aveugles-nés.
Unidor, qui n'admet pas de différence
Entre le monde des morts et le monde des vivants,
Continue son œuvre: il se fait ce qu'il désire.
De ses yeux aveugles il refait la femme qu'il a perdue
En allant ainsi dans le monde du vrai rien.
Il la fait ici de ses yeux aveugles
Comme là il l'a faite de ses yeux faux-clairs.
Elle s'appelle Amulette, bien belle elle est,
Petite image en chair morte de la mort—
De l'idée obsédante à laquelle il ne pense même pas
Pour en faire sa petite pareille à lui.
Unidor se tient sur une mer d'indifférence.
Mais pour Amulette il a fait une petite terre en l'air
De sorte qu'elle puisse se trouver aussi bien ici que là.
Les grandes mains jalouses de Romanzel la convoitent,
Bien que sa tête soit cachée dans les arbres incomplets—
Tout ce qui rappelle le monde vivant le rend fou,
Lui le malheureux poète des désaccords passionnés.
Quant à Mortjoy, notre doux favori,

Il sait bien qu'il est mort, et que ça lui plaît!
Et qu'il voit bien, malgré l'aveuglement mortuaire!
Il voit avec les yeux fermés, manière de voir
Plus innombrablement que quand, les yeux ouverts,
Il s'expliquait un seul pauvre objet à la fois.
Fouillant dans la robe si simple et sinistre
De la marchande solennelle de plus grandes illusions,
Il s'empare, en une fois, des trésors non à vendre
Qu'elle garde comme des antiquailles égyptiennes
Contre les yeux dédaigneux des trop riches touristes.
Il en fait son théâtre, une comédie éternisée
En courtes histoires tragiques, en petits contretemps.
Sur un tapis qui les rend raides et calmes il range
Les poupées impressionables de la circonstance.
Mortjoy, c'est l'esprit des morts heureux:
Après la vie vient la vie plus longue,
Viennent les heures exigües, les scènes pour ne pas pleurer,
Qui seulement font penser 'Que vienne la prochaine.'
Vient le bonheur rapide et long, comme au commencement,
Quand il n'y avait que la mort—le long bonheur
Trop empressé pour mécontentement ou excès.
Double absolu où tout se passe et rien ne se passe—
Ah, la bonne mort, l'aujourd'hui classique,
Le temps avant le temps, et après!
Mortjoy, le doux favori, à genoux devant elle,
Poursuit son jeu comme un enfant précoce
En matière de guerre ou de géographie
Fait ses batailles ou ses voyages imaginaires.
La mort est plus pleine de vie que la vie.
Ce n'est que quelques chapitres que la vie
Pour faire peur à ceux qui ont les yeux trop petits
Pour ouvrir de grands yeux sur la grande, grande mort.
Mortjoy, doux et intelligent, a les yeux fermés,
Mais c'est la mort qui les lui ferme, pas la peur.
La mort ne lui fait pas peur. 'Encore, encore!' il crie.
Quand la mort ne sera plus qu'une seule horreur
Trop étendue pour se la figurer,
Alors crèveront ses yeux orgueilleux
D'avoir si scrupuleusement évoqué
Tous ces mystères intimes dont on ne parle pas.
Mais cela, c'est plutôt la catastrophe de Romanzel.

Mortjoy jamais ne ferait des scandales.
C'est comme s'il n'avait rien vu.
La mort est un secret bien fermé en se confiant à lui:
Il a les fines boucles d'honneur sur son front.
Et quant à Unidor, il ne se demande pas où il se trouve.
Il met son dos à la mort et, ne regardant que devant lui,
Ne voit que le même plaisir d'étre soi-même—
N'importe comment ça doive se finir.
Jusqu'au dernier moment, comme dès le premier,
Ses yeux se renouvellent en contemplant
L'ampleur magique de la friponne figurine
Qui chaque moment disparaît pour pouvoir reparaître.

The Three Men-Spirits of the Dead

Over the dead bodies of the dead,
Over the too live minds of the dead,
Prevails the unknown goddess, death itself.
And what indeed is death,
Muffled and mute in the mute thoughts of the dead?
Romanzel, luckless poet of the dead,
Hovers on her, soaring round in word-lust.
He has the wings of a vulture,
The head of a bird vain of its manhood.
His feet are of lost roads and endlessness,
Hollowed up with anger, devil-toed.
And blacker than death, his body—
The black of furious silences.
Romanzel, doubtful if such abstruse goddess be
Terrible to know, since only silence-mighty,
Thinking amid the grim confusions
Struggling ribbon-wise where seems her head
To find a poetry of living death, resurrection
Of all that dropped down false in life, impossible—
Romanzel, spreading his tormented wings,
Spreads the blank sky of the blank-eyed dead.
Unidor, indifferent to the change
From world to other world not seen,
Holds the same task, contents the same desire.
With his blind eyes he builds the woman again

That death's veraciousness made nothing,
Even as in the lying sun she nightly faded
And each day must be anew stood up
Before his lying eyes, artificing sight.
Her name is Amulette, and saucy-fair she is,
Little image of death, of dead flesh moulded—
Close image of the far obsession,
Though never has he looked on death, uttered the word.
Unidor walks an indifferent sea, firmly.
But Amulette walks on land; he has devised
A little world in air suspended, as she is used.
And greedily Romanzel's hands reach down,
Though hidden among the incomplete trees her head.
Whatever brings life to mind is instant fire
In Romanzel's luckless drought of soul.
But not so with Mortjoy, our gentle favourite.
He is well advised that he is dead, and well pleased.
And well enough he sees, though blind, as death makes.
For his eyes are closed, he loves their blindness:
Faithfuller the quick, tumbled spectacle
Than when open-eyed he consented
To one poor numbered picturing at a time.
Groping in the sinister simplicity
Of her shop-attire (this merchant of more solemn marvels),
In one confiding gesture he claims
Her private, worthless treasures, not for sale,
Tucked in her apron like Egyptian rubbish,
Lest moneyed tourists, laughing through their pearls,
Think her a doting graveyard wife, and misbehave.
Of such is Mortjoy's theatre, an earnest comedy
Complete of brief undoings, minute fatalities.
On death's travel-carpet, motionless and calm,
The once distracted dolls of chance succeed themselves.
Mortjoy is the man-spirit of the happy dead:
After live hours comes the longer time
Of narrowing hours, of scenes that hurry tears,
That move the lips with only 'And the next?'
The longer, timeless time runs on as once
When death was first and life need not have followed—
The longer time of lightning prophecies
Too fast-ensuing to bode surfeit or lack.

Exaggerated absolute, where all or nothing happens—
How prospers death, the classic present,
Time before time, and afterwards!
Mortjoy, the preferred, at her side kneeling,
Makes play as might a knowledgeable child,
In wars grounded and in maps precise,
Imaginary battles and fond voyages taste.
More life in death stirs than in life.
Life is no more than those few chapters,
Of fearsome name among the fearful,
That turn away such eyes as dare not open
Whole-circle round on death, blinding quantity.
Mortjoy, gentle and brave, turned death wide-open eyes,
And death closed them, but bounteously.
Death does not little him with fear. 'More, more!' he cries.
When death's a single horror, vast inundation,
Then may his bursting eyes spill over,
And the pride crash that made familiar with
The household mysteries of death, interior gossip.
But such, rather, is Romanzel's famed calamity,
Who had such pride, yet never came so near.
Mortjoy's pleasure is not the spy of fame.
Nothing's to tell, for all he gathers tales.
Death is the closed secret of his curiosity.
Ringlets of honour softly seal his brow.
And Unidor? He does not puzzle where, when, what, who.
His back is turned on death: staring straight before,
His eyes live by the conjured figurine
Whose sly, loose magic loses her each moment,
That the next moment she may show again.

Le Théâtre de Mortjoy

Mortjoy est certainement un garçon heureux!
Voyez donc: il a son théâtre à lui
Où, en grande image de papier mâché,
Il est le prince magnifique du spectacle
Qui ne sort jamais de la loge royale,
Qui n'a besoin de chercher ni les hommages ni les belles pièces:
C'est un curieux autour de qui s'empressent
Les menues merveilles égarées de la vie.
C'est comme une poche de magicien, son théâtre:
Des choses s'y trouvent qu'on aurait dit évanouies
Dans le trou invisible où tombe le superflu du temps
Chaque fois que les cloches sonnent puissamment 'Pouvons
        plus!'
Sur le plafond, des rubans déroulant de très petits gens
Font une tresse historique—tous les romans qui jamais jamais
Ne seront racontés. Tant mieux: jamais les cloches
Les feront taire—long bavardage silencieux.
Puis, dans les loges les plus près de la scène,
Pour bien voir qu'ils jouent leurs rôles avec assez d'entrain,
Se trouvent les mauvais génies du spectacle,
Ceux qui mettent fin chaque nuit aux fausses joies qui s'élèvent
Comme des anges enfantins sur la représentation vieillie.
Assise dans sa loge avec noble raideur—
Qui dirait que cette vertueuse douairière
Cache la reine-sorcière de l'hideux drame de mort
Qui se passe sur la scène: la sorcellerie et l'escroquerie
Se mettant en lambeaux pour la joie de se raccommoder—
Les deux pôles tortueux du destin, entre lesquels
Nerveusement filent les foules des mécontents énergiques.
Et qui dirait que ce monsieur si comme il faut,
Gardant sa place dans la loge inférieure
Avec la haute fixité d'un homme soigneusement instruit
Dans tous les tours délicats de la science de la scène—
Qui dirait que lui c'est le pitre-escroc lui-même,
Celui qui fait chanter les balles d'assassin
Autour du corps de coton de la poupée-sorcière.
Ah, quelle interminable facétie! et penser
Que tout le monde est parti—les places vides,

Les programmes flottant libres (on ne les a pas lus jusqu'au
   bout),
Les cannes d'ébène, les jumelles, les perles de la marquise,
La claque de milord, la trompette du beau nègre—
Tous survivant comme des falbalas de la danse
Encore ivres de la musique, les danseurs déjà au lit.
Mais la métaphore n'est pas tout à fait exacte.
Car, vraiment, ce morceau n'ose se commencer
Avant que tout le monde s'en aille chez lui:
C'est éxigé—d'abord a lieu le retour à la vie.

Mortjoy's Theatre

Surely is Mortjoy of the luckiest.
Just think: a theatre all his own!
And there he rules, Prince of the Play,
A solitary monarch set up in *papier mâché,*
Perpetual fixture of the Royal Box:
No need to saunter out in search of vassalage
Or the rare shows secreted from all eyes but his—
The lasting eyes, unblinking, of curiosity.
To his side come running the lost little wonders
That fell out of life, it seemed, into a giant nothing-hole—
The same that swallowed out of sight
The extra numbers on the clock
When the tired hours angrily intoned 'No more to go!'
His theatre is a magic pocket: turn but the lights on,
And see! the tangled ceiling, historic plait
Of tales that never, never will be told—
Never will the tired hours hush this silent chatter,
Persistent gibberish safe from clock-sense.
Then, in the boxes close against the stage,
To make perfect-sure they play their self-same parts,
Sit the two evil geniuses of the boards,
Those who each night belie the happy endings
That rise absurdly from the aged spectacle
Like childish angels from decrepit death-beds.
And who would guess this virtuous dowager to be—
Stiffly ennobled in her vantage seat—
The very queen of witches, the very hag of the play:

Where witchery and crime tatter each other
For the crooked joy of indestructibility—
These two crooked poles of fate between which
Stream the irritated files of outcast energies.
And who would know the worthy patron of the lower box,
Whose lofty stare bespeaks the Thespian connoisseur—
Who would detect the waggish villain there,
The same who makes the murderous bullets sing
Against the cotton witch whose bats squeak out of key.
What an interminable game it is! And to think
That everyone's gone home, the seats all empty,
The programmes fluttering idle (not read through to the end),
Ebony sticks, theatre glasses, the massive negro's trumpet,
The pearls of the marchioness, milord's opera-hat—
All left behind alive, like trappings of the dance
Still music-sped, though long the dancers lie asleep.
But the metaphor falls short, the truth is tidier:
This scene may not begin till everyone's at home—
A rule, this, clearly printed in the programme
Half-way down, just after 'Time for life again'.

La Transformation de Romanzel

Peu à peu Romanzel monte: pas au ciel.
Il n'y a pas là cette atmosphère si doucement terrestre
Où les poètes ont anciennement déployé leurs ailes
Et fait des illusions adroitement cachées de la vérité.
Le ciel de Romanzel, c'est une lourdeur montagneuse
Qui l'accable de bien près, qui devient de plus en plus
    rigoureuse—
En sorte qu'il se change en plusieurs démons-satyres
Courant de cime en cime d'un pas éperdument léger.
Et toujours, impossiblement là-bas, en danse
Moitié paradisiaque et moitié lascive,
Voilà la femme pour ainsi dire terrestre,
L'aimable Amulette, ouvertement sans soucis,
S'inquiétant, dans le petit bois tout à elle,
De rien qu'elle-même, comme elle est belle, comme elle
    est absolue.
Unidor dort à part: les solitudes d'Amulette,
Ce sont ses rêves plus purs, où rien ne se passe—
Sauf le noir, faible frémissement du blanc ennui
Que fait la mort dans la tête paresseuse d'Unidor.
Mais Romanzel, là-haut, comprend tout, il comprend trop.
'Il faut me tuer,' se dit-il dans tous ses corps—
'Il faut tuer mon âme, c'est ça qui vit toujours.
Ainsi ma chair et Amulette seront contemporaines,
Mes yeux et sa beauté se connaîtront
Comme jours du même siècle, bien que moi
Je sois un peu le sot vieux, et elle se joue de moi
En pensionnaire insolente qui ne s'entend pas à l'amour.
Et d'Unidor il ne restera qu'un petit cœur de nacre
Pour ouvrir comme un médaillon de l'enfance
Et y verser quelques larmes indulgentes—sans savoir
    pourquoi. . . .'
Et tout en pleurs, s'apitoyant du pauvre Unidor,
Romanzel se précipite là-bas. . . . Amulette danse,
Encore plus aisément; Unidor dans ses rêves
Sourit d'une plaisanterie obscure et éphémère . . .
Des restes de Romanzel—dispersés sur la terre
Comme les os rejetés d'un spectre fâcheux—

Ni Unidor ni Amulette ne s'en aperçoivent:
Les chagrins des morts morts—cela ne les regarde pas.

The Transformation of Romanzel

Romanzel through deep heights rises: not to the sky.
In death no air like that soft earth-blue whose hollow climates
Poets long filled with secret universes
Where truth in plaintive multiple was not itself—
A mountainous oppression is the sky of Romanzel.
It weighs upon him low and cloudily,
The too-sweet, plenary oxygen of suicide—
Till he's so many several demon-satyrs
Leaping in frolicsome despair from peak to peak.
And always, impossibly below, framed in a dance
Half-lewd, half-paradisial—dear Amulette,
Frank earth-illusion, a nymph within a grove of self
Musing her free dominion and her loveliness.
Near by sleeps Unidor: the privacies of Amulette
His purest dreams are, all like himself asleep there,
Save for the faint black fume which death, white boredom,
In the untroubled mind of Unidor stirs up.
But Romanzel, far above, sees sharp, understands too much.
'I must kill myself,' he says in every body of him—
'I must kill my soul, it is that which still lives.
Thus will my flesh be time-identical with Amulette,
Her beauty and my eyes will have acquaintance
Like days of the same century, though mine be but
The old fool's part and hers the saucy schoolgirl's
Pretending nunnish innocence of love.
Of Unidor the relic's then a little locket-heart,
Pathos in mother-of-pearl like childhood treasure
Sometimes to weep against somewhat—not knowing why.'
And with a tearful grace, pity of Unidor
Like metric slowness anatomizing the rash downtumbling,
Romanzel leaps; falls, leaps. . . . Amulette dances,

More briskly than before, indeed; Unidor, dreaming,
Smiles at some nameless humour of an instant . . .
And all that's left of Romanzel bestrews the ground
Like the discarded bones of a vexed ghost.
Amulette does not mark them, far less does Unidor:
The sorrows of the dead who die—such matters cannot
    give them pause.

La Naissance des Bébés Morts

Au-dessus du petit bois d'Amulette et d'Unidor,
S'appuyant sur le feuillage comme cabane de carton
Se trouve leur maison de mort—quel ménage folâtre!
Unidor s'est déjà levé: c'est lui qui construit
La grande ville chimérique dans l'ombre de laquelle
Se garde décemment leur asile, loin des bruits discordants
Mais pas trop sauvage—comme toute maison bienséante
    de famille.
Unidor ne s'occupe pas de ce qui se passe en dedans de la ville,
Il suffit qu'il y ait une ville à voir dans le lointain—
Amulette trouve ça trés chic et pas trop embêtant.
Au fond elle a des goûts assez simples.
Elle s'est mise dans ses meubles d'un seul geste pratique et
    riant:
On n'y voit que les lampes! Amulette dit très peu,
Mais tout ce qu'elle dit, c'est inoubliable.
Elle dit: 'La lumière meuble tout, même les coins,
Et ne fait pas de poussière, comme font les objets soi-disant
    utiles.'
Mais naturellement elle a un lit, un bon lit
Au matelas bien épais, comme a tout le monde.
Ça se tient contre le toit, sens dessus dessous:
Amulette aime toujours à voir tout—c'est pourquoi
Il n'y a pas de second dans sa maison,
Ni plus d'une chambre, bien que la nuit elle dise de coutume,
A l'heure de se coucher, 'Bien, Unidor,
Il faut penser qu'il y a, entre nous et notre lit,
Les mêmes marches innombrables qu'il y avait hier soir.'
Et le matin, après le départ d'Unidor pour la ville,
Elle garde son lit encore une demi-heure:
C'est cela qu'elle aime, avoir le lit entièrement à soi,
Et, les yeux grand ouverts mais tout de même ne pensant
    à rien,
Faire des bébés voluptueusement à son aise.
Ils sortent de sa bouche comme des bouffées de tabac;
En effet, on ne peut dire qu'elle y tient
Plus sérieusement que n'importe quelle femme
A sa cigarette d'avant-déjeuner.
Les bébés s'arrangent comme ils peuvent:

Ce ne sont que de minces fœtus qui dégringolent
A vites étapes d'enfance jusqu'au plancher exact.
Là ils ne perdent pas leur temps en badinant.
Quelques-uns s'arrêtent près de la branche de vigne
Qui se glisse secrètement dans la maison,
Pour en goûter le grain si mystérieux et luisant.
Mais Amulette les pousse impatiemment vers la fenêtre;
'Dépêchez-vous, voilà papa qui vous attend là-haut.
Allez, allez, il faut aider papa!'

Dead Birth

Above the grove where Amulette and Unidor make play,
Resting among the tree-tops like a cardboard cottage,
Stands their deathly dwelling—an absurd household it is!
Unidor is already up: it is he who builds
The large chimera-city in whose shadow
Their modest covert is safe from outer jangle
And yet not brutish—like any self-respecting family residence.
Unidor cares little what comes to pass within the city,
Enough that there's a city in the distance to be seen—
To Amulette the thing's great fun, not really boring.
Essentially, however, her tastes are of the simplest.
She furnished her house, for example, in one humorous sweep,
One efficient look-round, one fastidious provision:
Lamps, lamps and lamps! Amulette is by no means talkative,
But as unforgettable as rare her sentences.
She says: 'Light fills a room better than tables and chairs—
It furnishes the corners even, and makes no dust,
Unlike the household objects by reputation useful.'
But naturally she has a bed, a proper bed,
Thoroughly mattressed, such as everybody has.
It lies just under the roof, and facing downward:
Amulette likes to see always what's going on
In every spot her own—thus there's no second floor
And but one room, though each night when it's bed-time
She says with wilful habitude, 'Come, Unidor,
Don't forget that between here downstairs and up-in-bed
There's the same breathless count of steps as yesterday.'
And in the morning, Unidor off to city-making,

She lies abed a luxury-long half-hour:
This is her fondest greed, to have the bed all to herself,
And, eyes full awake yet not in focus of thought,
To bubble babies lazily from her mouth
Like idle smoke-puffs fanatically precise.
Indeed, one would not say her mind was on the business
More seriously than any woman's on the cigarette
That gently ushers in the discipline of breakfast.
The babies must get on as best they can—
Poor comic foetuses fast-tumbling to the ground
Through all the dateless turns and spans of infancy.
And there they waste no time in dimpled babble.
Some few linger at the mystery-vine that laughs at masonry,
A leafy spy on indoor secrets, its grape-eyes gleaming—
What are they looking at? What do they taste like?
But Amulette is impatient with fancy, or the colic.
'To the window, children, no dallying, out you go.
Be quick, papa's up there, and waiting for you.
There, there, now—that's a darling—run and help papa!'

A l'intérieur de la ville: de jour

En dedans de la ville se répandent joyeusement
Des horreurs assez risibles: les nerfs vifs des morts
S'y déchaînent, comme de malins esprits déjoués par eux-
    mêmes,
Pour se venger d'eux-mêmes. Ce qui n'est d'aucune
    conséquence:
Dans ce monde illogique personne ne fait droit à personne,
Mais, de l'autre côté, personne n'est trop sensible.
Tout est un faux semblant; la ville provient d'un caprice.
Les débris inquiets qui animent les tombeaux
Ont un seul cerveau électrique—si l'on jette un regard
De chirurgien en dedans, on voit la ville même dont je parle.
Les habitants en sont tous des sanguinaires plaisants.
De quel temps on ne peut dire: à quelques égards
Cela a l'air d'une ville du moyen âge—de gros rires, de grosses
    cruautés.
A d'autres égards, c'est une ville des plus modernes:
Les édifices ne font pas voir leurs fonctions catégoriques.
Çà et là on remarque un beau balcon fretté,
Mais il ne s'agit pas de la musardise des dimanches—
C'est plus probable que de temps en temps une victime
    réfractaire
S'y accroche avec triste entêtement, préférant
Les coups qu'on lui verse aux douleurs du pavé.
Dans la place centrale il y a tel balcon
Très en vogue pour de telles cérémonies piquantes—
Personne ne se soucie des usages ordinaires de la maison.
Tout en bas se dresse un lampadaire très connu—
C'est l'endroit favori pour les pendaisons impromptues.
On n'est pas trop pointilleux dans sa manière de torturer.
Les autos et les voitures de tramway passent leur chemin
Sans s'arrêter pour regarder, sans faire attention
Aux corps tourmentés qui quelques fois leur barrent le passage.
Le tour le plus fin qu'on y joue, c'est d'attacher l'infortuné
Au dos d'un auto et le laisser traîner au hasard—
Bien souvent le pauvre drôle a la chance de rester intact.
Les gaillards les plus étourdis sont les bravaches nouveau-morts.
Ils vont brandissant leurs épées comme des soldats en congé
Qui soupirent vaillamment après la guerre.

Il n'y a rien de plus épatant, de plus exquis,
Dans tout ce répertoire de bizarreries lugubres
Que l'adresse du sabreur en train d'équilibrer
Un sujet difficile à la pointe de son épée.
Le grand feu de joie au beau milieu de la place
N'est pas un spectacle pour faire perdre votre temps;
Là on brûle les sujets les plus insignifiants.
Tout près, sur la colonne, on isole un à un
Les citoyens sans reproche, les êtres ennuyeux.
Souvent, un mois entier s'écoule, avant que le pieux
S'extasie du martyre, pour faire place au prochain.
Mais, à vrai dire, ce sont des niaiseries
Auxquelles ne s'intéressent guère les morts eux-mêmes—
Comme dans les journaux des pays étrangers
On ne trouve pas des traités sur les mœurs indigènes.

Within the City: Day-time

Within the city merrily rage such grotesque horrors
As might be guessed: the tangled nerves of the dead
Run lunatic there, like evil spirits self-baffled,
Crying vengeance on themselves. A tangle of no consequence:
There is no logic in this world, no justice bargained,
But, by the same rule, no one is tender in his flesh or right.
All's a wild fraud there, the city a grim caprice.
The febrile fragments which animate the tombs
Form one electric brain, inside of which the surgical eye
Discerns the dolesome city that I tell of.
The inhabitants are a sprightly, vicious tribe.
It is not possible to say to what age they belong.
The city has, in some respects, a mediaeval air—
Gothic laughter, Gothic malignancy.
In other respects it is a bigot of modernism:
The buildings keep their categoric functions secret.
Here and there one sees a balcony of curling fret,
But no token this of the proud favours of Sunday afternoons.
More likely is the sight of some refractory victim
Dangling therefrom with piteous resolution, preferring
So to swing under blows than to lie tragical
On the inexorable pavement high below.

In the great square of the city such a balcony
Has had long fame in these sophistications—
No one thinks to ask of the inner drama of the house.
Before it stands an ancient street-lamp of equal honour—
Renowned convenience of impromptu hangings.
One is not over-nice in the proprieties of torture.
The motor-cars and tram-cars go their way
Without stopping to look on or make observance of
The writhing bodies that sometimes choke their progress.
The most delicate prank in vogue is to string the wretch
Behind a motor-car and let him trail to the traffic's random—
Often there's luck in this, the silly survives intact.
The most roguish galliards are the braves not long deceased.
They jaunt about, their swords unscabbarded, like soldiers
    home on leave
Valorously sighing for the battle-front.
There's nothing quite so prodigious, so wanton-quaint
In this whole hypochondriacal repertory
As the intent skill of a swordsman juggling true
Some difficult subject on his tidy sword-tip.
The great bonfire signalling the middle of the square
Is not a sight to claim much of your time.
One deals there only with the unimportant cases.
On the pillar not far off are left marooned
Those tiresome neighbours without foibles—one at a time.
Often a whole month goes by before the righteous one
Transpires in martyrdom, to make room for the next.
But, come, these are indeed palling frivolities
In which the dead themselves take little interest—
As in the newspapers of foreign countries
Treatises on native modes do not abound.

A l'Interieur de la Ville: de Nuit

Toute ville devient de nuit un café populeux.
De nuit la ville des morts devient un cadre resserré
Où courent en minaudant ces rôdeurs nonchalants.
Ils ne sont plus que d'apathiques automates de jeu.
Les ornements du dandysme, les robes de bal et de ballet—
Tout cela embellit pêle-mêle les sombres murailles,
Comme les croquis que font toujours d'une manière badine
Les anciens habitués en accès de tendresses.
Mais ici on n'est pas grand buveur, ni grand enthousiaste
Ou de la maison ou de la demoiselle de comptoir.
Bien entendu, c'est la dame de cœur elle-même.
Mais tous ceux qui fréquentent ce bar si froidement neuf—
De la pureté des cartes à jouer pas encore usées—
Ne sont que des cartes à jouer toutes neuves.
Ils connaissent cette dame assez bien; à son côté
Ils ont tous poursuivi leurs rêves insensibles—
Rien de plus émouvant, de plus intime que cela
Ne se passe dans leurs vies. Messieurs les Dominos,
Qui méditent austèrement sur les hasards funestes
De la petite table de jeu, font encore moins d'imprudences.
Mais plus près de l'entrée on n'est pas si triste.
Des pièces d'échecs s'ébattent lestement là-bas
Au son d'un gramophone géant
Dont la main harmonique paraît presque vivant—
Grand ouvrage de cire jouant des disques avec un tact
    accompli.
La danse a lieu sur un vrai échiquier,
Les danseurs sont de vraies pièces d'échecs.
Ils se meuvent conformément aux règles de jeu.
Le gramophone ne se fatigue pas.
La même main qui en joue le remonte au moment voulu.
Eh bien, à quoi mène tout cela? Et si ça dure toute la nuit?
Il faut comprendre que les cartes ne sont que des cartes,
Messieurs les Dominos ne sont pas vraiment sortis de leur
    boîte,
Les pièces d'echecs sont des curions désœuvrés.
Et le gramophone? C'est assez connu de vous, je crois:
C'est la musique que font les races qu'on n'a pas eu le temps

De fâire entrer dans les évènements combles
Qui rendent la vie si douce, la mort si encrassée.

Within the City: Night-time

At night a city narrows into a populous café.
At night the city of the dead becomes a shrunken framework
Into which pour mincingly those uninspired wanderers.
All are but apathetic game-automata now.
The foppish trimmings, the wasted spangle of ball and ballet—
Such hang in brazen melancholy on the walls,
Like the fond sketches of habitués bygone
Immortalizing bouts of myopic tenderness.
But here the guests are not warm students of the glass,
Nor do they dote upon the management
Or wage profoundly the cult of the bar-girl.
True enough, she is the Queen of Hearts herself.
But all who hover near the spotless varnish of this too-new
    bar—
As chaste as shop-new playing-cards not yet dealt out—
Are little more themselves than fugitives of the pack.
The lady is not, indeed, a stranger to them;
They have lain next her in those frigid intimacies
Through which cards doze till there's a game. The gentlemanly
    dominoes,
Brooding austerely on the dreadful chances turned
By one small gaming-table, are not less discreet.
But there's more spirit toward the entrance-way.
A whole set of chess-men is at earnest sport
To the tune of a giant gramophone
Whose eloquent, harmonic hand seems half-alive—
Great waxwork symbol reeling off the discs with practised
    virtue.
And the dance moves expertly over a real chess-board,
The dancers are the impeccable counters of the game.
They circulate in patient form, according to the rules.
Nor does the gramophone at any time run down.
The same hand that plays it winds it up at the slack moment.
And what's the point of all this? And does it last the night
    through?

You must understand that the cards are mere cards,
The dominoes have not really left their box,
The chess-men are but idling curios.
And the gramophone? I believe you are familiar with it:
It is the voice of all those races that time has not admitted
Into the lavish happenings and courses
That make life so full of interest, and death so foul.

Le Banquet des Morts

Les jours de fêtes les morts se trouvent sur une grande table,
Une barque qui court d'un bout du monde des morts à l'autre.
Mais on s'en occupe rarement, comme jamais on n'y est trop
    content,
Jamais ne s'y passent des choses pour s'en réjouir.
De sorte que la table vogue comme une barque ensorcelée
Sur une mer ténébreuse—le flux indistinct
De regrets postiches: car les morts ne peuvent dire précisément
Ce dont ils ont envie, ce qui leur fait défaut.
Tout de même, il y a là des jours de fête, pour se féliciter
Des bonheurs improbables, sans nom, effrontément amorphes.
On ne s'assied pas—les chaises sont des épaves flottantes.
Même on ne mange pas: ce n'est qu'une promenade
Tout le long de la table prodigue pour en voir les délices:
Un verger chargé des fruits de choix; de gras animaux
Paissant à leur aise—avant-goût des mets ravissants;
Au milieu une fontaine où bondissent des poissons comestibles.
Mais les couverts et les autres articles du service
Ne sont que de grossiers dessins réalistes
Damassés subtilement sur les plis de la nappe.
Non, cette illusion de banquet n'a pas une suite alimentaire.
Bientôt la table s'envolera dans l'étendu blafarde
Où meurent les visions fictives des morts
En longs soupirs de faux contentement.

When the Dead Banquet

On notable days the dead mount a mighty table,
A barque that sails their world from one end to the other,
But which they rarely look to, since never fall to them
Extreme occasions fit to make joy and revel of.
Wherefore the table sails as might a magic barque
Riding a vacant sea—the garbled flow
Of sham regrets: for the dead cannot well utter
Precise passions, or call their wants by name.
And yet such notable days betide, to celebrate
Unlikely, clouded raptures, brazenly enigmatic.
No sitting down here—the chairs are floating derelicts.

Nor does one really eat—rather a hungry stroll
Along the table-edge, in prodigal anticipation:
An orchard excellent in fruits; plumped animals
Ranging prosperous—earnest of mouthsome roasts;
A fountain in the middle where play the fish most sweet of
    flesh.
But the knives and forks and plates and other table-things
Are but close patterns damasked against the cloth-hem to the
    life.
No, this promissory banquet has no dietetic sequel.
Soon the table will fly off into the wan expanse
Where the feigned visions of the dead expire
In slow-heaved sighs of false contentment.

La Musée de l'Aube

Quand vient le jour, les longs rayons
De cette chaleur comme des glaçons dans la mémoire,
Les morts s'enfuient, s'enterrent dans leurs tombeaux;
Ils cherchent une crypte au-dessous de la neige brûlante
Du trop soudain soleil qui leur fait voir
Comme ils sont morts au même moment qu'il fait
Prédiction de vie instantanée.
Au-dessous des plus bas nuages de l'horizon
Il y a une crypte couverte de jour comme si de la neige,
Ou comme si de longs glaçons—de telles fortes cryptes
Il n'y en a que dans les religions.
Sans bruit, sans s'éveiller, les morts se glissent
Dans les petites caves cellulaires qui forment
Les murs et carreaux creux de leur frayeur—
D'après les idées fanatiques des morts
Sur ce que veut dire la lumière vive:
'Pendant le jour, il faut paraître des cadavres,'
Se disent-ils. 'Le jour est ce diable si connu,
Qui pense nous inspirer de fins talents,
Des métiers bouffons, pour nous conduire
Hors du désœuvrement dont la mort dote les morts
Dans un royaume où tout n'est que fatigue,
Fatigue et maladie d'agir ni pour soi-même,
Ni pour les autres—royaume du grand Pourquoi.
Mieux vaut faire semblant de ne pas voir,
De ne rien sentir, comme de pauvres ossements
Qui ne demandent que d'être ce qu'ils sont.'
Mais quelques-uns, contre se sage conseil,
Montent faiblement les marches déceptives
Qui, plus on les monte, plus donnent de l'énergie,
Mais seulement pour se transfigurer
En belle sculpture, dès le premier perron:
Une lutte majestueusement pas fini—
Lutte avec ses soi-mêmes sans savoir ce qu'on veut.
Ou, si l'esprit prend feu aussi bien que le corps,
Et le soleil révèle l'étage doré, sans toit,
De cet enchantement en forme de musée—
Ah, dissolution en pensées oubliées,
On n'est plus soi: promenade à cheval,

Une femme joliment mise, dans un bosquet privé;
Ou une famille à table, des plats au goût ouvrier;
Et, où les murs sont presque ciel, le ciel
En peinture presque ciel, à peine le téméraie
Qui s'est évaporé ainsi en se laissant aller
Vers l'aube, l'extase de monter dans le jour
Qui ne vient jamais dans ce monde-là—vers la fatigue
De jouir du futur qui déjà est passé.

The Galleries of Day-break

When the long freaks of light (new time still somewhere)
Reach into memory like fresh morning icicles,
The dead shiver between hot and cold,
Find their marked places in the grateful crypt
Where lying still decides all feeling well or ill.
Under the feverish snow of sudden day,
Stony refuge from the sun's maddening prophecy
Of instantaneousness (life to the living
But to the dead, death again, false pang)—
A crypt, darkened by daylight heavily,
Keeps death in snowy hiding obdurate
To the long icicles of memory
That no thought's quickening in death can melt.
Such angry monuments of indestructible calm
Lie underground only where near overhead
Religion fortifies the pride of skeletons
Soothing all envy of what never dead men owned.
Noiselessly, lest wakefulness overtake them,
They clamber to the cellulate recesses
And drop into the hollow, chequered pavement—
This their vindictive lettering of the sun
In the illegible dialect of tombs.
'To natural light let us seem natural corpses,' they say.
'Light is a devil that once like sprightly fools we followed.
Swift cunning and clownish crafts he teaches,
And now to play such sciences would lose
The homely learning that death without a lesson
On the homely dead bestows—to do not, yet be wise
In so profiting of idleness by idleness.

For that's a death not death, weariness only,
A sick tossing, a country of no purpose
Where the deed comes first, then the reason of the deed,
And none to give it reason, the doer least—
Country of the great Why, and of whylessness.
Let us therefore be as irredeemable bones
When the day comes, to make us into souls
That cannot be our own, vain resurrection
Into an actuality of lost to-morrows.'
And yet some few, impatient of such wisdom,
As secretly as others to their tombs
Up dawn's deceptive stairway creep
And, feeble with rebellion, seem to grow strong
At each step left behind, but strong in folly only.
For, at the first step mastered, the memorial soul
Transfixed in sculptural battle with self and self
In a blind niche leaves off majestically,
Immortal ravel of distracted wills.
Or, if the mind has taken fire with body along
And the sun lights up another flight where roofless
This museum-like enchantment blends into sky
With golden flash and bright invisible spectra—
Ah, dissolution into forgotten thoughts,
Truly one is no more oneself then:
A woman prettily upon a horse,
Delicate her habit, solitary the grove;
Or table of the poor, a family supper,
Dishes in the humble style, tasting of plenty;
And, where the walls are nearly sky, the sky pictured,
Nearly sky, scarcely that most reckless one
Thus become deathly mist in yielding to the dawn . . .
The ecstasy of rising toward a future
That never to that world descends, all hope there
Being but of things long gone, and better not missed
Lest death float up and like aspiring smoke
Lead into nothingness greater than itself.

La Déesse qui Plaisante

Dans tout ce qu'ils font, les bons morts,
Comme ils sont sérieux, pas de blagues!
Au contraire, la déesse qui les protège,
Qui leur inspire leur grave empressement:
C'est une grande drôlesse, elle!
Regardez, dans les plis si sombres
De son gigantesque habillement,
Comme elle est petite et si gaie,
On dirait une chatte emmêlée dans ses jeux à soi,
Une chatte fainéante—n'importe les rats,
Qu'ils soient vivants ou morts.
Ah, qu'elle est douce pour ses enfants-rats,
Cette divinité comme une chatte
Qui leur laisse se croire être aimés
Pendant qu'elle fait de la philosophie.
'Ah, les pauvres,' se dit-elle, cette mère parodique,
'Demain il faut les manger—ne sont-ils pas les fruits
De mon génie raillant?
Demain je les mangerai, déjà ils s'embêtent
D'être plus réels qu'ils ne le sont.'
Ah, qu'elle est contente! Ah, le joli repas de demain!
Elle y pense toujours, d'y penser même est assez
Pour s'en rassasier jusqu'à l'ivresse et la révulsion,
En faire des hiers gratuits, mesquine infinitude,
Des creux dans le néant, regorgeant de vie.
Ainsi les veines vides des égouts anciens
Nourrissent les rats immortels du futur.
Ainsi, fou de mort, un cœur sec palpite,
Se félicite d'être tout de même cœur,
Si ce n'est que la mort qui palpite,
Si ce n'est que le cœur d'une déesse qui plaisante
Et prétend, dans les plis de sa robe trop grande,
Porter un cœur comme un monde vivant,
Plein de veines, plein de gens—un vrai monde
Paraissant, comme elle, éternel.

The Playful Goddess

And with what stern conscience, honest fellows,
The lifelike dead their living lives reclaim! No pleasantries!
But not so that goddess by whose wit and patronage
They cry unchallenged their mournful ecstasies:
A gay rogue, she!
Who would believe, under the tall sombre folds,
A toying inner creature, mind and mischief
Of the gigantic all-ghoul, Death?
Cat-seeming, in lazy thought-games tangled
While the rats teem, children of sterile breed—
Little difference, be they caught or spared.
Ah, the divine tact and felinity
Of Death towards the dead!
They, her philosophical pets,
Think love alone prolongs them.
'Ah, the darlings,' to herself confides our mother-parodist,
'To-morrow they must be eaten, embarrassed fruits
Of my perverse, time-prolonging humours.
To-morrow I shall eat them: over-real, too much themselves,
They know their madness, already are sane.'
Ah, the pretty notion! Ah, to-morrow's immense suppering!
She has not forgotten, anticipation fills
And makes a nauseous plenty—
Excessive yesterdays, paltry infinitude,
Cavernous nothing, tumid with life.
Thus in the still veins of ancient vent-ways
The immortal rats bespeak the future.
Thus beats, in false-earnest, a dry heart once a heart,
Rejoicing to be heart, however dead,
However 'tis only Death's jocose agitation,
However but the heart of a goddess at play,
Pretending, in her large make-believe of vesture,
A heart like a world a-toss, a live heart,
A veinage of people like a live world seeming—
Seeming, like her, eternal.

1933.

APPENDIX

APPENDIX

I.
Note On 'Midsummer Duet', p. 141

This poem was composed for *The Year's Poetry: A Representative Selection*, an anthology compiled by Denys Kilham Roberts, Gerald Gould, John Lehmann (John Lane, The Bodley Head, London, 1934). The editors' aim was described as being 'to select . . . the poems which best represent contemporary tendencies and poets whose work they regard as significant.' The poems were described in the preface as arranged according to the age of their authors, with 'the necessary exception' of this poem, 'which is printed at the end of the book'. It is stated there that the volume includes a large number of poems not hitherto printed. The poem is one of these: it was written *for* this anthology. Since the conception, the spirit, the format, of the poem originated with me, and grew from the initiating two stanzas delivered by the First Voice, I had necessarily, in the duet-partnership, an invisible backstage editorial role. It was naturally agreed on between my duet-partner and myself, when we were planning each a 1938 *Collected Poems*, that the 'Duet' should appear in mine. Despite the varied personal and literary acts engaged in against my credit in the following three decades by my partner in this duet, I retain it incorporated in *Collected Poems*, to keep faith with the pristine spirit of its inclusion in the original volume. The version of the duet that appeared there, and appears here, differs by some incidental revisions, made in partnership agreement, in the 1934 anthology version.

II.
Saturday Night
See Page 11 of the Introduction

On Saturday night, downtown, the farmers' wives
Who have come in to stretch their eyes and buy
Pink soaps and flower bulbs and pincushions
For ten cents each, go slinking between corners,
Their skirts a little long behind, wearing
Bright feathers in their hats to say they've left
Their corn and know as well as anyone
The proper way to pay respect to stores
With windows filled with dresses they can't buy
And to townfolk who look in store windows
Quite differently, as if they mean to buy,
And don't keep pigs to kill when the moon's light.

The farmers' wives and all the wives in town
Walk up and down the streets on Saturday night,
Shuffling their tiredness straight ahead of them,
Wondering how much there will be left to spend
On Sunday dinners, and worrying about
The price of everything they'd like to have.
And yet I think that they must bear in them
Some other unperceived inquietude,
So white and mournful on their sombre stalks
They move in melancholy back-and-forth.

The men are looking somewhere, too, for something,
Leering on street corners in their best suits
Like lamps a little awkward of their lights;
Like banners, also, on a holiday,
Unfurled to an elate significance.
And yet I must believe that they are not
Forever signalling to all the women
That pass them by with feathers in their hats,
For feathers may be pennons too—and still,
The young men and the husbands have not stopped
Their signalling on corners on Saturday nights.

The farmers' wives and all the wives in town,
The husbands, the young men who watch the feet
Of women as if they were afraid that they
Might blush through looking at the rest of them,
The old men spitting kindly at the gutters,
And all the sad Salvation Army folk
(There must be more than faith to keep the voice
Of that Salvation Army lass so high
Above the crowds that pass indifferently),
And yet besides, bewildered dogs and children—
I wonder if they like to think they've come
To heaven at last, that they parade vaguely
Among themselves like ghosts, knowing that ghosts
Are silent and unseen, and they themselves
Bedimmed in the store shadows on Saturday nights.

There is a pain upon the air, and hearts
Are restless under unbuttoned coats, and eyes
Are troubled and timorous with fear and joy,
As if they were afraid the world might end,
Yet glad to have it end on Saturday night.

This poem was published in *The Fugitive*, December 1924. I have made but one revision in the version printed here in the third stanza. The original reading was:

> Like lamps a little awkward of their light;
> They do not move but idly stand and wave
> Like banners hung out on a holiday.

I was 22 or 23 years old when I wrote this poem. It has for background scenes that had remained vivid after about seventeen years in my memory-pictures of experiences of my childhood—when I would make free to slip away on Saturday nights from my parents' place of business in a Pennsylvania town for peeks at what was going on in the streets.

I am moved to join here to this poem an early poem of my husband's, for its bearing on the matter of birth-placement, and the personal reality of being an American. It too has something of the character of an Americana item. Perhaps, if he had ever gathered his poems together for publication, he might have excluded it from the collection. But he cared about it; and, a good many years before his death, he took time to change the title from 'U.S.A.' to 'Our Dear U.S.', the new title suggested to him by a radical-minded friend's writing to us in gloomy political lament over 'our dear U.S.', he turning the phrase to this love-of-country use. He also, later, noted the following possible alternatives to 'Unbroken': 'Previsional'; 'A prospect-arch'; 'Conceptual'.

Our Dear U.S.

> To claim a noble name 'did' much
> In the old world, but in the new
> It shows you're saddled with a crutch.
> Not who you're born but where you grew
> Is what's considerable about you,
> From Back Bay to the Golden Gate,
> Where those are noble who are true
> To their geographical estate.
>
> O early land discovered late,
> Whose soil supplied the firstlings' corn,
> You, of your dignities, instate
> The heaven of the simply born—
> Unbroken arch of human prides
> Spanning all worldly Great Divides.

III.
Original 1938 Preface
TO THE READER

The reasons for which poems are read ought not to be very different from the reasons for which they are written. Why are poems written? Am I asking too much of my readers in expecting my reasons to be also theirs? Every poet should face this sort of question, and the readers of poems as well. An ambiguous situation arises when poems are read for reasons other than those for which they were written; or when the poet, conscious that the reasons of poetry are frequently not the reasons for reading poems, allows himself other reasons in order to have readers.

As a poet who has been persistently accused of 'difficulty', I feel that there is due from me an explanation of the baffling effect that my poems apparently have for a large number of readers; and that such an explanation comes appropriately here, where I present my poems in collected form, as the integrated whole of my poetic work up to the middle-point of my life. It would be unpleasantly disingenuous of me to publish this work without acknowledging a complaint which I know to be common. I do not think that the complaint is a legitimate one; but, on the other hand, I am not indifferent to it. No poet genuinely moved by the reasons of poetry can be indifferent to the accusation that her or his poems make inaccessible that which it is their function to uncover.

Why does one read literature of any kind? One reads to uncover to oneself something that would otherwise remain unknown—something that one feels it is important to know. Certain things are obviously more important to know, in an absolute sense, than other things. But people vary in their circumstances, characters and powers of attention. Even where there is general agreement about what is and is not important, there is great variation in the time devoted to serious as against trivial reading. Comparatively few people devote any time at all to the reading of poems; yet many would agree that the realities uncovered in poems are extremely important to know. This raises the question: why so many people do not read poems.

Some people do not read poems because it embarrasses them to try to be as serious as the reading of poems demands. Others disbelieve in the sincerity of poets, feeling that they affect a humanly impossible seriousness. Then there is a large class of people who have a vague good will toward poetry and poets, but who feel that the rewards are small compared with the amount of time and energy necessary—that reading poems is much too hard work.

Some people have a natural and wholesome disinclination to read poems, which deserves to be respected; as we respect those who, conscious that they lack the proper qualifications of experience or judgement, modestly refrain from advancing opinions on some controversial subject. But there are many who, from their education and sensibility of mind, might be expected to be readers of poems, and yet are not. The strongest single reason why they are not is miseducation as to the reasons of poetry. They have acquired the impression that poetry is based on fancied experience and yields only a fanciful kind of knowledge, or the impression that the wisdom to be found in poetry can be obtained in ordinary ways, without the tediousness of interpretation.

Is it not astonishing that, *because* I am a poet who writes strictly for the reasons of poetry, I am in the position of having to justify myself for not having other reasons, for not appealing to readers who read poems for reasons other than those of poetry, even for not appealing to those who do not read poems?

Is it not astonishing that the literary education of people gives them such a false account of the reasons of poems that they either do not read them at all or read them mostly for the wrong reasons? So that, if one writes poems for the proper reasons, one must teach one's readers what these are?

My poems would, indeed, be much more difficult than they have seemed if I did not in each assume the responsibility of education in the reasons of poetry as well as that of writing a poem. Because I am fully aware of the background of miseducation from which most readers come to poems, I begin every poem on the most elementary plane of understanding and proceed to the plane of poetic discovery (or uncovering) by steps which deflect the reader from false associations, false reasons for reading. No readers but those who insist on going to poems for the wrong reasons should find my poems difficult; no reader who goes to poetry for the right reasons should find them anything but lucid; and with few other poets are readers so safe from being seduced into emotions or states of mind which are not poetic.

But what are the right reasons for going to poetry—and, if there is so much miseducation, do most of the people who read poems read for the wrong reasons? And—a still more pressing question—are the poems that find a large number of readers likely to have been written for the wrong reasons? Can a poem written for the reasons of poetry serve as reading-matter for people who go to poetry for other reasons?

The right reasons for going to poetry cannot be very different from those that a poet must have if the poem is to be a poem and not reading-matter interesting on other grounds than those of poetry. A poem is an uncovering of truth of so fundamental and general a kind that no other name besides poetry is adequate except truth. Knowledge implies specialized fields of exploration and discovery; it would be inexact to call poetry a kind of knowledge. It is even inexact to call it a kind of truth, since in truth there are no kinds. Truth is the result when reality as a whole is uncovered by those faculties which apprehend in terms of entirety, rather than in terms merely of parts. The person who writes a poem for the right reasons has felt the need of exercising such faculties, has such faculties. The person who reads a poem for the right reasons is asking the poet to help him to accentuate these faculties, and to provide him with an occasion for exercising them.

The poetic faculties should exist in fairly clarified form in the constitutions of all sensitive and properly educated people. Readers may reasonably expect some assistance from the poet, who exercises the poetic faculties more habitually than people who are poets only in acts of deliberate concentration and difference from their ordinary selves (that is, in the reading of poems). But corruption of the reasons of poetry sets in—in both the reader and the poet—when too much emphasis is laid on assisting the reader: when the reader goes to poetry with no notion whatever of the faculties required, and the poet is more concerned with stirring up the required faculties than with presenting occasions for exercising them.

The history of poem-writing and poem-reading is in large part a history of such corruption. In poem-writing and poem-reading the stirring up of the poetic faculties has been a greater preoccupation than their proper use; the excitement of feeling oneself in a poetic mood has come to be regarded as adequate fulfilment both for the reader and the poet. Hence the frequent vulgarism 'What is this poem *about*?'—when the reader feels that there is an element in a poem beyond that designed to evoke in him the flattering sensation of understanding more than he knows.

I am willing to stake whatever authority and credit I may have as a poet on the following assertion: that when a poem is attacked for obscurity it is either because the reader has gone to the poem in order to be put into a poetic mood (not to have reality uncovered for him as it can be uncovered alone in poems)—or because the poet has been concerned neither with providing a poem nor with stirring up a poetic mood in his readers, only with enjoying the display of his own faculties. The poem that has the reason of flattering the author's vanity deserves to be called something worse than obscure; and when people use the term they generally mean something worse—vain, arrogant, snobbish. The reply to the charge of obscurity, from the poet who writes poems for the reasons of poetry, can only be: my poems represent so much poetic learning, and you can learn from them as much as I have learned —if you admit the reasons of poetry.

This is my own reply to the charge of obscurity—with an intensifying qualification: if you admit all the reasons of poetry. I wish to make no omission here that could be regarded as unfrank. Not only am I aware of the effect of extreme difficulty that my poems have had for the majority of readers, but I offer voluntarily the statement that, in one sense of difficulty, more difficult poems would be difficult to find. My awareness of exactly how difficult they are (in this one sense) gives me, however, the right to say why they are so: because they have been written for all the reasons of poetry. In fact, you cannot even begin to read them unless you admit that poems can have all the reasons of poetry as well as a few. If you accuse me of difficulty after an honest attempt to read my poems for the reasons of poetry, you are saying that poems should be written only for a selected few of the reasons of poetry. If you approach my poems without restricting poetry and yourself to the standardized reasons of literary education, you will not only see that my poems are not difficult: you will discover in yourself reasons for reading poems that you have largely neglected in previous reading. I can demonstrate this; any reader with a full potentiality of poetic attention can demonstrate it for himself. Which is to say that my poems are indications of the full scope of poetry, as well as being poems. Indeed, to say that a poem is an indication of the scope of poetry is to define what any single poem is by itself.

I have learned from my poems what, completely and precisely, the scope of poetry is; and any reader may learn the same. Is this to claim too much? If you feel so, it will be either because, having read my poems and gone with me as far as I go, you find that there is still much to learn about the complete and precise scope of poetry—in which case I should agree with you; or because you are instinctively antagonized by anyone's taking upon herself voluntarily a large share of the work of the world, or of poetry. Even with the people who govern you, there must be the pretence that the work is being urged upon them, and that it is only by the weight of mass persuasion that their natural delicacy is overcome. The most arrant dictator does not quite dare to do without this sort of pretence.

Antagonism to the large claim is generally of an animal kind, bearing no relation to evidence of capacity or to the need for someone capable of assuming a large share of the work; and a civilized pretence of delicacy is necessary where the large share is seized from animal greed—the gluttons for work must humanize their animal greed in order to tame animal antagonism. It becomes me to do no more, in answer to any feeling you may have that I am claiming too much, than to agree with you that there is still much to learn about the complete and precise scope of poetry.

But you may, on the contrary, say that the end of learning the complete and precise scope of poetry is an insufficient poetic end. Very likely you will say this rather than the other: that such an end is dry and narrow and becomes the critic rather than the poet. To which I should reply that the study of the scope of poetry *is* poetry, and requires all the reasons of poetry for its pursuit. To explore reality as a whole, to be not merely somewhere but precisely somewhere in precisely everywhere: this is a study in scope, and at the same time an achievement of scope, and that level of existence which is poetry. And in order to achieve poetic scope, and poetic existence, one must have all the reasons of poetry in one's heart, as well as in one's mind the realization that there is such an end to attain.

What are the reasons of poetry—the reasons for writing poems, and for reading them? The physical answer would be: a tremendous compulsion that overcomes a tremendous inertia. It is quite true that when someone sits down to write or read a poem the amount of inertia to be overcome is greater than with any other activity. It is greater than with the most distasteful activity conceivable, with the activity that one knows before-hand will be most unpleasant in performance and most unprofitable in result. But to describe poetic motivation merely as a compulsion is to conceal the larger part of the story. It is enough to say that one does something as a result of a compulsion when the reasons lie outside one-self. When one feels compelled to do something because one wants very much to do it from one's own point of view, then it is dishonest to put the onus of compulsion on some outside force—one only does this by way of excusing one's failures.

Such dishonesty accounts for much of the neglect of the reasons of poetry. Poets have attributed the compulsion of poetry to forces out-side themselves—to divinities, muses, and, finally, even to such humanis-tic muses as Politics. Thus W. H. Auden, unwilling to conceive that a large-scale compulsion may originate in the poet, has told me that I am 'the only living philosophical poet'—my muse is, presumably, Philosophy, as his is Politics. On leaving our respective universities, it seems, we respectively chose these subjects as our literary patrons—I the more serene academic one, he the more burly quotidian one, according to our temperaments. And T. S. Eliot, on leaving his university, wandered free without a muse until, his reasonlessness becoming unendurable to him, he made himself a tailor's-dummy muse of Religion. The nineteenth-century lament was: 'Where is the Bard?' The twentieth-century version is: 'Where is the Muse?' In America: 'Where is the Myth?'—in other words, let us invent new reasons of poetry, Red Indians or Columbus or John Brown or Brooklyn Bridge, some exciting subject that has the reason of not having been used before as poetic material.

Then as to readers: properly, the compulsion to read poems consists of reasons within the reader himself. There is something that he wants to do very much, and it can only be done in poetry. Yet in order to go to poetry he must overcome an extremely heavy inertia—as the poet also must. The inertia is not a resistance as to something forced on one from without; it is a sense of the extent of one's ambition in going to poetry, either as writer or reader. To go to poetry is the most ambitious act of the mind, and the preliminary inertia one feels is the emotional measure of the extent of this ambition. One does not feel this inertia from modesty: to have a poetic consciousness of existence at least some of the time, in at least some phases of experience, is the normal human dignity. Inertia toward poetry is the healthy question to oneself: 'Can I do it?' But because there are, behind the question (if it is asked at all), reasons of one's very own for wanting to do it, the answer is in the internal command: 'I must at any rate try, merely to try is in some way to succeed.'

What a happy picture I draw of the reader's approach to poetry, and what a fortunate state human dignity would be in if the picture were a true one! It is not a true one statistically; as, statistically, human dignity is in a low state in spite of our being wise in its nature and possibilities. My picture is true, however, for anyone who of himself approaches poetry, and would be generally true if the fervour with which people assert that they 'love poetry' were matched by a fervour of compulsion. The trouble is that as poets have transferred the compulsion of poetry to forces outside themselves, so readers have been encouraged to transfer their compulsion to the poet: the poet in turn serves as muse to them, inspires the reasons of poetry in them. And the result is that readers become mere instruments on whom the poet plays his fine tunes (not even original, since 'inspired' by his muse—which is why they are tunes, songs, musical pieces rather than poems) instead of being equal companions in poetry.

The 'reasons' that can be communicated by this method of inspiration —from muse to poet to reader—are limited in number and kind. In number they can duplicate only the emotions that external objects or scenes inspire—such as wonder, fear, admiration, scorn, tenderness, amusement, and so on. And they are limited in kind to the reasons of drama: to the reasons for which people desire illusions. Most people read poems in order to be inspired with emotions which differ from their ordinary emotions only in being more exaggerated, and to enjoy illusions which their ordinary life does not permit—to get a more unlicensed form of drama than they could possibly get within the conventions of the theatre. This is to read poems for the wrong reasons; and the poems which can so be read have been written for the wrong reasons.

The frequent complaint about the unreadability of my poems is so much evidence that they cannot be read for the wrong reasons. Go for reasons other than those of poetry to any poem written for the reasons of poetry, and you will be unable to read it. Poems will not serve as reading-matter when you want detective fiction, or a play, or anything but poems; a cow will not serve when you want a horse, nor sugar when you want salt. It cannot be, because this is not—let us be grateful—that kind of world.

To write or read poems for the wrong reasons is, however, very different from writing or reading them for a few, rather than all, of the reasons of poetry. There are right negative reasons for poetry, and right positive reasons. If one writes or reads poems for the negative reasons, then one has a few of the reasons of poetry. If one's reasons are positive, then one has all the reasons of poetry. By negative reasons I mean the need

412]

of protesting against false values which every good-minded person feels.
A poem written for negative reasons teaches what is false, destroys the
power of falsity by demonstrating that it is false. The negative reasons
for poetry are inevitably but a few selected reasons, since the effects of
falsity are few in kind; few of these effects can be removed by poems,
because there are few. Indeed, there is only one effect—the false effect
that the false is so—multiplied into a number of painful consequences
by the reasons for which the false is allowed to seem so. The reason for
identifying a falsity that has been allowed to pass for truth is always in
the recovery of the power of protest that was temporarily suspended by
the power of falsity.

A great part of the poems of the past had reasons of this kind, the
autobiographical or historical reasons of recovery that succeeded the
reasons of weakness: the poet concentrated in himself the period's
strength of recovery from false impositions. Poets of the English classical
period seem giants to us because they were poets by a power of protest.
We see them in terms of physical size; their poetic experiences were en-
counters with and victories over falsity—hence the physical impression
they make and the negative character of their achievements. So it had
to be, more they could not have done. Theirs was the spectacular—but
negative—rôle of challenging the power of falsity. Until that was done
there could be no positive reasons of poetry; poetry positive cannot
include the dispute with falsity. The romantic figures were giant-like
in another way. They renounced the muscular energies of their classical
predecessors, and the dispute with falsity. Thus disarmed, they were
deliberately and hugely weak; but in their weakness they dreamed hugely
of a future in which existence was poetry positive, all of truth. They
were giant-like by their dreams, prophetically swollen with dreams; in-
stead of writing poems, they drew a swollen outline of poetry, which was
their assertion of faith in poetry as something more than the negation
of falsity. So it had to be, more they could not have done. But these
are other days. These are days for neither dispute nor dreaming, but
for poetry positive, poetry actual. These days are, by the laws of
temporal and of poetic succession, that future in reverence of which the
romantics eloquently did nothing.

And what are *we* doing? What use are we making of the freedom con-
ferred on us by the past to write and read poems for all the reasons of
poetry? The very phrase 'all the reasons of poetry' provokes in you,
surely, the demand for a list. But I am not going to give you a list of all
the reasons of poetry. I am going to give you poems written for all the
reasons of poetry—poems which are also a record of how, by gradual
integration of the reasons of poetry, existence in poetry becomes more
real than existence in time—more real because more good, more good
because more true.

I am now no longer speaking of 'difficulty,' literary problems, the state of mind in which to approach poems, and in which to write them. I am speaking of the good existence. This is the same as to speak of poems, but you will not understand that (if you do not already understand it) except in poems. By describing poems as incidents in the good existence I may trick you into vulgar curiosity as of a mystical show. That at least is a purer reason, in its innocence, than any of the reasons for reading poems induced by literary miseducation. I am speaking of the good existence which is immediately possible; which was implicit in the poems of the past—when conflict with falsity and prophetic relaxation from conflict were the historically appropriate reasons of poetry—but could not be realized because those were not reasons enough. We need to read the poems of the past in order to know that such conflict and relaxation have literally been lived through and that we are now literally in the present of poetry; to know also that poems now written for those reasons desert our own immediacies.

Literally I mean: our own proper immediacies are positive incidents in the good existence which is poetry. To live in, by, for the reasons of, poems is to habituate oneself to the good existence. When we are so continuously habituated that there is no temporal interruption between one poetic incident (poem) and another, then we have not merely poems—we have poetry; we have not merely the immediacies—we have finality. Literally.

Francis of Assisi is said to have ascended a mountain to formulate a more precise Rule for his Order. Then he wrote the Rule down, and gave it to his vicar Elias. But Elias either lost the Rule, or secretly destroyed it, finding it too severe. So Francis ascended the mountain again. While he was meditating there, Elias and a group of brethren appeared before him, to protest that they wanted no severe new Rule. Whereupon Francis appealed to his Holy Conscience, which, speaking in the air, affirmed that the Rule must be observed 'literally, literally, literally, without gloss, without gloss, without gloss.'

And so I say, not within the supposititious contexts of religion but within the personally actual contexts of poetry: literally, literally, literally, without gloss, without gloss, without gloss. So read, so exist: with your very best reasons. Any other reasons are not reasons, or no longer reasons—mere compulsions from without, or mere glosses upon night-mares long ago ridden off the map of experience.

It is less difficult to read or exist well than to read or exist ill.

This book begins with my earliest poems, and its arrangement corresponds with the development of my poetic activity. I have omitted those poems which seemed to fall outside the story and made revisions wherever a poem innocently obscured or belied the sense of the whole. The poems of the first part were written mostly in America; those of the second part mostly in England; those of the third and fourth parts, mostly in Spain.

IV.
Excerpts From Preface To
Selected Poems: In Five Sets, 1970

My history as one who was for long a devout advocate of poetry, and then devoutly renounced allegiance to it as a profession and faith in it as an institution, raises a question of consistency. Those who know my poems—those who have cared for them, those who have not, those who have drawn from their inner attitude and their linguistic qualities propulsive force for attempts to transcend (in their own poems) mere period-modernism—have for the most part (as the indications go) shrugged off my change of view of poetry as exhibiting an inconsistency so bizarre as to be explicable only in private-life terms. This notion has seemed justified by my protracted public silence on the subject. By 1962 I had made but a single statement on it in print, and that, coming before I had explored all the significances of the new view, was a cautious generalization. The impression that my break with poetry might not be a critically responsible act was strengthened by the infusion of colourable insinuations into the flow-ways of literary rumour.

When at last I began to speak explicitly on my changed view of poetry, the question of consistency was my first concern, but not in relation to myself as one who had lapsed from it extraordinarily, mysteriously. The story I had to tell was of my becoming so much aware of a discrepancy, deep-reaching, between what I call the creed and the craft of poetry—which I might otherwise describe as its religious and ritualistic aspects—that I perceived the impossibility of anyone's functioning with consistency in the character of poet. Two exceptions to this impossibility must be made. There is a formal consistency possible in ever-prolonged evasion of the challenge to honour with which poetry confronts its practising devotees, and there is an organic consistency up to a point in consistent endeavour to meet the challenge where awareness comes (as come it must, in such endeavour) of an ultimate impossibility of meeting it and remaining a poet.

I can make here only a meagre identification of the challenge poetry holds: what compatibility can there be between the creed offering hope of a way of speaking beyond the ordinary, touching perfection, a complex perfection associable with nothing less complex than truth, and the craft tying the hope to verbal rituals that court sensuosity as if it were the judge of truth? Straining of effort to achieve compatibility between these will lend moral coherence to the effort, and for long employ a native will in a poet to consistency. If poets strain hard enough they must reach the crisis-point at which division between creed and craft reveals itself to be absolute. If, with intuition of final trouble ahead, they slacken the strain to a slow, morally comfortable rate of subsidence, neither they nor their public will feel anything worse to be happening than a tempering of moral intensity to the dignity of advancing maturity. The backing-away of poets of better-than-average conscience from extreme testing of the possibilities of consistency in the poet-rôle passes unnoticed because no poet before me has gone to the very breaking-point: there is nothing in the poetic corpus to suggest the pertinence to poetry of a higher standard of scrupulosity than that observed in its historic best. Someone cited Rimbaud to me in this connection; but it was not in the cause of consistency that he abandoned the poet-rôle. (I shall speak of him again.)

I have distinguished a formal consistency as peculiar to certain poetic procedure. In this procedure there is also a straining of effort, but the challenge to honour is never answered in this straining: all effort is expended in problems of craft. Such straining can be highly intense, and simulate, in its intensity, straining of the kind aimed at keeping a moral proportion between poetic craft and the sacred poetic motive; and it can seem to be blessed with success because the results appear to be 'good' poems, the actual tinkering being concealed under carefully mixed and applied literary polish. Further, a sanctimony of seriousness about poetry always accompanies craft-straining, and, functioning as a guarantee of good quality, excites a predisposition to confidence: though the procedure does not rise above poetic journalism, the steady-handedness with which it is conducted has the noble appearance of moral care. The difference between such industry and the moral strenuosities of those who try to make one sense of the two senses of poetry has never been distinctly appreciated, and has become obscured in the thickening opacity of the problem of poetry as a problem in the field of language of extensive human importance.

The work of poets taken in period-mass is very difficult to order qualitatively for any one period without arbitrary critical differentiations. It probably presents more confusion, characteristically, than a period-mass of the work of other literary professionals, or of the professionals of other areas of 'culture'-activity, poetic performance being of its outspeaking nature more personalized and more subject, thus, to individual variation. I venture the observation, at any rate, as one able to contemplate the immediate poetic scene (against the background of antecedent poetic vistas) with the objectivity of a non-competitor and a critic having only general human, extramural, affiliations, that never before has there been so great a variety of individual poet-styles, and so much poverty of thematic content of the kind the word 'poetry', in the entire virtue of its meaning, signifies—religious (to use the word again) in magnitude of scope and purity of interest-value. The total display crackles with craft-individualism, but there is no sparkling, no brilliance: all is suffused with a light of drab poetic secularity. [. . .]

The last poems I wrote are contained in my *Collected Poems* published in 1938. I can be seen, in that book, to be striving to find at once the poetic extreme *and*, the mark of human fulness of utterance—and to be heading towards finalities of proof of poetry, and of the poet-rôle itself. There is also to be seen there a movement of developing sensibility, above the personal or professional, reflecting consciousness-at-large of the approach of human life in the whole to a term, and of there being, to come, *something after*. The relation of the sense of a something-after to the striving is, precisely, that of religious sensibility giving itself into the keeping of poetic sensibility, which has a partial identity with it, but is, also, otherwise engaged. Poetry invites vision of a lasting, living fact awaiting our arrival at a state of grace in which we know it, *speak* it; it is also the patron of a historic love of the patterning of words with a physically ordered nicety, pleasing to human pride. I forced the issue, in my poems, of the spiritual serviceability of what has been regarded in all past human ages, and automatically continues so to be in this, as the universal type of the spiritual best in language. [. . .]

The taint of complaisance stands out sharply in the backward look at poetry. Generally, in the composition of human customs, there is a self-complaisance that obliges aspiration to yield immediate satisfactions to pride. The craft-requisites of poetry accommodate the urgency, in it. [. . .] I know of no one besides myself and my husband Schuyler (who, a poet, but, beyond that, a scholar of poetry, familiar as a brother with the yearning mansoul in it) who has put feet across the margin on the further ground—the margin being the knowledge that truth begins where poetry ends (or, as I said in introducing a BBC reading of my poems, that, for the practice of the style of truth to become a thing of the present, poetry must become a thing of the past). I have initiated enough poets into the idea of linguistic discipline for truth's sake, in the past, to know how verbally insensitive to considerations of truth poets can be, though behaving as persons born privy to it. In recent time, a few poets have professed agreement with my later view of poetry, and returned to their desks believing they could beat the impossibility that they had acknowledged. [. . .]

Readers will, I hope, better understand my poems, and the sequel to them as well, for my stressing, here, the conflict in poetry between the motive of humanly perfect word-use and that of artistically perfect word-use—though I know how difficult it is for people to see the latter, which seems so much an innocent contributor of loveliness, as a parasitic partner in the poetic enterprise, taking an unholy share, ever over-large, in its management, and the honours. [. . .]

[Presented here by the courtesy of Faber & Faber, England; and Norton & Co., U.S.A.]

V.
Excerpts From A Recording (1972), Explaining The Poems

A word on my feelings towards my poems. They are not either stand-offish or neutral. I honour my poems for their happiness in the words they are, and for their never stealing themselves from me to be strangers. We are friends as far as we went. And I did not renounce *them*: and, as I was their breath, they did not renounce me.

As far as half-way along in *Collected Poems*, and even beyond, there is to be found, with much variation of subject and experience-area, a repeated pointing to and acknowledging of the Given—by which I mean the Given in the large. This is the basis of what can be taken, in some of my poems, for a folkloreish mixture of savvy and bonhomie; elsewhere it shows as an equanimity testing itself against unminced potentials of the sombre, the indeterminate, even the catastrophic. However severe the tests, the Given is always treated as essentially untragic: some happiness of loyalty to it is always evident.

To comment on the poem 'The Troubles of a Book': lest it be mistaken for an exercise in poetic playfulness, I pause to characterize it as one that rises through stages of sense of the queer nature of a book, as a hybrid of external and internal actualities, to perception of its essentially tragic nature. I should not have thought such a comment necessary had not the editor of *The New York Times Book of Verse* (1970) presented the poem—to my astonishment—in a group labelled 'In A Lighter Vein'. The treatment of it there shows that even it, ending as it does, can be answered with letters and bookishness. . . .

Past the half-way mark, historically, in my poems, and up to a last phase, I am much preoccupied with the effort to make personally explicit the identity of myself poet and myself one moved to try to speak with voiced consciousness of the linguistic and human unities of speaking: I am restive insofar as this identity is only an implicit principle in my poetic speaking. There is also at work at the same time an effort to intensify in specificness the comprehensive reference I intended generally that my poems should have. The two heightened impulsions, working to bring within the poetic frame an explicitness and a specificness that it cannot contain and to which it cannot expand, produced within the poems themselves a struggle between compression and completeness of utterance. I cannot briefly make the explanation of the peculiarities of this phase easier.

Two points of particular counsel may be useful. The first is generally applicable. Nowhere should I be taken as speaking by what are called 'symbols'. If, for instance, I say 'the sun which multiplied' or 'the moon which singled', as I do in one poem, I am endeavouring to indicate actualities of physical circumstance in which our inner crucialities of human circumstance are set. My moon may look like the old tired poetical symbol, and I like an old tired poetic romanticist, but I truly meant that the moon's being what it is where it is intervenes in our outer circumstances as a negator of the sun's fostering excessiveness in our regard, both lush and destructive—as a tempering counter-agency, relatively little but near. However foolishly mystical this may seem, nothing so far learned by scientists or experienced by astronauts disproves this. The second point of counsel concerns my use of the word 'woman', and introduction of the fact of woman, in poems of this phase in particular. My use was literal on a large scale. I meant the common identity, woman, of women. I conceived of women under this identity as agency of the intrinsic unity-nature of being, and knew myself as of the personality of woman—as of this identity: and I endeavoured to make poems include expressly the sense of this as it was actively present in me. But neither in nor out of my poems have I degraded my seriousness about the nature of woman, and of poetry, with such goddess notioning as that into which my thought in and out of my poems—borrowed, as such things are called—has been mis-shaped.

Nor did my awareness of my partaking of woman-identity declass me as a poet to one especially to be considered as a 'woman poet'. Some curious effort has been made to make such a declassing of me a critical permanency with a cement of magniloquent praise, honour-bright in colour. The most foolish instance of critical segregation of me I have encountered puts me in a group of possessors of a sensibility praised as the female counterpart to that possessed by a number of masters of English light verse. (This was by W. H. Auden, introducing a book of poems by Phyllis McGinley). . . .

A certain relaxing of the complex preoccupiedness I have described is perceptible in the very last phase. Here that equanimity in the Given of which I have spoken is matched by a calm in the To Be. But there is still the difficult calm in the Not Yet—calm at this end of the poetic journey is divided against itself. But after that comes equanimity in the Next. For Next is also of the Given. . . .

To speak now of the supplementary section of my *Collected Poems*, which has the title 'Histories', and consists of three long poems all written well before the last phase of my poetic writing. I shall make a résumé of them; I have never before done so. They are poem-picturings of three different examples of liveliness stranded in history. The first is of the phenomenally lively personage Voltaire. The second is of myself as standing sensibly still on an island floating in history. The last pictures a period of modern life, and of modern art and literature especially, in which liveliness seemed moribund, and a lie of life was breathed into death, in the name of reality. Utterly different in subject, these three long poems, each a distinct work, have a same purpose of showing unlikeliest subjects to be poetically treatable, with fidelity. Whatever their failings, they are prides of the workshop, rightly so, I think—placed diffidently apart, rightly so, I am sure. . . .

To comment finally on an early poem, 'The Quids', that has had much circulation, and confused understanding. Its spirit is not that of philosophical irony. It was an expression of personal dissociation from, rebuff of, the automatic existence-processes. In its earlier form it went on for two more stanzas.

> But I know, with a quid inside of me,
> But I know what a quid's disguise is like,
> The gymnastic device
> Being one myself,
> That a quid puts on for exercise.
>
> And so should the trees,
> And so should the worms,
> And so should you,
> And all the other predicates,
> And all the other accessories
> Of the quids' masquerade.

(From *The Fugitive*, February 1924)

This close formulates almost fiercely the turning of sheer young bodily sang-froid to the impersonal physical countenance of the universe. (The personal story is different.)

*   *   *   *   *   *

I concluded this recording with a reading of some passages from *The Telling* (1970). I said, in introduction of them:

> My meanings have not changed, there, fundamentally, from what they were in my poems. . . . I attained there, I believe, to degrees of personal explicitness, and of specificness combined with comprehensive references in the verbal delivery of meanings, that poetry closes out. The attractive ingenuity of poetic devices obscures the fact that they serve an eloquence that does not allow expression to exceed, much, the suggestive.

[Spoken for Lamont Library, Harvard University]

L. (R.) J.